ATLANTA,
Cradle of the New South

CIVIL WAR AMERICA
Gary W. Gallagher,
Peter S. Carmichael,
Caroline E. Janney, and
Aaron Sheehan-Dean, editors

ATLANTA,
Cradle of the New South

Race and Remembering in the

Civil War's Aftermath

William A. Link

The University of North Carolina Press
Chapel Hill

*This book was published with the assistance of the
Fred W. Morrison Fund for Southern Studies of
the University of North Carolina Press.*

Set in Minion Pro by codeMantra
Manufactured in the United States of America

The paper in this book meets the guidelines for permanence and
durability of the Committee on Production Guidelines for
Book Longevity of the Council on Library Resources.

The University of North Carolina Press has been a member
of the Green Press Initiative since 2003.

Library of Congress Cataloging-in-Publication Data

Link, William A.
Atlanta, cradle of the New South : race and remembering in the
Civil War's aftermath / William A. Link.
pages cm. — (Civil War America)
Includes bibliographical references and index.
ISBN 978-1-4696-0776-4 (cloth : alk. paper)
ISBN 978-1-4696-2655-0 (pbk. : alk. paper)
ISBN 978-1-4696-0777-1 (ebook)
1. Atlanta (Ga.)—Race relations—History. 2. United States—
History—Civil War, 1861–1865—Influence. 3. African Americans—
Georgia—Atlanta—Social conditions. 4. Memory—Social aspects—
Georgia—Atlanta. 5. Atlanta (Ga.)—Social conditions I. Title.
f294.a89n4454 2013
305.8009758′231—dc23
2012044361

For my graduate students, past and present

Contents

Table, Map, and Illustrations

ATLANTA,
Cradle of the New South

Introduction

In 1886, civic booster and newspaper editor Henry W. Grady became one of the most successful popularizers of what he and others called a "New South." Grady wanted to hasten the South's rebirth. The specific locale for his call to arms was post–Civil War Atlanta. Destroyed by war, in two decades the city had rebuilt itself and became a leading, dynamic urban center. Grady emphasized the city as a center of a newly industrialized South that had abandoned the economic bases of the old slaveholding order. His "New South" incorporated some powerful notions that were reflective of Atlanta's new self-image. Especially among whites in the growing city, there was a strong sense that they had rebounded from the war and were at the leading edge of dynamic economic tendencies. An early historian claimed that the city was "everywhere regarded as the leading representative city of the New South" and that there was "no place in the South . . . more thoroughly American." It was a city, he wrote in 1905, where different people "meet, fraternize and unite in one harmonious whole" in a spirit of "toleration in thought, speech and conduct."[1]

Sixty years ago, C. Vann Woodward described the New South as nothing more than "a slogan, a rallying cry." Behind the slogan lay an ideology that embodied a faith in the future combined with a passion for the past, alternating between a "forthright recantation to an affable and uncritical optimism." Woodward urged historians to examine critically the lingering effects of a New South mentality in order to understand its significance and power.[2] In 1970 Paul Gaston, taking up Woodward's call, described a "New South Creed," a set of ideas serving as an exercise in mythmaking. The Creed became part of the postwar South's attempt to redefine itself. It spun a version of an Old South past and a New South future that were, according to Gaston, both "genuine social myths with a social power over the way in which their believers perceived reality." These myths were composed of images and symbols that reflect popular perceptions of truth. It was no coincidence that, as southerners reconsidered their past, their view of the future underwent a metamorphosis. The New South Creed described "not what ought to be or would be, but . . . what already was."[3]

During the 1980s, historians reexamined the concept of the Lost Cause. Defeat, wrote Gaines Foster, brought "pain and confusion" to white southerners, but their understanding of their immediate history fed into a New South ideology. Charles Reagan Wilson maintained the importance of southern commemorations of the Civil War, as they became a sort of "civil religion," which white southerners used to define themselves.[4] Thereafter, scholars reconfigured the subject around the theoretical notion of "memory" and examined ways in which remembering the Civil War became an exercise in power relations. Memory studies provide a structure for interpreting how the South's memorialization of the Civil War related to its ideological reconstruction after the 1880s. During the past two decades, historians have described how memorialization, the writing of history, and public remembrance combined to reshape public understanding of the Civil War. In particular, scholars have paid attention to gender and race and to the contested nature of memory.[5]

David W. Blight's *Race and Reunion* (2001) defined the field of Civil War memory studies. Unlike previous scholars, Blight portrays the Lost Cause as part of a larger, national debate about the meaning of the war. This debate involved three competing narratives: reconciliationist, white supremacist, and emancipationist. He found that in public discourse, North and South, the movement toward reunion "both used and trumped race."[6] The dominant memory of the war, in other words, was that southerners and northerners shared a sense of common nationality. This sense of reunion obscured the memorialization of the war as a war against slavery, fought to liberate 4 million enslaved African Americans. Blight describes the Civil War as the event that determined how Americans understood themselves, defined their nation, and shaped a vision for the future. At the center of this story was the fact that race was scrubbed clean from the memory of the war.

Despite an outpouring of scholarship about the South after the Civil War, historians are still trying to understand the most devastating war in our history. The war's meaning directly related to the shaping, branding, and self-identity of Henry Grady's New South. That concept was rooted not in the 1880s but in an evolving redefinition of the experiences and meaning of the war itself, a redefinition that extended over a long period of time. Robert Penn Warren once described the Civil War as the "greatest single event in our history." Its significance not only lay in what people remembered about the events of the war, but also in how it was "lived in the national imagination." According to Warren, the white South devised the "Great Alibi," and the North, "the Treasury of Virtue," to explain, condone, and transmute the meaning of the Civil War.[7] Unpacking these legacies requires understanding how southerners, white and black, came to understand their past. This involves expanding our understanding of the Civil War's aftermath beyond concepts of memory to a comprehension of its meaning.

This book considers a central question about the South in the aftermath of the Civil War: What was the relationship between war and the emergence of a "New South"? How did the struggle over the defining moment of the lives of nineteenth-century southerners—devastating, destructive, and disorienting warfare—shape the ways that they constructed their future? Inevitably, the ways in which the war affected southerners were far from uniform, but the stakes were high in this ongoing struggle to define what it meant. While whites embraced the concept of the Lost Cause—and a version of the past that eliminated the significance of slavery and race from the war—black people remembered the war as a central event in their history because of the destruction of slavery and their ensuing liberation. The war's meaning evoked contested versions of the past and the platform from which people argued about the shape of the future.

Atlanta provided a battleground in a larger, national struggle. In the aftermath of war, the city's white boosters trumpeted the "New South" as a slogan defining the city in a context of defeat, destruction, and rejuvenation. Leaders such as Henry Grady wanted to abandon the economic aspects of that old order but not its racial component; their version of the future assumed that economic progress would be accompanied by white supremacy. Grady and others wanted to reimagine, update, and reposition the social ethic of the Old South, which rested on white supremacy, in a new post-emancipation, free-labor, industrializing South. In many respects, this contradictory concept—involving rosy progress combined with caste-based subordination—was created and marketed from postwar Atlanta, which represented a path for development. The New South was a concept distinctively associated with the city, which blazed a trail in showing postwar whites how they could modernize, attract outside capitalists, and provide for stable social development.

Although Atlanta was exceptional because of its keen orientation toward a world capitalist system, in most ways the city resembled the rest of the South. As went Atlanta, so went the post–Civil War South: the city's history embodied the social, economic, and cultural trends of the late nineteenth century. Nonetheless, the Civil War defined Atlanta's history as it did that of few other

communities in the United States. From a small crossroads village springing into existence during the late antebellum period, Atlanta emerged as a
major depot of the Confederacy. William T. Sherman's successful campaign
to conquer the city provided a crucial victory for the Union cause. Destroyed
during the Confederate defense and Union siege and occupation, Atlanta
recovered, growing into the most important interior town of the post–Civil
War South. Relying on its strategic position as a railroad hub, the city also
benefited from the activities of an aggressive group of booster-entrepreneurs
who relentlessly promoted urban growth and development and marketed
the concept of Atlanta as the "Gate City."

The destruction and rebirth of Atlanta came to symbolize the rise of the
New South. Everywhere, the city was being "built (or rebuilt) with feverish
energy," wrote a newspaper correspondent in October 1865. Like the mythi-
cal phoenix, Atlanta rose from its own ashes. The city's "crumbling walls and
scattered and blackened chimneys" were remade into "new edifices." This
great city, destroyed by fire, immediately rebuilt and redefined itself. Months
after its destruction, Atlanta became known as the "Phoenix City."[8]

But this master narrative about Atlantans' war experience—focusing
on Sherman's Atlanta Campaign of 1864, the burning of the city, and its
reconstruction—wrote race out of the story. Though largely ignored by New
South boosters such as Henry Grady, African Americans succeeded in building an autonomous community that existed even while the city participated
in the post-emancipation rebuilding of white supremacy.[9] In the twentieth
century, Atlanta became a strategic center of African American leadership
during the civil rights movement. In the twenty-first century, it is the center
of black America. Atlanta's roots as an African American center date from
Reconstruction, when the city provided a safe haven for black people to establish an enclave in the Jim Crow South. Black Atlanta did not always directly challenge white supremacy, but what was said and debated there set
the pace for African American leadership across the country.

Atlanta's sense of identity and history was rooted in race. Founded on the
fringes of the slave system, the city changed radically during the Civil War
with the influx of enslaved and free black populations. After the destruction
of slavery, thousands of contrabands came to the city because of the Yankee
military presence. In the social crisis that followed emancipation, the violent suppression of African Americans occurred throughout Georgia, but
Atlanta became a sort of refuge because of the military presence in the city.

Invasion, destruction, and occupation had a distinctive meaning for freedpeople in Atlanta. We know something about how emancipation affected life

in the postwar South thanks to work by scholars such as Ira Berlin, Lynda Morgan, and Susan O'Donovan.[10] But we know less about emancipation's impact in urban areas and about the interrelationship between emancipation's urban impact and its impact on neighboring north Georgia counties. Equally important, we know little about how African American people responded to Grady's New South vision, an ideology that excluded consideration of black freedom and discounted the significance of emancipation. Like enslaved people elsewhere in the South, African Americans in Atlanta during the Civil War greeted northern invaders as liberators; and, as slaves left their masters and joined Sherman's army, a sense of betrayal gripped whites. Whites and blacks alike realized that northern invasion meant black emancipation, though they understood this change differently. Atlanta underwent a wartime boom, which opened new opportunities for enslaved residents. But masters and slaves both understood that the war promised freedom. Slaves certainly knew the stakes. Describing one Atlanta slave, an African American commented: "He was just like every other colored man— loyal. I never found one yet, who was not."[11]

What Stephen Kantrowitz calls the "reconstruction of white supremacy" forms a central theme in the postwar South. In Atlanta and in the counties surrounding it, whites operated under older, untenable assumptions. White Georgians' rebuilding of the racial order was tied to how they considered the wartime destruction and devastation, and, like other white southerners, they built a version of the past's meaning in which blame for this destruction was placed on white northerners and black southerners. White violence against black people, endemic during the Reconstruction years, became central to this rethinking.[12]

The northern occupation of Atlanta also provided some measure of protection for the city's black community, though whites and blacks still groped for the meaning of freedom.[13] Atlanta became a center for another kind of northern invasion, the establishment in late 1865 of an outpost of the evangelical and abolitionist American Missionary Association (AMA) and its program of African American education. This northern political and cultural invasion, though not always entirely sympathetic to freedpeople, fostered a distinctive environment. For ex-slaves, the meaning of freedom remained ambiguous, as white violence reinstalled white supremacy throughout Georgia. But, as elsewhere, freedom and the end of the Civil War provided enclaves of difference and exceptionalism. Atlanta provided a distinctive locale for encounters between northern whites, ex-slaves, and native-born whites. White supremacy reigned supreme in the city, yet African Americans migrated there in large numbers, seeking jobs and refuge. In the antebellum period, Atlanta had been a fortress of white solidarity. In the postwar period, the city provided a stage on which the meaning of race in postwar America played out. There, freedpeople gained a toehold for what would subsequently become a center of black cultural, economic, and political power.

The struggle to define meaning helped to shape what the New South became. Sherman's invasion, together with the events of the war's immediate aftermath, made the experience of destruction and renewal, redefinition and remaking, critical to forming the identity of the region and the era. And the definition of a New South that existed apart from the slaveholding South, yet retained many of its central characteristics, became a motif for the people building it. At the same time, the New South was not born out of consensus and uniformity, but out of a struggle for power through identity. Remembering the war had a real meaning for whites and blacks because remembering so deeply influenced how the social and racial order was emerging. The contest over remembering the war was more than an argument about memorialization, for what occurred in Atlanta helped to define the contours of the post-Reconstruction American South.

ONE

A Troublesome Thing

Invasion

During a clear winter day, late on the afternoon of January 3, 1861, residents of Atlanta, Georgia, experienced an unusual event: a ten-second tremor, probably a small earthquake. Seismic activity in northern Georgia was rare; local residents feared a dark augur. "Who will account for it in this latitude?" asked the *Atlanta Daily Intelligencer*. "May not its coming and passing away so easily, with the clear and bright sky," it asked, "be symbolical of the present political convulsion in the country, which, in the South, will pass away so easily, leaving the spotless sky behind?"[1] Six months later, city residents were similarly amazed when they witnessed the appearance of a comet, with some speculating that it offered another ominous sign of war and bloodshed.[2] In early 1861, Atlantans feared for their future. On January 2, elections were held for Georgia's secession convention, and state leaders began a quick march toward disunion, culminating in the enactment of an ordinance of secession on January 19, 1861.

Few people realized, of course, how much of a cataclysm secession truly would be. Atlanta faced an uncertain future involving privation and disruption, social disorder, invasion, and the collapse of slavery. Nonetheless, the Civil War made modern Atlanta. The war spawned a sustained boom, and by 1864 the city had become the Confederacy's most important economic center, supplying its western armies. At the same time, the war boom also brought on a host of problems, exposing a fragile social order. The approach of Sherman's massive army during the spring and summer of 1864 amplified the significance of Atlanta's tentative emergence as an urban center; both the Union and the Confederacy realized that the impending battle would be crucial. Sherman's conquest of Atlanta resulted in the city's destruction, the meaning of which, for years to come, continued to define the city's identity.

TWENTY YEARS BEFORE SECESSION, Atlanta was little more than a backwoods town on Georgia's northern frontier. After removal of the Cherokees in the 1830s, land-hungry white settlers rushed into the region. In subsequent decades, railroads linked north Georgia with the rest of the state. In 1837, the new town of Terminus came into existence, where Peachtree Creek empties into the Chattahoochee River. Terminus was so named because it marked the southern end of the state-financed Western & Atlantic Railroad, which would eventually connect north Georgia with Chattanooga, Tennessee. As the first railroad penetrating the upland region, the Georgia Railroad reached Atlanta on September 15, 1845, to the wild celebration of local farmers arriving for the event in one-ox carts. The Macon & Western Railroad reached Atlanta in 1846, the Western & Atlantic a year later. In 1854, the newly built Atlanta & West Point line opened up markets to Alabama and beyond.[3] Terminus, with 30 inhabitants, renamed itself Marthasville in 1843. Two years later, the growing town adopted the more ambitious name of Atlanta, and the legislature awarded it a new charter in 1847. Claiming 2,500 residents in 1850, it had reached a population of nearly 10,000 by the Civil War's outbreak.[4]

An early resident remembered Atlanta as "a thicket—all woods," while another called it "too small to be called a village," with rough country roads rather than streets. Most of the homes were log cabins; the town had a frontier feel.[5] A northern visitor described the town as the "most unattractive place that I had seen."[6] But Atlanta's backwoods character changed quickly, as its growth exemplified how railroads remade interior American cities during the nineteenth century. Each of the four railroads operated depots, machine shops, and freight warehouses, and, by 1861, forty-four passenger and freight trains passed through town every day.[7] Streets ran parallel to railroads rather than on a grid; railroads were located according to the ease with which they could traverse the hills and ridges south of the Chattahoochee River. By the late 1840s, four major thoroughfares—Peachtree, Marietta, Whitehall, and Decatur—converged in the town's central mercantile and transportation center.[8]

With an energized group of boosters leading the way, antebellum Atlanta internalized values of growth, enterprise, and industry. Like other dynamic southern urban entrepreneurs, Atlantans exhibited an insistent capitalist ethos that tapped into the global market system. Bolstered by railroads, the town solidified its economic position as a transportation hub, dominating the region's agricultural hinterlands. Atlanta meanwhile also began to build and expand a manufacturing base. During the 1850s, its population grew by about a thousand people per year, making it one of the fastest-growing towns in the South.[9]

Much of Atlanta's success reflected the success of boosters in luring rail-roads and in solidifying its regional economic dominance. But boosters also faced obstacles in moving their city forward because of its reputation for dis-order and lawlessness. In the early 1850s, Atlanta boasted nearly fifty stores that made money by selling whiskey to thirsty residents. Bars, saloons, and drunkenness characterized life. In the notorious Snake Nation and Morrell's Row districts, the town became known for its prostitutes, thieves, gamblers, and murderers. A Moral Party, which was dedicated to cleaning up the town, competed with a Rowdy Party in municipal elections in 1850. Maine native Jonathan Norcross, a millwright who ran a sawmill and dry-goods store and speculated in cotton, won election as mayor on the Moral Party ticket.[10] But the Rowdies, rather than surrendering easily, fired a small cannon loaded with grass and dirt at Norcross's office, demanding that he resign. Norcross responded by organizing a posse of one hundred men, which suppressed the rebellion and arrested its ringleaders. The Rowdies were "taught a les-son," remembered a local historian, who wrote at a time when many of the participants in the Moral-Rowdy showdown still lived.[11] By 1855, the *Atlanta Weekly Intelligencer* could comfortably agree that "honest men" triumphed over "rowdies, bullies, and assassins."[12] Despite this rosy portrayal, antebel-lum Atlanta continued to have an unsavory reputation. Insults to honor fre-quently resulted in violence. "A rougher village I never saw," remembered one resident. At the same time, townspeople remained acutely aware of their fragile past—and of the need to stabilize the social and political order.[13]

A hierarchical racial order provided one way to stabilize Atlanta. But the institution of slavery remained less important in Atlanta than in the rest of Georgia; in 1860, only 5 percent of the city's slaveholders owned more than twenty slaves, while more than a third owned two or fewer.[14] Only nineteen free blacks lived in Atlanta in 1850; a decade later, thirty-one. White artisans, believing in a whites-only social and economic system, feared the competi-tion of a larger black population, and, in 1855, the city council imposed a $200 fine on free blacks entering the city. Hired slaves also seemed threaten-ing to the white population. A group of white workers complained to the city council in March 1858 about "Negro mechanics whose masters reside in other places" and who "underbid the regular resident citizen mechanics of your city." The white mechanics appealed to the city council to limit the use of unsupervised black labor.[15]

That Atlanta lay on the margins of the slaveholding regime raised the stakes during the sectional crisis. White boosters were eager to demonstrate their loyalty. After Georgia seceded, municipal leaders quickly embraced the

Confederate cause—even advancing a case to make the town the capital of the new southern nation. Dissenters were repressed; the community quickly rallied around the Confederacy. In March 1861, when Atlanta resident J. A. Stewart announced his loyalty to the Union, he faced enough public pressure and threats to persuade him to change his mind.[16] The only choice in regard to secession, concluded the *Atlanta Daily Intelligencer*, was "subjugation or independence."[17] With the South facing invasion by "Northern vandals," it added a few months later, there was little difference between the "most violent hater of the old government and its former most helpful admirers."[18]

On February 16, 1861, Confederate president Jefferson Davis visited Atlanta, speaking before an enthusiastic crowd of five thousand at the city's largest hotel, the Trout House. That spring, streams of volunteers joined the local militia units, the Atlanta Grays and the Gate City Guards; by the summer, Fulton County had produced more soldiers than any other county in Georgia.[19] After Virginia seceded, on April 17, 1861, Atlanta's businesses shut down, cannons fired in celebration, courts adjourned, and church bells rang in what one historian has called a "joyous din."[20] News of secession brought "quite a lively time in the city last night," wrote one young Atlantan. "I hope we will not have war," he added, "for I am certain I do not want to go."[21]

The town's location in the Confederate interior, removed from the northern invasion, proved an advantage. After the fall of Nashville to Union forces in 1862, Atlanta grew in importance as a transportation, manufacturing, and depot center. The city was "one of the best resorts during the invasion in the South," trumpeted a newspaper early in the war, and "will no doubt be crowded with strangers during the winter."[22] The city also served as a hospital center, with ten hospitals in Atlanta treating 75,000 soldiers by war's end. In 1862, Atlanta housed the Confederacy's Commissary Department, the Quartermaster Department, and the medical headquarters of the Western Department.[23] Two years into the war, the city had become, according to the *St. Louis Republican*, the "most vital point in rebeldom."[24]

Atlanta also became one of the Confederacy's most important manufacturing centers, second only to Richmond in strategic significance. On the city's western side, an arsenal produced 75,000 rounds a day and employed over 5,400 workers by August 1862.[25] Workers manufactured field pieces, shell casings, casting shots, fuses, tents, and swords, as well as whiskey, clothing, shoes, saddlery, leather goods, and belt buckles. Gunsmiths milled and rifled barrels; the Western & Atlantic shops produced the famous Joe Brown Pike, named for Georgia's governor. Flour mills fed Confederate armies and produced hardtack. Railroad shops manufactured cars and serviced them.

Atlanta's furnaces and foundries produced iron for Confederate gunboats and ironclads, along with other war supplies essential to the cause. The Atlanta Rolling Mill became a leading producer of rolled and rerolled rail, which sustained the Confederate transportation system. The economic boom drew in migrants, some of them refugees from Yankee invasions, mostly because of jobs created during wartime. Atlanta's population doubled during the war to about twenty-two thousand people. By early 1862, the city had become what one historian called "one of the most important workshops of the Confederacy." Atlanta had been transformed from a frontier town into a vital urban-industrial center of the Confederacy."[26]

Testing the ability of the city fathers to govern, the wartime economic boom strained Atlanta's social fabric. The railroads became overwhelmed with passengers and freight. Traffic clogged the railroads, and military needs competed with the demands of civilian passengers and freight. Tracks and rolling stock were so overused that maintenance became impossible. Western & Atlantic trains ran so closely together, according to one historian, "that there appeared to be one continuous line of box cars and locomotives from Atlanta to Marietta."[27] Wartime expansion fanned antebellum Atlanta's culture of speculation. Shortages of critical resources—raw materials, labor, and housing—became endemic. "Times is very hard here," wrote one local woman.[28] As early as October 1861, the DeKalb County grand jury complained how ordinary folk suffered "for [want of] many things which are essential to their comfort and welfare in life." Shortages and dislocation resulted not only from "enemies without," the grand jury charged, but also from "enemies within"—rapacious speculators.[29] Civilians suffered from rampant inflation. Lucy Hull Baldwin, who spent her childhood in wartime Atlanta, remembered how her father pulled a $100 bill out of his pocket and told her to buy a stick of candy.[30] Speculation, declared the *Atlanta Daily Intelligencer*, was "now the curse of our country," owing to the actions of a "set of vampires, who will neither fight for the South nor contribute a cent to the support of those who are in the field."[31] The *Intelligencer* worried especially about the rising price of salt, an essential ingredient in food preservation. The "heartless extortion" of the salt supply badly affected rural Georgians, who "must perish" if speculator-driven price inflation continued.[32]

In May 1862, Atlanta became a military post, a step that formalized the city's strategic importance. Col. George W. Lee, in charge of protecting military property and supplies and maintaining order, imposed a curfew and tightened restrictions over bars, billiard halls, and livery stables.[33] On August 12, 1862, Gen. Braxton Bragg declared martial law in Atlanta, expanding the power of the Confederate provost marshal to regulate civilian activities by requiring passes and mandating that hotel guests register their presence. The military post exercised broader control over transportation facilities.[34] Bragg also appointed Atlanta's mayor, James Calhoun, who had been elected in January 1862, as civil governor.[35] Increasingly, military needs crowded out civilian ones. By 1863, the military was requisitioning horses, for example, at the expense of civilian transportation, something diarist Samuel Richards denounced as "high handed and dishonest."[36]

As Union armies pushed forward, refugees streamed into Atlanta.[37] "You have no conception of the anxiety & fear that *pervades some* in our community," wrote one resident in November 1861. She described "*many, very many* citizens" fleeing Savannah, "& still they are coming."[38] Three refugee newspapers—the *Chattanooga Rebel*, the *Knoxville Register*, and the *Memphis Appeal*—moved to Atlanta. After Yankees occupied Nashville in February 1862, John and Annie Schor relocated to Atlanta, where they expected to remain "until we can drive back the hated enemy and return victorious to our dear old home."[39] John owned two factories in Atlanta, and the Schors feared invasion. If Union forces captured the city, Annie predicted, the Schors would most likely lose their factories.[40] Annie and her husband found the city a challenging place to live.[41] Temporary housing sprang up in tents, lean-tos, old boxcars, and even passenger depots.[42] Diarist Sallie Clayton told how her family had to give up a rental house on Mitchell Street because it was sold. They found a new place to rent, but the quarters were so cramped that they had to find additional space.[43]

As in other parts of the South, conditional Unionists in Atlanta had opposed secession until the bombardment of Fort Sumter and the onset of northern invasion. Diarist Sam Richards declared that secessionists were nothing more than "professional men and young squirts who have little or nothing to lose."[44] At the same time, some Atlantans also belonged to what historian Thomas Dyer calls a "small, but significant minority" of "Secret Yankees" who remained unconditional Unionists. Dyer estimates that perhaps a hundred people fell into this category.[45] These Atlanta residents were often suspected of disloyalty. The *Atlanta Daily Intelligencer* warned of subversives in the city, some of whom might become incendiaries. Southerners worried about arson even in the pre-secession era, though the perpetrators they most often feared then were resistant slaves. During the war, white fears shifted to traitors who might burn their businesses and homes. "The people, in country and town, should keep a bright look out for these prowling scoundrels," said the *Intelligencer*. These people were "to be found almost every where." The *Intelligencer* so feared incendiaries that it favored hanging them on the spot if caught in the act.[46]

Unionists operating in wartime Atlanta provided some basis for Confederate paranoia. Abbey Stone, a Vermont native who had moved to the city with her husband in 1854, participated in a network of underground Unionists and kept a detailed diary of her activities. The Unionists kept to themselves, avoiding conscription officers, and they offered some support to the Union cause by informing northern spies about Atlanta's fortifications. They also secretly cheered the Yankees' advance, on occasion openly defying Confederate authorities.[47] Unionist James L. Dunning refused to permit his Atlanta Machine Company Works to be used in the war effort. Confederate authorities responded by seizing the facility. When Sherman occupied the city in September 1864, Dunning climbed up on a pole and raised the Stars and Stripes. Most Unionists in Confederate Atlanta, less bold than Dunning, kept their views to themselves. There was "no safety in talking in public," recalled one of them.[48]

RISING CRIME AND DISORDER—a throwback to Atlanta's frontier days— threatened the city's social order during wartime. According to one estimate, there were as many as eight to ten thousand draft dodgers in the area, foraging for food and terrorizing residents in the suburbs.[49] Some residents complained about "loafers," vagrants who appeared in the city.[50] Thieves grew more audacious, complained the *Southern Confederacy* in February 1863. "When will a stop be put to this? Have we any law?"[51] The city's jails became too cramped to house a growing number of inmates. By 1864, local authorities heard a rash of complaints about a perceived crime wave, especially among young people. There were a "large number of idle and vicious boys strolling about the City," the Fulton County grand jury charged in April 1864, who appeared "to be under no control." They frequented "many places of vice, corrupting and . . . [being] corrupted."[52]

As crimes such as theft, counterfeiting, assault, and murder became common, the citizenry lost confidence in local law enforcement. Occasionally, outraged residents took the law into their own hands. In November 1863, two men caught pillaging the trunk of a guest in the Trout House were jailed. A biracial mob appeared and, in a "unique and grotesque processing," marched the accused thieves through the streets, with a drummer and fife player providing martial music, followed by a "promiscuous crowd of negroes and white boys." The men had their heads shaved; one of them was tarred and feathered; and both wore a sign that read: "Trout House Thieves."

This provided proof, commented the *Atlanta Daily Intelligencer*, "of the in-efficient manner [in] which the city police and the city affairs in general are governed." In no other city in the Confederacy, the newspaper believed, would such a mob outbreak have been permitted.[53]

With wages unable to keep pace with prices, labor unrest periodically erupted. In October 1862, workers at the Confederate arsenal struck for higher wages, but the strike collapsed when authorities threatened to con-script the workers. Similarly, a printers' strike in 1863 failed in the face of threatened conscription.[54] Spurred on by rising prices and food shortages, civil unrest led by women erupted in 1863 in Richmond, Virginia; Salisbury, North Carolina; and Macon and Augusta, Georgia, especially among sol-diers' wives. On March 18, 1863, as many as twenty Atlanta women stormed local grocers, seizing bacon, meal, and vegetables. They took food because they needed it; "their suffering condition," they explained to onlookers, justi-fied their actions. Although the women attracted sympathy for their actions from some Atlantans, others worried about a breakdown of law and order. The women took property in the same way as the government had seized it, commented Atlanta's *Southern Confederacy*, and their actions imitated governmental tyranny. Was it any wonder that people had become "imbued with a spirit of lawlessness?"[55]

Anxieties about crime and social disorder combined with white fears about Atlanta's black population. During the war, slavery had become a criti-cal ingredient in the wartime boom. Slave dealers ran a highly profitable business, with rising prices and skyrocketing demand.[56] Although the Afri-can American population in antebellum Atlanta remained small—especially compared to that of coastal or central Georgia—in sheer numbers the city became blacker, increasing from 20 to 46 percent African American between 1860 and 1870.[57]

The war also presented new opportunities for black Atlantans. Roderick Badger, a free black dentist, became the subject of white protests because of his "professional pretensions," but he succeeded in amassing property dur-ing the war. Similarly, six black barbers also acquired wealth.[58] In 1861, Polly Beedles, a free person of color, married Henry, a slave who was the property of the Georgia Railroad Bank. During the course of the war, the Beedleses accumulated property in her name.[59] Jefferson Simons was an Atlanta slave and blacksmith whose services came into high demand once the war began. Hiring his time from his master, "I owed nobody," he recalled. Buying his tools in 1860 and a wagon the next year, Simons later paid $325 in Confeder-ate currency for a mule and $200 for a horse. By the end of the war, he owned enough property to make a claim for compensation from the U.S. government for a lost mule, horse, wagon, and tools.[60]

Other slaves achieved greater autonomy. Joseph Holland, owned by banker and railroad man E. W. Holland, worked in Atlanta as a drayman. He acquired enough property to purchase himself and his wife from his master. In addition, Joseph saved enough money to buy his own stock—two mules and a horse—which he used in his hauling business. As a result of wartime prosperity, Holland also bought a house and lot. A decade after the war, the Southern Claims Commission certified that Holland's ownership of property was "fully & satisfactorily proved." In September 1864, when Sherman occupied Atlanta, although Yankee soldiers confiscated Holland's mules and horse, Holland followed the northern army, working for them as they marched through Georgia and the Carolinas.[61] Prince Ponder, enslaved before the war, bought his freedom out of profits from a successful grocery business, where he sold provisions, tobacco, and whiskey. A local white described him as "unusually energetic, industrious & money making" and owning "as much if not more property" than any black Atlantan. Julius Hayden, a local judge, owned Ponder's wife, Emma, and they lived on the Hayden farm about three miles from the city. In August 1864, once Sherman laid siege to Atlanta, Judge Hayden fled the farm, leaving Ponder in charge in exchange for his serving as caretaker. Ponder owned a substantial amount of property: two mules, a bay horse, a horse and buggy with harness, and a wagon, along with stores of whiskey, tobacco, wheat, rye, hogs, and bacon. By 1870, he described himself as a wheelwright, and the census taker reported him as having $600 in real property.[62]

Whites were not happy about African Americans' economic freedom. There were widespread fears, in particular, about a rising population of hired slaves. The city council, which sanctioned slave hiring in 1853, banned it two years later, though the law remained mostly unenforced.[63] Particularly troublesome was the common practice by which masters permitted slaves to hire themselves out. Self-hiring was frequently condemned by whites. On January 4, 1861, the Atlanta City Council prohibited the practice of hiring "Negro Mechanics" who belonged to people outside the city limits. Fears about an unregulated hired slave population grew after 1861. In September 1862, fifteen male slaves were arrested when they were discovered unsupervised in quarters above a downtown storehouse. "That negroes, slaves, should be permitted to hire rooms to sleep in, away from their owner," said the *Atlanta Daily Intelligencer*, was a "new feature of toleration in our city." The newspaper called for officials to suppress the practice of permitting slaves to hire and board themselves. As late as April 1864, the Fulton County grand jury maintained that self-hiring was "on the increase and constantly abused."[64]

During the Civil War, whites confronted the consequences of an expanding, unregulated black population. "In this vicinity we could well spare a free negro and mulatto," said the *Atlanta Daily Intelligencer* in October 1861, "whose presence in our midst is quite a nuisance." Most black people, it claimed, were "seldom found working, but dress fine, drink whiskey, and smoke cigars all day long."[65] "I am disgusted with negroes and feel inclined to sell what I have," Richards wrote in February 1864. "I wish they were all back in Africa, or Yankee Land. To think too that this cruel war should be waged for them!"[66] Whites worried about the loyalties of their slaves, who made clear their sympathies. "My only fear is [that] there may be some trouble with our negroes," wrote an Atlanta woman in November 1861. She warned of a "*diabolical* plot" intending to increase the numbers of free blacks "to try to excite our slaves to rebellion."[67] Slaves' sentiments were more complex, however. When slaves heard Union cannon fire, they excitedly reported it to their masters. "Did you hear them cannon last night and early this morning?" an enslaved man asked his white mistress in late May 1864.[68]

Whites made various attempts, mostly unsuccessful, to restrict black autonomy. In 1863, the city council prohibited slaves from renting horses or carriages without their owners' approval. The council also banned slaves and free blacks from selling beer, cakes, fruits, or confectioneries and prevented them from walking with a cane, club, or stick and from smoking tobacco in public places.[69] The mayor's court, which regulated petty crime, cracked down on self-hiring erratically and inconsistently. In May 1861, ten slaves were charged with "living separate and apart from their owners and hiring their own time," and the court responded by fining their masters. Similarly, in February 1862, the court fined a white man twenty dollars for "allowing your slave to hire her time and enjoy the privilege of labor for her self & c." The court avoided prosecuting self-hiring because of the law's ambiguity and because of the difficulty of enforcement. By early 1862, the court had decided that there was "no penalty prescribed by the ordinance against the hiring of their time, by slaves to be inflicted upon the Slave for such offence."[70]

A basic problem in any crackdown was that many Atlanta whites profited from the underground economy. In February 1862, the mayor's court fined a white man, Thomas Clince, ten dollars for "allowing your slave Nancy to keep an eating house & c."[71] In August 1863, another white, Harris Fuller, was fined ten dollars for permitting his slave, Louisa, to maintain an eating house "on her own account or the account of another person."[72] The generally lax attitude toward self-hiring, combined with the fact that whites paid greater attention to the existence of independent black entrepreneurs than to self-hired slaves, continued during the remainder of the war.[73]

Whites knew that black economic independence had profound implications: they had only to observe the many Atlanta blacks who succeeded in acquiring property. Austin Wright, an enslaved tinsmith, self-hired himself and ran a tin shop in the city. Originally from a plantation west of Atlanta, he found city life to his liking. His master, Thomas Latham, stopped collecting his hiring wages during the war, and, by 1863, Wright regarded himself as free and as working "in his own name." He also became an important leader in the black community and, after 1867, a Republican Party activist. During the war, he lent money to other enslaved and free African Americans in Atlanta. Early in the war, moreover, Wright helped to organize three "negro balls," ostensibly to raise money for Confederate soldiers and their black servants. In December 1861, the *Atlanta Daily Intelligencer* charged that the "negro balls" had "become so frequent in our city, that they amount to a nuisance." At the balls, a "big buck negro, with a gold watch in his pocket, and a gold chain around his neck . . . acts as master of ceremonies." The *Intelligencer* complained that the money raised rarely benefited soldiers but that holding the balls had become a pretext for local black leaders to accumulate capital.[74] In the minds of many whites, the "negro balls" had gotten out of control, and, in 1863, the city council prohibited them.[75]

The expansion of Atlanta's black population also aroused white fears about crime. Many blamed an epidemic of theft on "negroes [brought] from a distance . . . who are too frequently left in the charge of no responsible party."[76] About the rise in theft, the *Atlanta Daily Intelligencer* commented: "We have no doubt that most if not all this pilfering is done by negroes."[77] In another indicator that whites found the public presence of blacks disturbing, the city government attempted to prevent the sale of liquor to black people. In July 1861, when Randall, a hired slave, was charged with selling liquor to another slave, Isaac, the mayor's court responded with the harsh sentence of thirty-nine lashes.[78] In February 1864, another slave, Edward, was convicted of a similar crime and received an identical sentence.[79]

White fears grew in response to perceptions of an increasingly defiant and resistant black community. To whites, freedpeople simply seemed to be more assertive than slaves were. In March 1861, John Parker, a free black man, faced charges of unruliness and received twenty lashes.[80] Disorderly conduct on the Atlanta streets became a common charge before the mayor's court.[81] A rising incidence of blacks' defiant disregard of racial etiquette—what whites called "impudence" and "insolence"—was especially disturbing to whites. In October 1861, a slave, Lucy, was charged with "disorderly conduct by using impudent language to a white person & c." She was sentenced to thirty-nine lashes.[82] In February 1863, a hired slave, Bill, who rode a horse on the sidewalk and used insolent language, received fifteen lashes.[83] In February 1864, another slave, Stephen, was charged with yelling at midnight and "mocking the Policeman."[84]

The war forced masters and slaves to confront each other on a different basis, raising new questions about the institution of slavery itself. At the same time, black people profited from the wartime boom, as did whites, and they exploited opportunities as they became available. But African Americans also faced hardships. Confederates arbitrarily impressed them to construct fortifications and dig trenches, regularly exposing them to harsh conditions and military danger. During the late stages of the war, the northern invaders imposed hardships on whites and blacks with little distinction, and in spite of the prospect of liberation, African Americans also confronted danger, deprivation, and loss.

ATLANTANS REALIZED THAT THE CITY'S IMPORTANCE AS a strategic economic center made them likely targets of the Union war machine. As a southern newspaper announced in 1864, if Atlanta—the "gate city from the North and West to the Southeast"—fell to Yankee invasion, the results would be catastrophic. A correspondent for the *New York Herald*, David Conyngham, agreed with this assessment. Militarily, Atlanta was of vital strategic importance. Key to the railroad network of the Gulf South, Atlanta served a crucial role as a depot and manufacturing center. The city was "the cradle from which the southern armies drew their supplies."[85]

In tandem with Ulysses S. Grant's efforts in 1864 to capture Richmond, Sherman's Atlanta Campaign became an important chapter in the history of the American Civil War. By 1864, there was little possibility that the South could win the war; the odds were stacked in favor of Union victory. But Union victory in Atlanta would put an end to the Confederate military's ability to sustain itself and transport men and supplies across the railroad system. Atlanta occupied a crucial position militarily. It was as important to the Confederacy, according to Governor Joseph E. Brown, "as the heart is to the human body."[86] As one historian has written, Atlanta was the "inner back gate" to the interior South, the "foundation of the hostile power and will of the Confederacy."[87] Sherman, assuming command over the Western armies in March 1864, received his orders from his old friend Ulysses S. Grant on April 4, 1864. Deliberately avoiding specifics, Grant instructed Sherman to attack Gen. Joseph E. Johnston's army, "to break it up, and to get into the interior of the enemy's country as far as you can, inflicting all the damage you can against their war resources."[88]

Some Atlantans were confident that the geography of northern Georgia would protect them. "Numerous mountains, spurs and ridges present an almost impossible barrier," the *Intelligencer* assured its readers in April 1862.[89] Some Confederate soldiers, such as Georgia militiaman P. C. Key, believed that God's "almighty power" was behind their cause.[90] Others were less sanguine. "Every thing looks dark & gloomy enough now, and the clouds still gather thick and fast," wrote Annie Schor in the spring of 1862. "Never until now," she wrote, "did I feel hopeless of our success."[91] Once the fighting began, Atlantans hoped for miracles. On June 10, 1864, Mayor Calhoun announced a day of fasting, as Sam Richards recorded in his diary, to seek divine protection from the invaders.[92]

Sherman had visited north Georgia as a young army officer in 1843, and he recognized how daunting the challenge of overcoming this mountainous, semiwild territory was. Yankee invaders, wrote a newspaperman accompanying Sherman, passed through a "rough and broken country" that was blanketed with dense forests and high mountains whose passes and gorges were easily defended and whose rivers blocked the path of invasion.[93] Even while fighting against a hostile geography, Sherman maintained a long supply line. His strategy was to outflank and eventually overwhelm his opponent, General Johnston.[94] In contrast, Johnston followed a purely defensive strategy that was designed to conserve his resources and draw Sherman into costly frontal assaults.[95] Beginning in May 1864, Sherman's forces slowly moved south in a series of engagements fought under a ferociously challenging physical environment. After two months of fighting, in July the Yankees advanced across the Chattahoochee River, flanking Confederate forces and moving toward the center. By late July 1864, northern forces were besieging Atlanta.[96]

Sherman's commanders ran a highly efficient organization that transported supplies, repaired and rebuilt bridges, laid rails, and maintained telegraphic communication. The army also provided reliable intelligence. Jacob Cox, commander of the Third Division of the Twenty-Third Corps of the Army of the Ohio, described the local topography as "almost unknown." Existing maps, which were "erroneous and misleading to a degree that was exasperating," gave only the outlines of counties and the town and village

William T. Sherman during the Atlanta Campaign (courtesy of the Library of Congress)

names. Smaller waterways were randomly drawn and usually wrong. Maps of existing country roads proved so erroneous that "every attempt to calculate distances upon them or between them was sure to lead to trouble." Cox adapted to the situation, assigning an officer in each division to serve as acting topographer, who would report to the engineers at corps and army headquarters. Acting topographers constructed an itinerary for every march that sketched the local geography in detail. Information was consolidated at the division level, where working maps were created and distributed to the field officers.[97] As important to his army as maps, according to Cox, was the superiority of the Union's transportation and communication logistics. Col. W. W. Wright and his corps of two thousand men oversaw the Western & Atlantic Railroad; they quickly reconstructed wooden bridges and built new ones. Their effectiveness provided a crucial advantage that, according to Cox, was "beyond praise."[98]

Along with Grant's campaign to capture Richmond, Sherman's invasion of north Georgia constituted a struggle of "true Napoleonic dimensions," according to Atlanta's *Southern Confederacy*.[99] The northern invaders faced an enemy that was dug into hostile, mountainous terrain.[100] Confederates threw up breastworks "like enny thing," wrote one soldier.[101] Yankees were no less skilled. Northern soldiers, wrote an Illinoisan, were "as expert in the use of the spade and the ax as with the rifle, and two hours' work made a very fair protection."[102] During the long, three-month campaign, the two sides often lay in close proximity. "We can see very distinctly from our works," wrote one Georgia militiaman, "portions of the enemy's lines, and they can see us."[103] "Our entire front, go where you will, from right to left," wrote a northern correspondent, was a "world of fortifications."[104] By August 1864 Union trenches and rifle pits were located about two miles from Atlanta's city center, the approximate location of the city limits. Rebel defenses were composed of a succession of rifle pits and forts located on high ground in the Atlanta hills. A no-man's-land of about a half mile separated northern and southern lines.[105]

From the outset of the Atlanta Campaign, Johnston's strategy was to retreat in order to find a favorable location to engage Sherman. Outnumbered, Johnston relied on what an Indianan called the "decided advantage" of superior Confederate fortifications.[106] Both sides mastered the ability to exploit north Georgia's hilly terrain. The Confederate defenses at Kennesaw, according to a later description, were "the most superior system of defense ever employed in battle up to the time they were used." Immediately after the war, Prussian officers visited the scene in order to learn more about the science and technology of trench warfare.[107]

The fortifications became the soldiers' home, the place where they lived, ate, and died. Alonzo Miller of the Twelfth Wisconsin Regiment spent his Fourth of July, 1864, in the following manner: "In the morning I had the hard tack given me, small piece of pork, a little sugar and coffee for one day's rations. In the afternoon we moved 1 mile. In the eve I went after spades and built breast works all night, and the 5th we made a charge. It seems nothing like years that have passed and gone, but be as it is, if I only am spared my life, that will be all I will ask."[108] "Here we eat to live," another soldier wrote his wife, "& not live to eat."[109] A. T. Holliday, a soldier in the Georgia state forces, dreamt that he had returned home to bacon, ham, beans, squashes, cucumbers, apple pie, fried peach pies, chicken pies, and buttermilk. Instead,

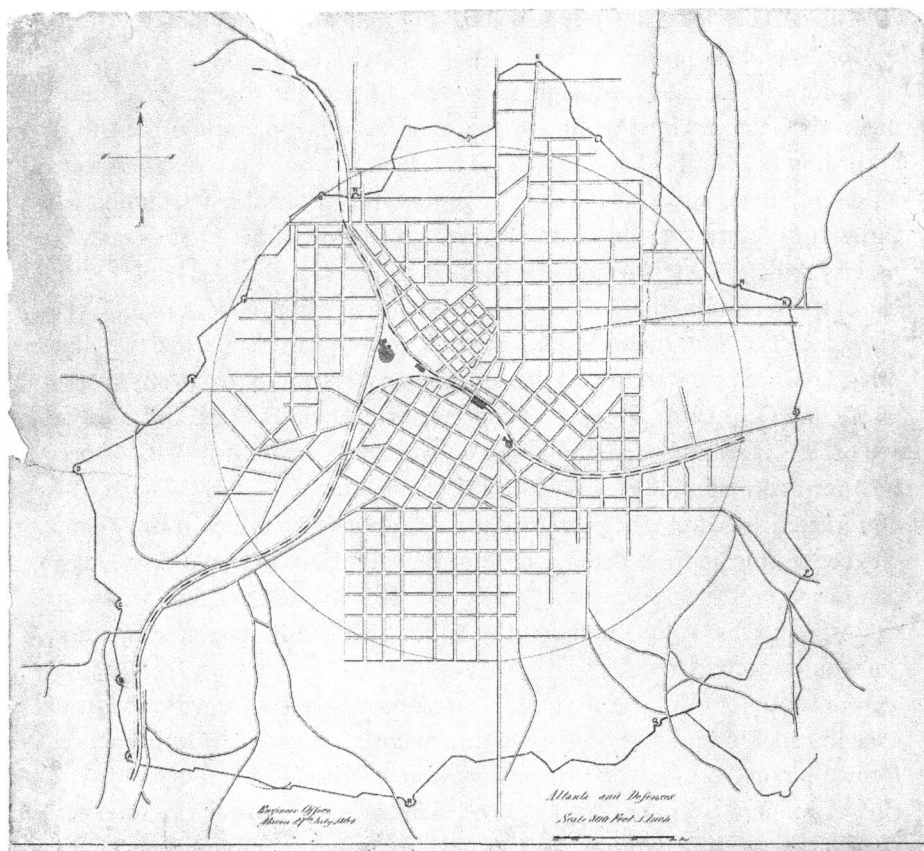

Atlanta's line of defenses, 1864 (courtesy of the Atlanta History Center)

he woke up and found himself in a five-foot ditch, and rather than "my own family to look upon I found as far as my eyes could see in both directions a nasty set of white men like myself."[110] "I have plenty of war to do me and my family and my children's great grand children's children," he wrote in early August. "I have lived in the ground until I have turned to be nothing more than a gopher or a mole."[111]

Constructing fortifications and inhabiting them became the soldiers' routine. When not taking enemy fire, wrote a northern soldier to his wife, soldiers "were digging a great deal of the time." The people back home "would hardly know us as we are poor and look care worn."[112] Wisconsin soldier William Wallace described to his wife how his company had constructed twenty different fortifications between May and August 1864 in their march through north Georgia. Once Sherman's forces laid siege to Atlanta in late July 1864, Wallace and his comrades spent an evening advancing twenty-five rods in front of the old works. They immediately began constructing new fortifications. "Digging after night through stumps and roots is no easy job," he wrote, "and when daylight came the rebs was not very pleased at our impudence in getting so near them."[113]

The Confederate forces depended on slave labor for this kind of military construction, a job that authorities impressed on an often unwilling black population. Diarist Abbey Stone described how southern officials rounded up black labor and how she aided slaves who were trying to avoid the press gangs. The runaways begged Stone to shelter them. "We don't want to make no fortifications to keep away the Yankees *our*selves. Let folks build their own fortifications. The black'uns they have got, are dying up like any thing, for they work 'em so hard, and half starves 'em besides." For two days in June 1864, she wrote, she served as a "jailer," hiding four enslaved men.[114]

Slowly advancing, the Yankees constructed fortifications or took over those already built by the Confederates. "We set to work at our spades & picks & by morning we had neared a work not to be sneezed at by the Rebs or anyone else next night," wrote Edward Allen of Eau Claire, Wisconsin. The digging continued whenever there was a lull; as soon as the firing ceased, he wrote, "we went to work & built another picket fence 20 feet out side of the other."[115] Life in the trenches on both sides was, as one Yankee put it, "very disagreeable."[116] Yankee trenches, commented a Confederate who was viewing captured fortifications, were "heavier and stronger than our own," but they were also "badly policed and very filthy."[117]

Inside the pits and trenches there was relatively little danger, according to a Georgian, who reported that four men occupied a narrow space between poles with earthworks around them.[118] But if soldiers left the safety of the trenches they risked sharpshooters. "Minie balls whistle over us continuously," wrote a rebel soldier.[119] As one commander later said, "No one could say any hour that he would be living the next."[120] Soldiers were expected to stand at arms and be prepared for combat at all times. Artillery barrages, sniper fire, and canister attacks were commonplace, day or night, and the average soldier slept uneasily. Once firing began—with "a roar that bursts upon the still night air like the sound of a hurricane"—the soldier instantly took to his feet, "instinctively grasping his faithful musket." The night was "rendered hideous," sleep having been "driven from all eyes."[121]

The late spring and early summer of 1864 were especially rainy months in north Georgia, a fact that compounded the soldiers' misery. It was raining on a day in mid-June when Alonzo Miller wrote to his parents "and has rained every day since we stepped our feet in Georgia."[122] Describing the fighting at New Hope Church on May 25, 1864, a member of the 102nd Illinois Volunteer Infantry remembered how the rains grew "as darkness set in, and the night was most dismal." Rain and the smoke of battle rendered the darkness of the night impenetrable, while confusion ruled and "pitilessly the rain came down, saturating our clothes through and through."[123] Robert T. Wood of Washington County, Georgia, wrote to his wife that soldiers stretched blankets over themselves during downpours. "We are the dirtyest set you ever saw," he declared. Lice infestations had become common.[124] A. T. Holliday, who complained of daily soakings, called his tent a "rail pen covered over." Sometimes the men's hunger was so desperate that, despite the brackish drinking water, they were willing "to eat maggots and meal without sifting and no complaint." War was a "troublesome thing sure."[125]

LOSING PATIENCE WITH JOHNSTON'S cautious defensive strategy, Jefferson Davis installed John Bell Hood as the new Confederate commander on July 17, 1864. Hood, who had lost a leg at Chickamauga and an arm at Gettysburg, went on the offensive. The result, however, was a rebel defeat on July 20 at Peachtree Creek and another at the Battle of Atlanta two days later, followed by two unsuccessful and costly assaults. After one of these assaults, a Union soldier observed that some of the Confederate dead had as many as forty bullet holes created by the terrible effects of canister and case shot. "A man could not remain long wounded in such a place," he wrote.[126] Rebuffing Hood's assaults, Sherman spent much of his time regrouping and restoring supply lines. His engineers so fully reestablished rail service on the Western & Atlantic link to Chattanooga that one Atlanta resident complained that in the city he could hear "the whistle of the Engines when they arrive . . . blowing in defiance to us."[127]

The opposing sides warily sized each other up in late July 1864. Confederate troops enjoyed the advantage of an elaborate system of fortifications designed by Confederate engineer and Atlanta resident Lemuel P. Grant. Completed in October 1863, Grant's fortifications consisted of a seven-and-a-half-mile line of redoubts, rifle pits, and trenches. These included twelve to fifteen centers located on high ground, around which the works were constructed.[128] By July 22, the two armies were in position, a mass of humanity so large that a Georgia militiaman facetiously claimed that "half the people in the world are here."[129] The center of Atlanta lay within range of Sherman's artillery, a line of men that extended fifteen miles in length. A reporter

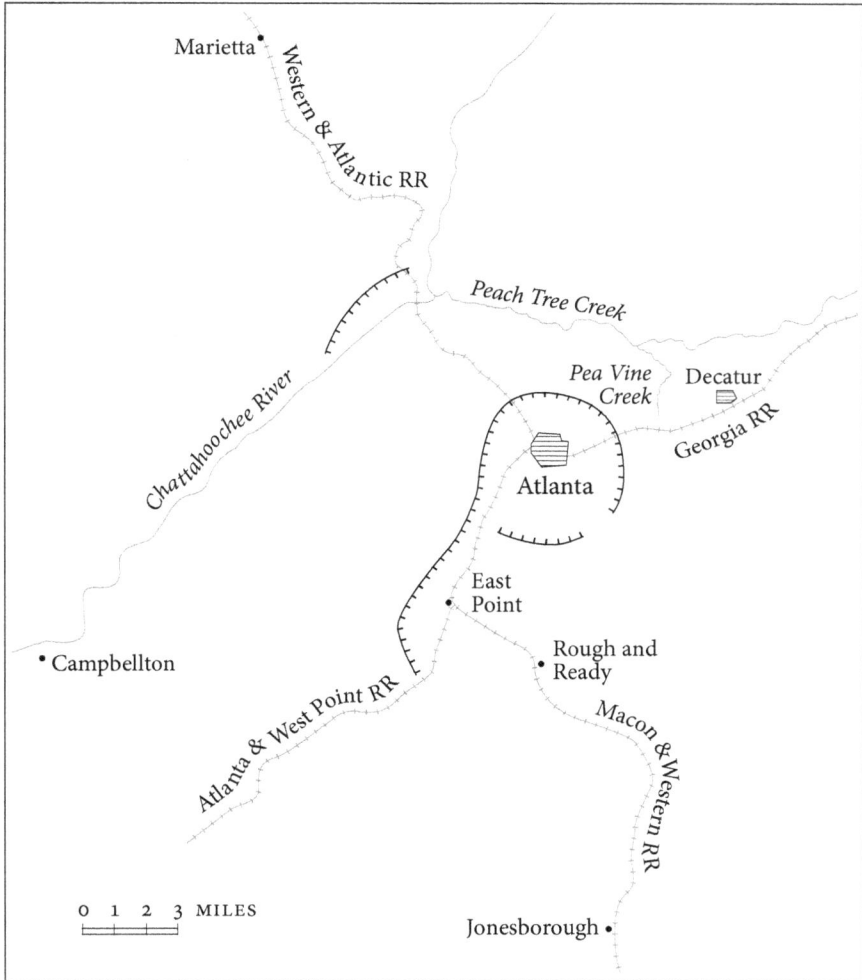

Final stages of the Atlanta Campaign, summer 1864

described the scene. Before Sherman's army lay Atlanta, "plainly visible," protected by rebel forts and earthworks that were "thronged with men in gray." The northern army maintained its own breastworks "winding mile after mile, over hill and valley." Thousands of blue-clad soldiers, "as busy as ants," moved in the rear of the main line. Artillery fire created "light wreaths of smoke," punctuated by the "deep, dull roar of artillery, far away, right and left." Behind the Yankee lines were small white shelter tents; behind these were long lines of red earth, over which the army had advanced. Even further to the rear were long wagon trains and clusters of hospital tents. Footmen, horsemen, teamsters, orderlies, generals, and staff officers clogged the roads to the front.[130]

As the two armies battled during May and June 1864, residents of the city heard distant artillery fire. "A little nearer each day," an Atlanta diarist recorded in early June, "and each day the cannons are heard more distinctly." By July, she reported that "booming cannons have long been our sunrise anthem, and lull-a-by at night."[131] War came home in July, once Sherman's forces encircled Atlanta and sought to cut off the remaining rail lines in the south and west.[132] The Union artillery dug in within range of the city, preparing for attack. "When we get our forts finished," wrote a Yankee artillerist in late July, "we will play them such a tune as they never heard."[133]

In order to soften up Confederate defenses and reduce their resistance, Sherman launched a punishing bombardment.[134] The first shells struck the city on July 20, landing at the corner of Ivy and Ellis Streets, while other shells hit the city hall square, the Female Institute, and the car shed.[135] An eyewitness wrote nearly a quarter of a century later that residents heard a "hideous, shrieking, whizzing noise" that was "unearthly and blood curdling."[136] Mollie Smith, a teenager at the time, recalled that the report was "so much louder than the usual cannonading that it attracted our attention." "What a big gun!" remarked one of her brothers. Another brother, a veteran of the First Battle of Manassas, corrected him. "That is a shell," he said. "They are going to bombard the city."[137] After July 22, Yankee artillerists were ordered to keep up their fire on the city day and night.[138] A northern soldier wrote two days later that the shelling was "enough to make a man deaf." In early August, a newspaper correspondent described how hundreds of cannon erupted, day and night, with "iron missiles of every shape and size . . . sent screaming, hurling and bursting." The air seethed with "the battle storm."[139] An Illinois soldier wrote that the big siege guns seemed to "shake the earth," making sleep impossible. Atlanta was on fire with "flames fleshing up to the very skies."[140]

During the bombardment, Sherman stood outside the city, carefully monitoring the artillery reports. He ordered one of his generals to position two 30-pound Parrotts to target buildings in the city center.[141] On August 10, a day after the 4½-inch siege guns had arrived from Chattanooga, Sherman urged his artillerists to "keep them going" with a "steady, persistent fire"; time was "too valuable to be wasted." Sherman was informed that the guns had been firing every five minutes, and that this rate would increase.[142] Northern cannon targeted buildings, keeping up their fire to prevent Confederate efforts to extinguish the blaze. Union artillerists nicknamed the Parrotts that were lobbing shells into the city "the Atlanta appeal," and they were, according to one soldier, "fun to us but death to them."[143] Some of shells landing in Atlanta were inscribed with biblical verses in Hebrew.[144] Watching the bombardment from a hill in the northern lines, an observer described it as "sublimely grand and terrific."[145]

The sights and sounds of Atlanta's bombardment fascinated Confederate commissary agent Benjamin J. Semmes. He described the shelling as a "beautiful sight . . . looking precisely like meteors or shooting stars." Semmes descriptively catalogued for his wife the incoming fire. Some shells sounded like a railroad train moving through the air; the shells screaming overhead mimicked the express train to Macon. Other shells possessed musical qualities, singing "'flibbety gibbety' in a very loud and fearful manner" as they flew toward their target. Still others offered a hissing noise before exploding on impact.[146] Mollie Smith's family thought themselves protected from the bombardment, but soon found that they were badly mistaken. While she was seated at breakfast, a 32-pound shell crashed into her home. Exploding above the dining room, the shell opened up a three-foot hole in the wall near the piano, wrenching off one of its legs and carrying it across the room. The sofa was torn to pieces, every pane of window glass was destroyed, and blinds were smashed. Pieces of shell tore into an adjoining closet, damaging clothing and burning bedclothes, while other fragments hit the floor. The family fled the smoke-filled house.[147]

Lasting five long weeks, the bombardment wreaked significant physical damage. The psychological damage—the fear and brutalization that were felt—was perhaps even more significant. To soldiers and civilians alike, the siege seemed interminable. As one Confederate soldier observed on August 2, Yankees continued to "shell the place every day, but without effect only making holes in the houses."[148] The bombardment accelerated decidedly during the second week of August. On August 7, Semmes informed his wife that he was "living in danger hourly and daily," with shelling coming "heavily and rapidly." He predicted a "a very hot fire" over the next days, though he assured his wife that "I do not feel any anxiety, but on the contrary a firm trust that God will protect me."[149] Semmes's prediction proved accurate. On August 8, Sherman urged Gen. Oliver O. Howard to position his artillery so as to "make a sad havoc in Atlanta" and fire shells into the city center and "reduce it to ruins." Sherman further ordered that all of his batteries that could reach Atlanta "fire steadily on the town" and that each gun use fifty rounds of shell and solid shot.[150] The next day, gunners fired as many as 5,000 rounds, at peak rates of sixty per minute, with shells bursting throughout the city.[151] Three days later, on August 12, Semmes described spending a "sleepless night, disturbed by clouds of mosquitoes and the crashing of 20 pound Parrott shells every minute during the night." The northern invaders kept up "a constant fire now, day and night."[152] This was a "spiteful fire," Semmes later wrote, and, though Yankees who were taken as prisoners claimed that the Union army was shooting only at military fortifications, he witnessed batteries shooting over the fortifications to reach the heart of the city.[153]

Civilians, in fact, were randomly killed and wounded. The superintendent of the gas company and his six-year-old daughter were killed while lying beside each other in bed when artillery struck their house at Elliott and Rhodes Streets. On North Pryor Street, a woman was hit by a shell and killed while she ironed clothes. At Whitehall and Alabama Streets, a barber was struck by a shell that ricocheted off a lamppost; his leg was amputated, but he died from shock. A woman en route to downtown Atlanta was hit in her back and killed. A Confederate soldier standing in front of a Forsyth Street house was struck by a bursting shell, as was a young boy with him. Soon, both bled to death.[154] Semmes reported how he dined with a young man from Alabama on August 24; two hours after dinner, his new friend's leg was amputated on the same dinner table. All told, a local surgeon informed Semmes that he had performed 107 amputations on civilians during the shelling.[155]

Although city firemen had been exempted from military service, their work was as dangerous as that of soldiers on the front. Big fires burned in Holland's cotton warehouse on Alabama Street, near the railroad; in eastern Atlanta, in three large private homes; and there were even larger fires on Marietta and Lloyd Streets.[156] On August 13, Union artillery opened fire from six batteries on Marietta, Peachtree, and Williams' Mill Roads, in front of the Medical College and the Atlanta Rolling Mills, in an artillery attack lasting from 8:00 P.M. to 4:00 A.M. About midnight, a shell hit a storehouse on Marietta Street, setting it on fire. After the fire bell was rung, a fire engine appeared on the scene. But Union artillery concentrated fire, while firemen stood their ground despite the shelling and prevented the fire from spreading to a large warehouse.[157] When the federal bombardment ended on August 25, craters littered Atlanta's streets, and in the central and northern parts of the city every house was hit numerous times.[158]

Civilians constructed shelters known as "bombproofs" and learned how to dodge incoming fire. Typically constructed in makeshift fashion in pits protected by logs and dirt, bombproofs dotted backyards across the city.[159] Under the railroad beds, Atlantans dug a network of holes, while bank vaults provided additional shelter. Residents spent a third of the time in the "bowels of the earth," according to one account, "burrowed under the ground like moles."[160] An early Atlanta historian wrote that residents calmly prepared for the worst, with men moving about the "streets as usual, discussing the topics of the day, and dodging an occasional shell." Women "busied themselves with their household matters, with their ears on the alert for the well-known sounds of danger." Often a woman unceremoniously dropped her sewing and made a "wild and precipitate plunge for the backyard, where the family would quickly disappear into the bowels of the earth, there to remain until there was a lull in the storm of lead and iron."[161]

Rather than pounding Atlantans into submission, the shelling solidified civilians' resolve. "We have had a considerable taste of the beauties of bombardment to-day," Sam Richards wrote during the second day of Union bombardment. He condemned the shelling as "a very barbarous mode of carrying on war, throwing shells among women and children,"[162] although Sherman contended that the city was unoccupied. Many residents had fled Atlanta in July, once it became clear that the northern army was approaching, but several thousand residents remained during the siege. The reliable and accurate Union intelligence network had probably informed Sherman of this fact. To eliminate any doubt, in August 1864 Hood dispatched messages under a flag of truce, making it clear that civilians still inhabited the city.[163] A *Mobile News* reporter described the chaos in Atlanta as residents fled. Wagons, loaded with furniture and possessions, "crowd every street." "Every train of [railroad] cars" was "loaded to its utmost capacity."[164]

Some historians have described the bombardment of late July and early August as "light." And the estimated number of deaths resulting from Yankee artillery fire would seem to bear this out. Observers wildly exaggerated casualties and carnage from the bombardment. In his careful analysis, Stephen Davis concludes that only about twenty civilians were killed and two hundred wounded.[165] Nonetheless, with time, the perceived cruelty and brutality of the Yankee bombardment loomed large in the psyche of Atlanta whites. Many saw Sherman's Atlanta Campaign as a ruthless, vindictive effort to punish defenseless civilians, with a devastating impact on the social order. The bombardment of Atlanta marked the beginning of Sherman's reputation as a cruel invader, a reputation that became firmly established after his March to the Sea. Despite the relatively low number of civilian deaths in Atlanta, no doubt many survivors were traumatized. The significant psychological trauma that occurred perhaps approximates the modern definition of post–traumatic stress disorder (PTSD). For many years afterward, white Atlantans' views of the northern invasion and occupation were shaped by this experience.[166]

DURING THE LAST WEEK OF AUGUST 1864, Sherman began a flanking maneuver, in which he moved six of his seven infantry corps—sixty thousand men—to a position sixteen miles south of the city between Rough and Ready and Jonesborough. Hood's unsuccessful assaults earlier had exposed the Confederate defenses, creating an opportunity for the Yankees. Sherman's main objective was to destroy the Macon & Western, the only remaining rail link that extended south out of Atlanta. In a battle on August 31, the northern forces succeeded in capturing the railroad.[167] Once this last connection was closed, Atlanta's fate was sealed, and Confederate forces withdrew from the city on September 1, 1864.

Not fully aware of their disastrous loss at Jonesborough, some Atlantans and rebel soldiers believed that the Confederates had carried the day. The Yankees "have all retreated from the immediate front of Atlanta," wrote a soldier from Louisville, Georgia.[168] But Hood's sudden withdrawal then caused a panic; confusion reigned. Streets were clogged with wagons, and looters ranged throughout the city, with stragglers and desperados plundering stores and homes. In July, the Confederate command had shipped out much of the capacity of Atlanta's war production. Now that Atlanta was defeated the rebels took steps to ensure that the city's remaining vital resources would not fall into enemy hands. A thousand bales of cotton held in the southern suburbs were torched, along with the city's magazines and siege guns. Rebel authorities sent four trains with a total of eighty-three railroad cars that were filled with ammunition on the Augusta Railroad about a mile from downtown Atlanta. The engines were separated and were then crashed into each other, while soldiers exploded the ammunition on the cars. The explosions made the earth tremble, with wood and iron fragments flying in every direction and the ground blackened for hundreds of yards.[169]

Maj. Gen. Henry Slocum had been left in command of the twelve-thousand-man Twentieth Corps on Atlanta's northern front, while the rest of Sherman's corps moved to the southwest to flank the Confederates. Slocum's troops, hearing explosions inside Atlanta, reported—as did Union troops southwest of the city—that the Confederate troops had withdrawn from Atlanta.[170] On the morning of September 2, Slocum dispatched three divisions to probe Confederate lines. Near East Point, on the northwest side of Atlanta, they encountered abandoned rebel fortifications, some half finished.[171]

Col. John Coburn's Second Brigade, of the Third Division, was the one of the first units that reached the city. He was met by Mayor James Calhoun, who offered surrender. Meanwhile, detachments from Gen. John W. Geary's division simultaneously entered with forces under the command of Gen. William J. Wood. The 2nd Massachusetts marched into the city with a band and military parade. Locals looked on "sullenly" or "peered timidly from behind blinds." Gen. George Stoneman, who arrived behind the advancing troops, took formal possession of city. The northern invaders hoisted the Stars and Stripes above the city hall. When northern troops asked what the gawking civilians had had to eat lately, one of them wrote that they replied: "30 pound parrott shells."[172]

The conquest of Atlanta meant, of course, liberation for the enslaved population. A few days after Sherman entered the city, Sam Richards complained about the "impudent airs the negroes put on, and their indifference to the wants of their former masters." The Yankees had insisted that the slaves be freed. "Our negro property," Richards lamented, "has all vanished into air." It was shocking to Richards how quickly slaves fled their former masters.[173]

Sherman did not enter Atlanta until the morning of September 3, quietly arriving from the southwest. Atlantans watched him, according to one account, "eager to catch a glance of the man whose name had now become so famous." One black man exclaimed: "I just wanted to see de man what made old massa run."[174] Atlanta, Sherman telegraphed to Gen. Henry W. Halleck, "is ours, and fairly won." He would later proudly report to Grant on September 6 that he was "feeding high on the corn-fields of the Confederacy."[175]

Atlanta's surrender on September 2, 1864, came after what a *Chicago Tribune* correspondent called "four long, wearisome, sleepless months."[176] The campaign, according to one observer, involved "continual fighting and incessant and exhausting marching," surpassing any "conception of man's capability of endurance."[177] "Our poor fellows," wrote a Yankee soldier near the end of the Atlanta Campaign, were "nearly worn out," since they had been "constantly on duty for 112 days, and a great deal of that time under fire, and when not under fire they were digging."[178] "The untold labor they have done is herculean," Sherman wrote in September 1864, "and if you ever pass our route you will say honestly that we have achieved success by industry and courage."[179] This great army overcame "earthenworks and mountains, and rivers and forest wilds," and now no longer feared anything else.[180]

GRANT CALLED THE ATLANTA CAMPAIGN the "most gigantic undertaking given to any general in the war."[181] Although Sherman failed to destroy the Confederate army, the fall of Atlanta constituted one of the Civil War's greatest Union victories. Atlanta's surrender dealt a blow to southern fortunes, bolstering Union morale and greatly aiding Lincoln's standing in public opinion on the eve of the presidential election in November 1864. For white southerners, the experiences of Sherman's Atlanta Campaign and his March to the Sea were especially traumatic. The invaders of southern soil were regarded as mortal enemies. A Confederate soldier remembered seeing his first dead body on a battlefield. "The man was an invader," he recalled, "and in my eyes deserved an invader's doom." Not disturbed by the sight of the death of his enemy, the soldier later remembered that "war has ever been concrete to me from that time on." Quoting a Greek poet, he remarked that "A sweet thing is war to those that have tried it."[182]

Invasion brought destruction to Atlanta as it did to other cities in the South. Although it is tempting to agree with Don H. Doyle's conclusion that the war treated Atlanta "with greater fury" than it treated "any other southern city—perhaps more than any American city ever,"[183] the shelling of Atlanta was perhaps no worse than the destruction in other besieged communities, such as Vicksburg, Charleston, Petersburg, and Fredericksburg. Although white Atlantans' memories of wartime destruction were selective and were colored by their own experiences, these memories played a critical role in forming their later attitudes.

White Atlantans today think of Sherman's invasion as an event that helped to identify their city's particular position in the Confederacy. Without question, memories of Atlanta's wartime destruction shaped postwar Atlanta's definition of itself. At the same time, destruction wiped away the old Atlanta. Already an economically dynamic, if socially unstable, community before the war—a place dominated by outsiders and newcomers—Atlanta after the war charted out the South's remaking of itself in the wake of defeat. Out of their wartime trauma, white Atlantans remade their memories in constructing a future that included economic rejuvenation and renewal.

Ocean of Ruins

Destruction and Rebirth

Sherman's conquest of Atlanta occupies a conspicuous place in the popular and scholarly understanding of the Civil War. Narratives of the Atlanta Campaign have influenced American ideas of the ways in which warfare affects civilians and have figured in the construction of both white and African American memories of the Civil War and of the southern economic rejuvenation that followed it. In many respects, the postwar narrative of the war's meaning in the South was white-dominated, a narrative that drowned out but did not entirely eliminate alternative narratives. Their version of the past unified whites, overcoming their social divisions and conflicts, in the forging of a new social compact. Atlanta figured prominently in how white southerners understood the war in large part because of the fact that the city was invaded and destroyed. Destruction, as a number of historians have pointed out, became a prevailing theme in discussions of the significance of the Civil War.[1]

Antebellum business leaders were well aware of the critical importance of railroads and other forms of transportation to hinterland trade, and, already possessing a community of northern transplants, avidly sought outside investment.[2] Subscribing to a culture of free-labor capitalism, Atlanta capitalists oversaw a smooth transition to a postwar economic order. But the particular characteristics of Atlanta's wartime destruction shaped how city boosters regarded economic and business development. Destruction provided an opportunity to start afresh, with a new industrial infrastructure and, more importantly, a new ideological framework that favored capitalist growth. As was true in post-1945 western Europe and Japan, Atlanta's wartime destruction provided a new basis for understanding and explaining economic development. Soon after the war, white Atlantans eagerly promoted economic expansion, and their recovery from wartime devastation became a point of pride, almost a marketing brand. Moving on from their anger and their sense of victimization, entrepreneurial Atlantans began to see the destruction as a symbol of how far they had come in constructing a post–Civil War South, a South in which their city held a special economic position.

Although Atlantans tended to remember the Civil War by focusing on its devastation, there remained a sharp divergence of perception between white and black Atlantans about the meaning of the changes brought by the war. White residents were frequently reminded that the traumatic invasion and defeat had brought the end of the slaveholding system and the collapse of the old social order. In the ensuing vacuum, the insistent reestablishment of the notion of racial supremacy came to define the rebuilding and refashioning of the South. The altered racial landscape required whites to rethink a host of old assumptions, among which sorting out the racial order took priority over everything else. The postwar South was consumed by a struggle among its black and white populations over the meaning of the war itself and what the postwar world would become. In this struggle, the issue of race loomed large.

ON SEPTEMBER 11, 1864, about a week after he occupied Atlanta, Sherman ordered the expulsion of 1,649 residents, who constituted a little less than a tenth of the city's original population. Determined that Atlanta not regain its strategic position, Sherman declared Atlanta a military camp that would be "exclusively required for warlike purposes." He further ordered his quartermaster to seize all buildings and either occupy them or tear them down for lumber to house his army.[3] Although Sherman later revised his order and permitted about fifty families to remain, most of them African Americans and Unionists, at first Sherman ordered that Union families move north and that "secesh families move on," presumably south. All of Atlanta's cotton, he declared, was "tainted with treason, and no title in it will be respected." Other agricultural stores, equipment, and war matériel were also subject to seizure.[4] Sherman informed Army Chief of Staff Henry W. Halleck of this decision, which enjoyed Halleck's full support. If Atlantans "raise a howl against my barbarity and cruelty," Sherman wrote Halleck, "I will answer that war is war, and not popularity-seeking. If they want peace they and their relatives must stop war."[5]

White southerners condemned Sherman's decision to deport city residents as prime evidence of the barbarous way he waged war. Much of this condemnation reflected what Virginian and Confederate veteran Basil L. Gildersleeve later called a tendency on the part of both sides—especially civilians—to depict each other in the "blackest colors." Even "ordinary" killing, he wrote, was deemed criminal if done by a "ruthless rebel or a ruffianly invader."[6] Along with former Confederates' intense focus on the civilian depredations wrought by the northern invaders, their depiction of Sherman as a modern Attila formed a theme in the popular understanding of the war. Sherman's war policies, according to this view, provided prima facie evidence of his unjust and perhaps unlawful war against civilians. Some historians of the campaign agree with this assessment. Yet, by the late stages of the war, as Mark Neely has recently argued, there was nothing exceptional in Sherman's policies compared with those of other Union generals.[7] Union sieges commonly employed artillery against towns and cities, such as Vicksburg, Charleston, and Fredericksburg. Northern commanders, including Sherman, held the Confederate military responsible for the safety of civilians if they permitted them to remain in occupied areas. The bombardment of Atlanta, Yankee military leaders believed, involved a legitimate use of military power. From Sherman's perspective, the southerners had started the war; Atlanta had profited from it. Now the fruits of these actions would have to be reaped.[8]

His military superiors felt that the general was operating legally in that he was protecting the security of his armies in a hostile environment far removed from secure supply lines and exposed to guerrilla attacks. In this sense, the rules of war as practiced in the 1860s fully justified Sherman's decision to expel Atlanta's civilian population. Sherman realized that if he were obliged to support a civilian population in the city, it would drain him of vital resources. His goal, ultimately, was to remove the Confederate military asset represented by Atlanta. On September 6, 1864, Sherman informed Hood of his decision to evacuate the city. Sherman offered to provide food and transportation out of the city by rail to Union supporters and to provide transportation by wagon for Confederate supporters to enable them to reach rebel lines. He promised that the civilians' removal would "be made with as little discomfort as possible," and he promised to transport their "moveable effects"; slaves could accompany their masters as long as they were not compelled to do so.[9] Sherman's letter to Hood was followed, a day later, by his orders to the Union armies. Atlanta was emptied of all civilians except those working for the Yankee cause. The Union quartermaster was empowered to seize all buildings and staples such as cotton and tobacco. Engineers were also authorized to "set apart for destruction" any buildings or homes that they needed to in order to fortify the city's defenses.[10]

Whether justifiable or not, Sherman's policy regarding Atlanta's civilians attracted bitter criticism. Hood agreed to comply with Sherman's logistical

Expulsion of civilians, *Harper's Weekly*, September 1864
(courtesy of the Atlanta History Center)

demands, but he attacked the morality of his policy, which, in a letter to Sherman, he described as transcending "in studied and ingenious cruelty, all acts ever before brought to my attention in the dark history of war."[11] More correspondence followed. Sherman pointed out that although both sides had removed civilian populations when it suited them and arbitrarily burned and destroyed homes, he had never accused Confederate commanders of "heartless cruelty." Hood exposed Atlanta's civilians to the Union bombardment, Sherman claimed, by defending a line that was too close to town. Sherman's removal of civilians from Atlanta was intended to protect them from "scenes that women and children should not be exposed to." It was Hood's Confederacy that had "plunged a nation into war—dark and cruel war." In due course, Sherman wrote, God would judge whether it was "more humane to fight with a town full of women and the families of a brave people at our back, or to remove them in time to places of safety among their own friends and people."[12]

Sherman and Hood offer a study in contrasting personalities whose approach to warfare fundamentally differed. While Hood embodied an older, more genteel ethos according to which war should be viewed as a conflict between armies, Sherman advanced a different, more "modern" perspective. Responding on September 12 to Sherman's claim that his actions were humane, Hood insisted that Sherman was practicing unusually cruel warfare. Confederate forces, Hood claimed, had never expelled civilians from their homes: Sherman's bombardment of Atlanta was wrong because he had provided no advance notice and ignored the safety of its civilians. Yankee artillerists were too skilled to miss their targets so often as was claimed. Rather than having provoked the Civil War, the South was defending itself against "insolent intruders" in order to resist their "claims to dominion over masters, slaves, and Indians." Sherman, Hood continued, expelled Atlanta's citizens and then added insult to injury by asserting that he had helped the "defenseless." Invading the South in order to subjugate "free white men, women, and children," Hood told Sherman, you made "negroes your allies," and tried "to place over us an inferior race, which we have raised from barbarism to its present position." Better, Hood said, for Confederates to fight to the death, even to "die a thousand deaths," than to "submit to live under you or your Government and your negro allies!"[13]

In response, Sherman declared that he had provided for civilians' departure with "liberality and fairness," care having been taken to prevent the suffering of women and children. But in a letter to Halleck he revealed that his true reason for the deportation was to confiscate all of Atlanta's houses for military purposes; to reduce the lines of defense to the city limits, rather than be forced to extend them out to the "vast suburbs"; and to escape the necessity of having to feed a destitute population. If the city were inhabited with a civilian population it would consume scarce military resources. In the end, it made "no difference whether it pleases General Hood and *his* people or not."[14]

On September 12, Mayor Calhoun and other city fathers wrote to Sherman to ask for a modification of Sherman's deportation orders because "helpless people" would be "driven from their homes to wander [as] strangers and outcasts, and exiles, to subsist on charity." Unsympathetic, Sherman reasserted the military necessity of the civilian expulsion from Atlanta. His forcing the civilians out was not "designed to meet the humanities of the case, but to prepare for the future struggles in which millions of good people outside of Atlanta have a deep interest." Both the national interest and the principle of military necessity required that "we must stop the war that now desolates our once happy and favored country." In the end, war was not a pretty business: "War is cruelty, and you cannot refine it; and those who brought war into our country deserve all the curses and maledictions a people can pour out." "You might as well appeal against the thunder-storm as against these terrible hardships of war."[15]

Though unfairly portraying Sherman as a war criminal, Hood had exposed a truth about his policies: he was little concerned with the welfare of Atlanta citizens. His main—perhaps his only—objective was to win the war. But as with other of his wartime actions, Sherman's expulsion of civilians was fully endorsed by precedent. In August 1863 Brig. Gen. Thomas Ewing had issued his General Order No. 11, which expelled all the citizens of four western Missouri counties in an action that one historian describes as "the most drastic and repressive military measure directed against civilians by the Union Army during the Civil War." Over time, however, it was Sherman who became the most vilified of the Yankees in the memories of southern whites.[16]

The deportation of civilians from Atlanta was, in truth, smaller than later representations of it suggest. In the end, between September 12 and September 21, 1864, only 709 adults, 867 children, and 79 slaves were deported from the city by rail and wagon to the rebel lines at Lovejoy's Station and from there on to Macon. African Americans—along with some loyal white families—were permitted to remain in the city if they refused to travel with their masters. Still another group of Atlantans, those deemed Unionist, left the city and went north.[17]

After the war, acutely sensitive about his image as a rampaging vandal, Sherman offered an explanation of his actions. In his memoirs, he deplored the depredations and destruction of civilian property as the acts of "bummers" operating on the fringes.[18] Rather than having deliberately destroyed Atlanta when he left in November 1864, Sherman claimed that he had intended only to burn the public buildings in the city center.[19]

Most white southerners came to disagree with Sherman's assessment. As Carol Reardon shows, they equated Sherman's invasion of the southern heartland with the war's worst devastation—and regarded it as representing Sherman's general disregard for civilians.[20] In late 1864, the *Atlanta Daily Intelligencer* described Sherman's campaign as an invasion by "barbarian hordes, under the leadership of their barbarous chief." "No vandal Captain of ancient times left a blacker, or more cruel record for the historian to indite, than he has done." Atlanta, the *Intelligencer* continued, had become the "most flourishing interior city of the South," a city that, by 1861, "bade fair to rival in population and wealth, as it did in commercial enterprise, any city in the Southern Confederacy." Sherman had destroyed this place in "one vast sheet of fire, the flames rising so as to light the country round for miles and miles" and then "ingloriously took up his march to the sea."[21]

Subsequent accounts by white southerners took a similar tone. In 1880, John Bell Hood wrote in his memoirs that Sherman's actions had violated the laws of war. Hood made a legal distinction: Atlanta, he said, was not a "regularly fortified city," but rather was defended during the war by "temporary breastworks," as opposed to permanent fortifications, which were constructed of iron and stone. Not having been a regularly fortified town, Atlanta was not lawfully subject to bombardment, and no extreme war necessities justified Sherman's all-out bombardment. His expulsion order also violated the laws of war, according to Hood. Atlanta civilians "gave no such cause for action on the part of General Sherman," he contended, "nor was the safety of the Federal Army in any manner involved."[22]

Hood's interpretation of Sherman came to prevail. In his *Rise and Fall of the Confederate Government* (1881), former Confederate president Jefferson Davis singled out Sherman's expulsion order for special censure. "Since Alva's atrocious cruelties to the non-combatant population of the Low Countries in the sixteenth century," Davis wrote, "the history of war records no instance of such barbarous cruelty as that which this order was designed to perpetrate." Women and children were expelled from their homes in a military order characterized by its "cowardly dishonesty." The ensuing devastation of the city "was in perfect harmony with the temper and spirit of the order." Davis described the burning of Atlanta as a wanton destruction of noncombatants' property, an act that was "as relentless as savage instincts could suggest."[23]

With most of its residents expelled, occupied Atlanta was stripped of its personality. It had become a city, wrote one newspaper correspondent visiting in October 1864, in which "a military man holds it; a military people rejoice over its capture, and internally, as well as externally, it is provokingly military." In every direction the observer looked, blue-clad soldiers were to be seen, and everywhere, "and in every conceivable habit and posture, you will see the national uniform here displayed as a uniform *nationale!*" Houses, emptied of civilians, were occupied by officers with the "broad straps and bright stripes of Uncle Sam's ponderous staff, looking their bluest." Local hotels overflowed with people in blue uniforms, while the city's Southern Medical College had become a "magnificent Northern Hospital." Atlanta's occupied condition was "more than enough to give any Southerner the blues." The occupiers continued to wreak havoc, and the city was "sadly marred by the chimneys of once happy homes, now standing alone, and

without aught else to mark the ruin and desolation of war's cruel hand."
With half the city destroyed, ruins "strew the landscape for miles around, . . .
cover[ing] the heads of the loyal soldiers of Sherman's hosts, and as often,
perhaps, interposing between the ground and their feet."[24]

In his Atlanta Campaign, Sherman avidly pursued military objectives that
led to the bombardment of the city and the expulsion of its citizens. In terms
of the military standards of the time, these two decisions, combined with
his fabled March to the Sea, were legitimate. It is perhaps unjust that his
actions earned him the enmity of white southerners for many generations.
But whether Sherman was militarily justified in waging his sort of warfare
is of less importance than the fact that he became a symbol for invasion and
destructiveness. The truth lies less in the objective reality than it does in
white Atlantans' perceptions. For there is little question that white Atlantans
rallied around the notion that Sherman's campaign meant invasion, and that
invasion meant destruction.

ON NOVEMBER 15, 1864, as the 33rd Massachusetts's band played "John
Brown's Body," Atlanta's northern occupiers left the city, torching the downtown and singing as they marched out of town. They left the city in ruins.
According to one estimate, during their departure the Yankees left four
to five thousand buildings destroyed, with only about four hundred un-
affected.[25] Describing the feelings he had had as he heard the music and
watched the city burn, a Vermonter later declared, "I have never heard that
noble anthem when it was so grand, so solemn, so inspiring." The heavens
were "one expanse of lurid fire."[26] Atlanta's burning, commented Sherman's
aide Henry Hitchcock, presented the "grandest and most awful scene." He
described "great tongues of flame, then huge waves of fire" shooting up beyond rooftops, while collapsing walls sent up cinders. From Union headquarters, Hitchcock watched "immense and raging fires, lighting up the
whole heavens." "The whole region for miles was lighted up with a strange
and indescribable glare," an Ohio soldier remembered. "Atlanta on fire—Ah
cruel war," echoed another Buckeye, "and cruel it has become."[27]

A recent study by Paul F. Paskoff shows that the extent of physical destruction caused by Yankee invasion has been exaggerated and, in particular, probably did not retard subsequent southern economic progress. Yet
Paskoff also points out the extensiveness of destruction in eleven locales
in the South, including Atlanta. Urban economic and political centers had
become military targets, and once besieged, they were more likely to suffer extensive physical damage. Atlanta, along with cities such as Richmond,

Charleston, and Columbia, stood as an example of war's devastating impact on the South.[28]

After Sherman left the city, Atlanta came to represent Confederate defeat and its consequences. Northern visitors portrayed Atlanta's ruin as a just retribution. The "Babylon of the South" had fallen, wrote a reporter, with its deserted "splendid houses and broad streets." Its future seemed clear: "The streets will soon be overgrown with grass, and sportive children will play through them and furtively peep through the piles of brick and the ruins of factories, foundries, and railroad depots, peopling the deserted halls with ghastly legends." Atlanta was nothing more than "a deserted city of ruins" whose "growing grandeur and loveliness" had disappeared. The city stood as a "lesson to rebels of the fruits of their wicked efforts to rend their country in pieces."[29]

The Union conquest of Atlanta, their two-month occupation, and their fiery departure all resulted in physical destruction. As the lifeline of Atlanta's economic existence, the railroad infrastructure had become a primary target. As they moved southward from east Tennessee toward Atlanta, Sherman's commanders ravaged the Western & Atlantic Railroad lines.[30] Sherman encouraged the devastation, giving specific instructions about how the rail lines should be destroyed. "Let details of men . . . begin at your very front and break up and destroy the railroad absolutely back to and including Decatur," Sherman wrote to Gen. John A. Logan in July 1864.[31] "I want you to do the best job of railroad destruction on record," he told another general. Sherman instructed that the cuts in the railroad lines be filled with logs and trees and then covered with dirt so that "we may rest perfectly satisfied as regards the use of this railroad during the remainder of this campaign."[32]

Observers frequently commented on how much havoc the Atlanta Campaign wreaked on the landscape. When Sherman's massive army left Atlanta, wrote memoirist F. Y. Hedley, there were few Union soldiers remaining between Atlanta and Chattanooga, where months before that area had been "alive with masses of fiercely contending human beings." After the "demon of destruction" had passed by, the landscape stood "still and desolate." Although most of the graves of the dead remained unmarked, noted Hedley, trees destroyed by cannon, along with destroyed caissons, testified to the "fearful struggle."[33]

When he arrived in Atlanta on September 11, 1864, Union photographer George N. Barnard visually documented the effects of Sherman's campaign. For the next month, he photographed empty battlefields, fortifications, denuded forests, barren fields, pockmarked houses, and the burned ruins of

Environmental destruction on the battlefield (courtesy of the Library of Congress)

downtown Atlanta. Barnard's images show how the invaders and defenders reshaped the forests, valleys, and farms that stood in the path of war. The city "suffered much from our projectiles," wrote a journalist who had accompanied Sherman, as a result of which bombardment many houses were burned out and destroyed. "Almost every house in the centre and the north and west ends of the town bear testimony to the skill and execution of our gunnery."[34] A reporter who visited the route of Sherman's invasion a year after his campaign noted that a stretch of 136 miles between Chattanooga and Atlanta was marked by ruined buildings and destroyed property, showing "what a desolation war is."[35]

Strolling through central Atlanta a year after its destruction, a reporter described what remained. The city hall had survived. The large, square, two-story brick building was occupied by troops and served as a jail, its ground windows barricaded with iron rails. Nearby, though located in the areas of the worst bombardment, five churches had fared well; only the Episcopal church had burned. The buildings around these churches bore the marks of war. City residents were still in shock, according to this account, "too exhausted or paralyzed . . . to have attempted anything toward rebuilding." One brick building was "covered rudely with boards," yet a barber ran his business there. With some exceptions, there was "nothing in Atlanta that deserves the name of business."[36]

Eyewitnesses' accounts agree that the devastation was widespread. A Richmond newspaper correspondent wrote in August 1864 that the Western & Atlantic route between Dalton and Atlanta had been devastated for four miles on either side.[37] The property of north Georgia was already completely destroyed, wrote a Wisconsin soldier in early June 1864; nothing could "escape the scrutiny of the boys." The country was "desolate" and "fearful."[38] "Our army is destroying all the Crops as we go along," wrote a soldier in the Ohio 94th Regiment.[39]

Both Union and Confederate armies were especially hard on forests. Both sides felled large numbers of trees to use for heat, light, housing, corduroy-road construction, and bridges. Denuding the north Georgia forests required large amounts of labor, most of which emancipated slaves accompanying Sherman's army supplied. On the Confederate side, armies of impressed slaves provided labor for arduous tasks. Both armies made heavy use of "pioneer corps" who did most of the heavy work of girdling and felling trees, a task with which slaves already had experience as plantation workers. Some of the remaining deforestation resulted from artillery fire; in fact, much of the war zone was denuded. Soldiers expressed mixed emotions about the environmental impact of war, as Megan Kate Nelson notes in her recent book. "Some soldiers and civilians expressed regret when they viewed the ruined forests around them," she writes, "but most observers admired the ways that war's technologies both destroyed landscapes and created new ones."[40]

An Atlantan who returned during the fall of 1864 described an altered landscape. Approaching the city from Kennesaw Mountain, twenty-five miles away, he was presented with a vista unobstructed by the dense forest that had once blocked the view. For many miles around the city, "scarcely a tree is standing, and near and within a few miles of the city *fire and the axe* have destroyed the habitations of the rich and the poor, and laid waste the ground." Animal carcasses lay everywhere, "while the stench . . . filled the air, producing a loathing on the part of all who ventured into the city, unutterably disgusting." On downtown streets lay the charred remains of railroad ties that were "so numerous and spread out to such an extent, as to remind one of the ocean when the waves are raised by a brisk wind." This was "an ocean of ruins."[41]

Without question, Atlanta suffered extensive environmental devastation that went beyond the destruction of buildings. A newspaperman writing in the aftermath of the Atlanta bombardment reported that the city was now

Downtown Atlanta after Sherman's departure, November 1864
(courtesy of the Library of Congress)

characterized by "mangled shade trees, distraught flower beds, [and] topsy-turvy summer houses."[42] The recent devastation contrasted with the natural beauty that had once characterized Atlanta. A correspondent for the *New York Tribune* described postwar Atlanta. Native growth included small oak and pines, while Atlanta arborists, in the "hand of culture," had planted china trees, grape, myrtle, roses, laurels, holly, honeysuckle, and plum, along with other shrubs. "The salubrity of the climate and the purity of its waters," the observer commented, together with its position on the "dividing ridge between the Gulf and the Atlantic," all made Atlanta's natural landscape appealing. It was a place where the "figs are now ripe and hanging on the trees, this being the second crop," and where "grapes grow in abundance, and wine is made of a delicious flavor." This natural abundance stood in contrast to the human destruction: everywhere were makeshift bomb shelters, homes disfigured with "marks of our shot, splintered cornices and doorways, shattered rails and chimneys, perforated walls and torn fences," all the result of Union cannon "whirling night and day over the doomed place."[43]

An acknowledgment of the extent of the wartime destruction came seven years after Sherman left the city, in 1871, when Congress established the Southern Claims Commission in order to compensate Unionists for property lost to the Yankee army. The commission denied most claims by applying exacting standards. In order to receive compensation, the claimants had to document both their lost property and their loyalty to the Union during the war—a difficult combination. Even though most claimants probably exaggerated their cases, collectively their claims suggest the prevalence of the damage.[44]

Many claimants described how the northern army tore down their houses—a common practice during Sherman's invasion of the South—in order to use the lumber for the army's housing or for fortifications. Elizabeth Grubb worked as a seamstress in Atlanta for most of the war. Expelled from the city in October 1864, she fled south to Thomaston, Georgia. Later, Grubb maintained that Union soldiers tore down her four-bedroom house, well house, and a picket fence surrounding the yard, worth $1,500 altogether. An eyewitness testified that soldiers, under the command of a Union officer, tore down the house, loading the lumber into wagons. The "soldiers just tore down the house and went to hauling it off." There were a "good many houses torn down in the city by the soldiers at that time." The claims commissioners rejected Grubb's claim, citing a lack of evidence to prove her Unionism, except, after the fact, "to regret the war."[45]

Among the large number of rejected claims was that of the petitioner Henry Holcomb, who, though he served during the war as the Atlanta City Council's clerk, as the city tax collector, and as city treasurer, claimed that he had supported the Union and been "cursed and abused" for his sentiments. During the siege, the Confederates seized about sixty acres of his timber from land just north of the city. When the Union army occupied Atlanta, they tore down Holcomb's house, cut down seventeen acres of timber, and erected a fort on his property. In April 1875, the claims commissioners rejected Holcomb's case, noting that he had occupied offices during the war that "no man loyal to the Federal government would have been permitted to hold."[46]

Other claims involved Union foraging and their ravaging of local agriculture. James Lamar, a millwright who owned a thirty-acre farm about eight miles north of Atlanta, was, he claimed, "an outspoken & well known friend of the Union cause." Lamar had harbored a Yankee spy, while his brother and two nephews had served on the northern side. Confederate authorities arrested him in the fall of 1862. He served forty-one days in jail in Marietta and was moved to Atlanta after a mob threatened to lynch him. In June 1871, Lamar petitioned the claims commission for compensation of $662. He asserted that on July 20, 1864, soldiers hauled off 350 bushels of corn, 50 bushels of potatoes, fodder, peas, and a bay mare from his farm. So large were these amounts that it took the troops about two days to complete the work. In a rare example of generosity, the claims commissioners declared in December 1878, "We rarely meet with a case as wretchedly proved as this." They awarded Lamar $482.50 in compensation.[47]

ATLANTA RESIDENTS RETURNING HOME IN LATE 1864 found a city that had become a hollow shell, with the surrounding countryside in a chaotic condition. A Confederate official who had examined the damage on the Western & Atlantic line reported devastation, while also noting the "utter want of law and order" in north Georgia. Residents, he wrote, could not "keep any kind of animals with safety, for farming purposes." Sadly, "every species of this property" was taken "indiscriminately, as fast as they are brought to the different counties, and unless some protection is guaranteed, the planting interest will suffer, and a great many farmers will not attempt to raise any surplus produce."[48]

Lacking a functioning government or post office, and almost devoid of stores and businesses, Atlanta was in no better condition than was the countryside.[49] Scarcely a house in the city was undamaged, according to one account, most of them having torn roofs and scarred walls.[50] "How this pretty city has suffered by the bombardment," lamented a newspaper reporter.[51] Cannon shot and unexploded ammunition lay everywhere in the cellars and streets. Garbage blocked the streets.[52] "Destruction's devastating doom" marked this "once flourishing city, the pride and boast of Georgia." Inside the destroyed city were scenes of "smoked and blackened ruins." Observers were "amazed and appalled at the savage ferocity of our yankee foes, and at the *fiery* vengeance" that they inflicted on the city.[53]

William Wallace, a northern soldier who toured the city after Sherman's troops entered Atlanta, described what he found. Nearly every house had shell holes; some were "completely riddled." The city possessed very few signs of life, most of its inhabitants having left it. Near the railroad yard were four large trains of cars and five locomotives, all destroyed, with pieces of the cars strewn on the track. Wallace described the melted grape and canister that lay on the tracks "like wheat about a threshing machine." Nothing remained of a rolling mill but the chimney. A pond in the city was filled with dumped ammunition, still in the boxes. Wandering farther downtown, Wallace found deserted storefronts, the stores emptied of their goods. Fancy garden fences throughout the city had been torn down for lumber. "Every where the beholder turns his face . . . it looks a waste place."[54] Atlanta, wrote another soldier, was "tore to pieces" after the shelling. What had been "quite a business place" now lay in ruins.[55] There was "not hardly a House in the City," declared a New York soldier, but "What is Full of Shell or Bullet holes."[56]

Whitelaw Reid, editor of the *New York Tribune*, completed a postwar tour of the South in late 1865 that included a stop in Atlanta. In his well-known account, he wrote that Sherman's mark on Atlanta was "still written too plainly to be soon effaced, in gaping windows and roofless houses, heaps of ruins on the principal corners and traces of unsparing destruction everywhere." Between Dalton and Atlanta—an area known as the "track of the destroyer," where fighting had been fiercest—"solitary chimneys and the debris of burnt buildings everywhere tell the old, old story." "Such waste and destruction all about us," Reid declared.[57] In the summer of 1867, a correspondent for the *Boston Daily Advertiser* followed the route that had been taken by Sherman's army into northern Georgia, going southward from Tennessee along the Western & Atlantic Railroad. The traveler described "a continuous swell of graves, rifle pits and more imposing breastworks." The landscape possessed a "weird and Dantesque ugliness that was almost overpowering." Atlanta itself was "a mass of ruins, rugged contrabands, and the most squalid looking herd of 'poor whites' it has ever been my fate to look at or listen to."[58]

Travelers to Atlanta after Sherman's departure described an experience that sounds much like the modern psychological diagnosis of PTSD. Inside the city limits, a Georgian encountered only ruins, which the "dead seemed to inhabit as with ghosts the streets."[59] Approaching the city from the South, another resident who was returning to the city described the Confederate breastworks and rifle pits, along with the torn shrubbery, scarred trees, and "hastily constructed" graves for the dead on both sides. Outside the city, "huge fortifications of red dirt" wound "snakelike around its whole extent." Animal carcasses lay everywhere. There was an "absence of all life in the town itself." The destroyed cityscape was "appalling," according to this observer. Atlanta now stood "like a grinning skull on the wayside; a fragmentary memento of a former life and greatness."[60]

The destruction of the battle was compounded by Sherman's two-month occupation. Businesses on Peachtree Street, Atlanta's main avenue, wrote a visitor in early 1865, were left "all a heap of ruins which the torch of the enemy has occasioned." The downtown business center lay in ruins. On Marietta Street, which ran parallel with the Western & Atlantic Railroad, all the businesses for a mile and a quarter had been obliterated. Downtown churches also suffered. The Presbyterian Church was shelled while it housed refugees trying to escape the bombardment. The Wesleyan Chapel, farther up the street, was still standing, though "horribly desecrated" and "left more in the condition of a hog pen than the house of God." Near the suburbs of the city, the occupiers had torn down houses for their lumber. The "fiends assigned to the work," wrote the reporter, "did their duty recklessly. Nothing but charred ruins are left to mark the spots of business houses . . . [and] private residences." Those familiar with Atlanta, he wrote, "will know what amount of destruction" had occurred. "The ruin is complete," the observer concluded.[61]

Looters arrived soon after Sherman's departure. A visitor in late November 1864 described wagons loaded with booty. People from surrounding areas engaged in "remorseless plunder." Littered with two to three thousand carcasses of animals, Atlanta felt like a morgue. Horses were turned loose in the city cemetery, where they grazed on grass and shrubbery. Northern soldiers, according to this account, had desecrated the graves, and the "crowning act of all their wickedness and villainy was committed by our ungodly foe in removing the dead from the vaults in the cemetery, and robbing the coffins of the silver name plates and tippings."[62]

When a northerner visited the city a year after Sherman's siege, he observed that the cityscape was "painfully saddening." "Wreck and ruin before and behind you," he wrote, "wreck and ruin on every side." The Confederates' burning of the stockpiles of war matériel before the Union occupation in September 1864, followed by the torching of the city by Sherman's troops in November, incapacitated the city. According to some estimates, half of Atlanta's buildings were in ruins by the time Union troops left, with as many as 5,000 homes, or 90 percent, having been destroyed within the city limits. Two-thirds of the city's shade trees were felled. The Atlanta suburbs, according to one account, "present to the eye one vast, naked, ruined, deserted camp."[63] Sidney Andrews, who toured the South in late 1865, wrote about "thousands of masses of brick and mortar, thousands of pieces of charred timber, thousands of half-burned boards, thousands of scraps of tin roofing, thousands of car and engine bolts and bars, thousands of ruined articles of hardware, thousands upon thousands of tons of debris of all sorts and shapes." Andrews also mentioned that cannonballs and long shot were lying around the streets. A year after Sherman had left, many homes remained "shell-struck," and from the center of the city one could still see "a dozen or more forts, and many a hillside from which the timber was cut so that the enemy might not come upon the city unawares."[64]

In some respects, these accounts seem to resemble dramatic descriptions rather than reflect any historical reality. Yet the vivid imagery of the city's wartime travails became iconic for the Confederacy's collapse: Atlanta became identified as a city uniquely devastated by the war, a symbol of how the Confederacy itself was upended. Northerners saw Atlanta's demise as just retribution for the South's rebellion, while many African Americans regarded it as just in light of the collapse of the slave system. Many black residents greeted the invasion as an act of liberation, a military danger they willingly endured in exchange for witnessing the end of slavery. Many would eventually abandon their masters and follow the Union army in large numbers as it moved toward Atlanta and beyond.

Exempt from Sherman's expulsion order, black people experienced conflicting sensations of liberation and ruin as they struggled to survive an apocalypse that ended their bondage but destroyed their surroundings. In 1864, Polly and Henry Beedles, a free black couple in Atlanta, enthusiastically greeted the northern invaders. Henry "was always for the old Government, preferred it to the Confederacy," Polly subsequently told the Southern Claims Commission. "We did all we could for the Yankees." When Sherman's troops arrived, some of them camped near the cabin that the Beedleses constructed and owned. "We were glad to see them, and treated them well," Polly remembered, and they provided provisions for the soldiers. But the troops wanted more, and they confiscated the Beedleses' meager possessions: a horse, all their chickens, a pet pig, a washpot, and "everything else they could get." About a week after Sherman occupied Atlanta, soldiers appeared and tore down the Beedleses' home, their stable, and their well house, taking the lumber to assemble housing for the troops. Polly "begged them but they told me they would take it." Soon troops appeared with wagons and saws, ordering the Beedleses out of the house, and they "tore all the house down." Despite the Beedleses' appeals, they were made homeless. "They took everything we had," Polly remembered, "fence posts, . . . houses & all. They broke us up we had nothing to eat & no house left." The Beedleses moved to Chattanooga, where Polly worked for the Union army as a cook. Eleven years later, in December 1875, the Southern Claims Commission paid the Beedleses $848 in compensation for their wartime losses.[65]

IN EARLY DECEMBER 1864, Mayor Calhoun and other city stalwarts returned to Atlanta; on Christmas Day, the Rev. H. C. Hornady preached in the

First Baptist Church.[66] By early March 1865, businesses were operating out of temporary quarters. According to a newspaper report, lots for new business came into great demand, commanding high prices. What one historian calls a "new instant city" was reemerging.[67] By spring, deportees returned en masse. "Every train that arrived was crowded with those, who, after living for months among strangers," wrote an early Atlanta historian, "were again seeking the familiar haunts of home." As early as June 1865, the *Atlanta Daily Intelligencer* reported a brisk trade in rebuilt downtown stores; gold, silver, and greenbacks "seemed to be in everybody's hands." By summer 1865, Atlanta counted perhaps eight thousand inhabitants; a year later this had swelled to twenty thousand.[68] Meanwhile, the city became an important location for investors. Although returning residents found "footprints of ruin and the marks of destruction"—traces of the "heartless vandal" who had destroyed the city—its residents resolved that Atlanta "should yet arise from her ashes and her ruins, and even surpass everything she had been in the past."[69]

In May 1865, about a month after the Confederate surrender at Appomattox, Col. Beroth B. Eggleston led a force of about eighty Union cavalry to Atlanta, where he took possession of the city and raised the Stars and Stripes over the city hall. When Confederate president Jefferson Davis was captured on May 8, 1865, he was held briefly under Eggleston's command in Atlanta. The Union troops imposed a curfew, administered loyalty oaths, policed the unemployed freedpeople, and distributed food and supplies to needy residents. The *Atlanta Daily Intelligencer* praised Eggleston for maintaining order.[70] Although the Union colonel maintained command for only six weeks, the city was transformed into a garrison town with a long-term northern military presence.[71] "We have become an overpowered and an armless people," lamented the *Intelligencer*.[72]

Since the antebellum era, agents had submitted reports to the offices of R. G. Dun in New York City, which provided assessments of businesses and evaluations of their creditworthiness to potential lenders. The Dun reports document the gradual reawakening of business activity in postwar Atlanta. The postwar Dun reports from Atlanta, which began coming in again in October 1865, were grim, most of them noting businesses that had been physically destroyed or were otherwise out of business. The Civil War fell hard on people like George Johnston, an Irish immigrant who ran several small hotels during the late 1850s. In October 1865, the Dun agents described Johnston's business condition as "broke bad."[73]

The firms that survived the war and were most likely to be able to return to Atlanta were those that had profited during the war boom. Some small operators, like O. H. Jones, who ran a livery stable during the war and was characterized as an "honorable man & a keen shrewd trader," managed to keep their businesses going despite the wartime destruction.[74] Other firms that had been active during the antebellum era also rebounded after the war. In the late 1850s, two enterprising railroad conductors had founded Cox, Hill, & Co., a highly rated merchandising firm. Like other businesses, this firm, though badly hurt by the war, remained viable and competitive after 1865. The lingering effects of the war boom were an important factor explaining the survival of some businesses. Some Atlantans had made handsome fortunes during the war because of their close relationship with the Confederate government in the areas of supply and distribution. In the instance of Cox and Hill, the merchants emerged from the war "probably with more than before" because of profits from the Confederate quartermaster business. Somehow, they saved this capital, perhaps by investing in gold abroad. The most successful entrepreneurs were those who, despite the collapse of Confederate currency, possessed capital that they could plow back into their businesses after the war. During the anxiety-ridden months just after the war, when the survival of businesses was very tenuous, the agent wrote that Cox and Hill remained in "every way reliable."[75]

Other successful postwar businesses in Atlanta preserved wartime profits. Merchant Ormond McNaught enjoyed a prosperous stock business and was reported in December 1859 to have the "finest storehouse in the State." McNaught also suffered when the war came, but the firm possessed a crucial advantage: like many of the firms that ultimately survived, it accumulated capital during the war boom and presumably saved it in gold. Immediately after the war, McNaught's business was in healthy financial condition, according to Dun, because the merchant had worked for the Confederate quartermaster and "probably saved some." McNaught regained good credit and the blessing of the Dun agent. "I look on this as as strong a firm as any here," he wrote in February 1866.[76] Still another example of an Atlanta entrepreneur preserving resources and surviving the war was that of A. C. Wylie, a merchant who financed blockade-running and accumulated gold reserves. According to the Dun agent, Wylie "made a great deal" during the war but "lost as much" thereafter in cotton speculation. Even so, with a small amount of preserved capital, he was able by 1871 to establish one of the largest mercantile operations in Atlanta.[77]

The connections between pre- and postwar economic successes also appeared in the instance of George Washington Adair, an antebellum capitalist who expanded his business after the Confederate defeat. Though a

Unionist prior to 1861, Adair enthusiastically adopted the cause, editing the pro-Confederate *Southern Confederacy*. Late in the war, he demonstrated his rebel credentials by joining the cavalry, serving under the fabled Gen. Nathan Bedford Forrest. Adair became one of postwar Atlanta's most successful real estate entrepreneurs, but the foundation of his wealth lay earlier. A railroad conductor who first moved to Atlanta in 1854, Adair began a successful trading and auctioneering business. But the Dun agent also reported a business about which Adair subsequently said little—slave trading. In January 1857, he and his partner were described as "negro brokers" who were "keen & shrewd traders" and were "good for all contracts." The wartime demand for slaves in Atlanta added to Adair's capital resources and provided a basis for his postwar business expansion and wealth.[78]

As the city had earlier in its history, Atlanta welcomed migrants in the postwar years, and, when residents' businesses failed, outsiders opened new enterprises. In the postwar years, Dun agents began to notice the presence of greater numbers of Jewish merchants in the city—a population that either did not exist in Atlanta before the war, or was largely ignored. The agents reported the arrivals of Jewish entrepreneurs with a mixture of envy, suspicion, and admiration. Typical was the case of Abram Rosenfield, who had come to Atlanta in 1865. Connected to a dry-goods business in Washington, D.C., Rosenfield did well. "Jews doing a good bus," wrote the agent dismissively.[79] Atlanta had traditionally been friendly to northern investors and businessmen, and this attitude continued during the postwar years. G. McGinley, originally from Paterson, New Jersey, had moved to Georgia in the antebellum era and become involved in owning and running hotels. During the war, he operated Trout House, the city's most important hotel. After having opened another hotel in Jacksonville, he occupied himself during most of the 1870s managing the Kimball House in Atlanta, which was the largest hotel in the South. Although "not a popular man" and known to be "slow to pay accounts"—perhaps because of the small profit margins in the hotel business—McGinley still became an important business leader in postwar Atlanta.[80]

Although northerners joined the ranks of migrants, many migrants to Atlanta were native-born white southerners. In 1865, Garrett & Bro. moved to Atlanta from nearby Campbell County. In good credit standing before the war, they invested capital "saved from the wreck," according to the Dun agent, who pronounced them "fair bus men" whom "I should not fear to credit."[81] Many of the new migrant businessmen arriving after the war were southerners who came from outside Georgia. W. H. Brotherton moved from Tennessee to Atlanta in 1865 to start a merchandising business. He was judged "a good bus-man" who had a "fine run of trade."[82] Similarly, J. F. Jenkins moved from Kentucky to start a druggist business in partnership with some people from West Point, Georgia.[83] S. R. McCamry moved from Chattanooga to Atlanta sometime in 1866. "A sharp shrewd trader," he was reported as having "considerable means which he has not lost." He began a merchandising business with partners from Athens, Kentucky, and from Atlanta. He was judged to be a "high toned honorable gentleman and worthy of credit"; his company apparently had a "fair run of trade and a large stock."[84]

DURING THE FIRST FEW YEARS AFTER THE CIVIL WAR, economic rebuilding and revitalization came to characterize Atlanta. Visiting in late 1865, Sidney Andrews commented on the city's "nervous and palpitating" energy.[85] It was a "devil of a place," noted another visitor. "The men rush about like mad, and keep up such a bustle, worry, and chatter, that it runs me crazy."[86] Newspaperman Reid wrote that the city was "adapting itself, with remarkable rapidity, to the new order of things." Despite "gaping windows and roofless houses, heaps of ruins on the principal corners and traces of unsparing destruction everywhere," the city was quickly rebuilding. The city's leaders were "pure Southerners," determined to make it into "the foremost of the interior cities of the Gulf States."[87] Atlanta's citizens were enterprising, wrote a northern teacher, and "the whole town presents a business air, *not* peculiar to Southern towns generally."[88]

The city's railroad facilities, decimated by the war, were quickly reconstructed. The roundhouse was characterized by an Atlanta newspaperman in November 1866 as a "model of architectural beauty" that was "greatly superior to the one destroyed." A new, three-story depot opened in December.[89] Northern visitors agreed that the city was thriving. An Ohio correspondent noted that the railroad's machine shop was "now equal to, its former state of proficiency," while the car factory hummed with activity. As he wandered the streets, the newspaperman found "life and bustle and activity . . . everywhere around" him, contrasting with "bewildering mazes" of ruins. The newspaperman predicted that Atlanta was "destined to be the business centre in the Southern world."[90]

ALMOST AS SOON AS SHERMAN LEFT THE CITY and residents began returning in late 1864, a new narrative about Atlanta began to emerge that formed the basis for the Lost Cause ideology. The characteristics that had made Atlanta important during the war, opined the *Atlanta Daily Intelligencer* in April 1865, could restore its former prominence. The city's strategic location as a railroad center, the "salubrity of its atmosphere," and the availability of clean and pure water supplies all made Atlanta "blessed." The railroads were back in business, and although much of the transportation infrastructure had been destroyed, "time and energy" would restore things. The future was bright, predicted the *Intelligencer*, and Atlanta would "rise from the ashes to which it was consigned by a ferocious and brutal foe." "No cloud," it concluded, shadowed "the faces of our people," and "despondency and gloom" had given way to "cheerfulness and resolution."[91]

In July 1866, two years after Atlanta's conquest, the city was busily engaged in the work of reconstruction. "From dome to cellar," declared the *Intelligencer*, "the work has been vigorously prosecuted, until we begin to recognize much of the beauty and . . . the familiar old building in former years." City residents' memories of the widespread wartime destruction remained acute. "Amid the smoke and carnage of war," Atlantans had "witnessed that labor of years swept into nothingness, while the agonized walls of a homeless and helpless population lingered around the 'blind goddess with her scales,' and ascended to the spire posts!" Atlanta's reconstruction stood as both "a silent spectator of our efforts at recuperation" and an attempt to remove the "foot-prints of war."[92] John H. Kennaway, an English traveler who retraced Sherman's path into the interior of the South a year after the war, described his first impressions. He hardly knew, he wrote of Atlanta, "whether to wonder most at the completeness of the ruin which had swept over it, or at the rapidity with which its restoration was being effected." The city's four railroad lines were back in operation. There was still evidence of destruction, including fallen brick walls and isolated chimneys that stood grimly, as if they were "ashamed of such prominence." But there was also evidence of intense activity: wooden-frame workhouses sprang up, and buildings of a "more substantial character were beginning to rise."[93]

This redemption narrative became part of postwar Atlanta's identity. A pamphlet describing Atlanta to northern investors, published in 1871, stated that an "angel of destruction" had once seemed to "hover over the apparently hopeless wreck, making it like Babylon of old, a fit habitation only for bats and for owls." Six years earlier, the only signs of life and business activity were, he said, newsboys and porters working near the railroad depot and "the whistling of the locomotives." But how matters had changed. Through "enterprise and indomitable industry," Atlantans had "manfully struggled to rebuild waste places." The city now presented a "scene of prosperity far more wonderful than the desolations of war, more difficult to describe, and scarcely possible to realize."[94]

Numerous visitors to Atlanta, curious about the destroyed city, adopted this idea of redemption. The city was "resuming its old business-like aspect," wrote a *Chicago Tribune* correspondent in May 1865, with "most of its former citizens having returned and gone to work." Rather than "sitting in despondency," Atlantans were "busy as bees in clearing away the wreck." Rail lines were restored, debris cleared, and new buildings erected.[95] A correspondent for a Louisville newspaper had a similar impression. Out of a "blackened waste" came a new, rising city. "Everybody is intent on doing something," he wrote. "Cincinnatus-like, every man is ready for the plough or Senate, as occasion may demand."[96] Atlanta's destruction opened up opportunities for northern capitalists, who had, according to one account, discovered new business opportunities.[97]

The term "phoenix"—based on the classical myth of a bird that was reborn out of the ashes of its own destruction—became an emblem of postwar Atlanta. "Taking into consideration the era and circumstances," as an early historian wrote, it was "doubtful if a parallel can be found to the magic resurrection of Atlanta within a year after the city was in ashes. It was the fable of the Phoenix re-enacted in real life."[98] By the early 1880s, postwar Atlanta represented the rising of the New South itself.[99] In 1887, when Atlanta adopted a new city seal, it featured a phoenix rising above the flames, with the Latin word "resurgens," or "rising again." The phoenix seal symbolized, as the official historian of the city wrote in the early 1950s, "the story of a resurrected city, rebuilt by dauntless citizens who refused to accept defeat and determined to make their city greater and more beautiful than ever."[100]

An early phoenix reference appeared soon after the war, in late 1865, when entrepreneur J. E. Williams erected the Phoenix Building on Decatur Street at the site of the destroyed Athenaeum building. "How appropriate the name," commented one observer. "Indeed the appellation might be applied to the whole city; for Phoenix-like, she is rapidly rising from her own ashes to a nobler destiny and a prouder history that was ever known to her in the former halcyon days of peace and prosperity." He predicted that the "Atlanta of the future" would "far eclipse the Atlanta of the past."[101]

Boosters embraced the phoenix metaphor because it represented a clean break from the past and would communicate an optimistic impression to potential investors from outside. Perhaps more than other southerners, white Atlantans looked toward the future. And the future meant capitalist expansion. Urging the extension of new rail connections to cotton-producing regions of eastern Alabama, a booster stated that the rebuilding of the railroads was an indication of Atlanta's rebirth. "Your city has risen, Phoenix-like, from her ashes, and has already built up the waste places caused by the late war." Atlanta's businessmen possessed both "capital and foresight" as they extended their arms, "Briareus-like, in other directions, reaching after trade and travel which have hitherto enriched other cities."[102]

Of course, the revival was real. As William Thomas observes, in 1865, immediately after the war, the U.S. Military Railroad Corps repaired and rebuilt the devastated Western & Atlantic, installing 140 miles of new track and constructing sixteen bridges. The effort relied on a massive expenditure of human and financial resources that the U.S. government provided, resulting, according to Thomas, in an "entirely redeveloped railroad network."[103] Business activity in other areas was also significant: 338 new firms were licensed in the city during the latter half of 1865 alone. Atlanta's retail district possessed 250 brick buildings by late 1866, most of them new or reconstructed structures. Railroads rebuilt depots and shops; new machine shops and foundries supported the railroad boom. The city's political leadership constructed two new market houses, enlarged and refenced the city cemetery, widened and improved streets, and removed the debris left over from the war.

Boosters eagerly promoted an interpretation of the city's past and future that was tied to economic development. In the two years after the war, Atlanta had "risen out of her own ashes" to regain the status it had had before the Civil War. *Barnwell's Atlanta City Directory* stated in no uncertain terms that the city should be regarded as a trailblazer for the entire South: "May we not again be cursed by the demoralizing and destructive tendencies of war," it proclaimed in florid style, "but continue, as a community, to march onward and up ward in every ennobling cause, until Atlanta shall have become one of the great cities of the continent."[104] Northerners also rushed to have a role in the city's redevelopment. Atlanta's postwar city fathers included a notable group of northern emigrés who had arrived in the 1840s and 1850s. After the Civil War, other northerners moved to Atlanta, and, by 1870, more than a third of the owners of the largest amounts of property were nonsoutherners.[105] Atlanta, for northerners and southerners alike, represented reconciliation and rebirth. Reid commented that Atlanta had become a hub of energy. City boosters had recreated a "city out of this desert of shattered brick—raising warehouses from ruins, and hastily establishing stores in houses half finished and unroofed." To many commentators,

Atlanta resembled Chicago: both were bustling transportation hubs, both were said to be among the "foremost of the interior cities," and for both a bright economic future was predicted.[106]

Sidney Andrews was one of those who compared Atlanta to Chicago. Atlanta, he wrote, was a "new city . . . springing up with marvellous rapidity." City streets had come alive with activity: "with drays and carts and hand-barrows and wagons, —with hauling teams and shouting men, —with loads of lumber and loads of brick and loads of sand, —with piles of furniture and hundreds of packed boxes, —with mortar-makers and hod-carriers, —with carpenters and masons, —with rubbish removers and house-builders, —with a never-ending throng of pushing and crowding and scram-bling and eager and excited and enterprising men, all bent on building and trading and swift fortune-making." "In her busiest days," Chicago could scarcely have matched Atlanta's dynamism. The city's railroads "groan with the freight and passenger traffic, and yet are unable to meet the demand of the nervous and palpitating city."

Andrews saw mixed blessings in the postwar boom. "Men rush about the streets with little regard for comfort or pleasure," he observed, "and yet find the days all too short and too few for the work in hand." Atlantans heard the "sound of the saw and plane and hammer" all day long, yet builders had more demand for their work than they could fulfill. Rents remained high, and there was a "most urgent cry for store-room and office-room." Four thousand mechanics were employed; another thousand could have found work "if brick and lumber were to be had at any price." The "one sole idea" for everyone was to make money, yet the frenzied speculation, Andrews be-lieved, portended an economic crash. The booming rebirth had its negative aspects: "The streets never were either neat or tasty; now, what with the piles of building material and the greater piles of *débris* and rubbish, and the vast amount of teaming and hauling over them, they are simply horrible."[107]

Like northern urban centers, Atlanta was consumed by commerce. The city was a "fast place in every sense of the word," a newspaper correspondent wrote in 1867. "Our friends in Atlanta are a fast people. They live fast, and they die fast."[108] "The most obvious characteristic of the place is the energy and life there is about its inhabitants," added another newspaper account in 1869. Atlanta was "totally unlike any other Southern city." A city "born of se-cession in her death throes," Atlanta had become a "Phoenix rising from her ashes." The city was a "fusion point after the war, of a great many hostile and opposing faiths." Its leadership possessed "more live ideas upon the subject of business and politics, and are less subject to old fogy prejudices on the one hand and carpet-bag ascendancy of any place in the South."[109]

Rebirth meant commerce and a pace of life not perceived as southern, commentators noted. "Men rush about like mad people," wrote one visitor, "and keep up such a bustle, worry, hurry and chatter, that it nearly runs me crazy." At dinner at a boardinghouse, "I could not eat for the noise," with boarders rushing in, quickly eating, and then rushing out. The hurried lodgers even wore their hats at dinner in order to save time. They looked "nearly worked to death," the observer noted, and "I have not seen a gentleman with a calm, placid face in the whole town."[110] Atlantans, commented a Macon resident, were the strangest people, "always in a hurry." A Milledgeville visitor declared that the "whole city seems to be running on wheels, and all the inhabitants continually blowing steam."[111]

New Atlanta had become a community without values. "There is little that is distinctively Southern in Atlanta; it is the antithesis of Savannah," wrote Edward King in 1875 in his travel account, *The Great South.* Atlanta had, he said, "an unfinished air; its business and residence streets are scattered along a range of pretty hills; but it is eminently modern and unromantic." Few traces remained of the war, and the rebuilt streets and residences exhibited a "smart, new air," which provided a "pleasant surprise after the tumble-down, unpainted towns of which one sees so many in the South." Atlanta's downtown business district exuded the "same canny air," and it seemed "to be boasting" of its "tidy looks and prosperity to the countrymen who come into town to market."[112] Even though located in the heart of Dixie, Atlanta more resembled a "hustling, thriving, growing city of the North and West," another northern reporter observed.[113]

Northerners were eager to buy what the boosters were selling—the proposition that Atlanta represented a new sort of South emerging out of the Civil War. The postwar spirit of economic development led some observers to conclude that the city had adopted northern ways. The city, according to a northern correspondent writing in May 1867, was "essentially Northern in appearance; a young Chicago dropped down in Georgia." A correspondent for the *New York Times,* writing in October 1866, told readers that one of the "mysteries in Georgia" was the growth of Atlanta as a dominant interior town. Atlanta's emergence as a paragon of the New South seemed unlikely. Situated in hills, without good rivers, and with no natural trade advantages, it had become the most important economic center in Georgia. One reporter maintained that Atlanta's dynamism resulted from its strategic location as a transportation center. "A railroad was as good as a river," he observed, and "in this fortunate junction . . . her commercial energy is found."[114]

Atlanta was attracting national attention, declared a North Carolinian in 1869. Rebuilt, it had become the "Chicago of the South."[115] Like Atlanta, Chicago was an interior town that had established dominance over the hinterlands through railroads. Chicago was also a new city that had come into its own about the same time that Atlanta emerged as an economic center. The *Atlanta Daily New Era* explained the city's renewal and growth. Atlanta successfully blended a busy capitalist culture—manifested in the "rushing together of men of varied characters and origins"—with a cosmopolitanism "unexampled in the history of any Southern town."[116] Why its thirty-five thousand inhabitants would "choose these hills for their habitation is a matter of curious inquiry," wrote a Louisville visitor in September 1875. Perhaps the reason lay in the fact that the city was "new and bright," with little to remind inhabitants of the past, the "time that tried men's souls." There was only a little evidence of "trenches and remnants of forts in the suburbs." Atlantans themselves were "impressed with the necessity of doing everything well."[117]

IN 1889, WALLACE PUTNAM REED described the "remarkable change" that had occurred in the first fifty years of Atlanta's history. The city's prewar economy contrasted with important socioeconomic tendencies of the Old South. Unlike the rest of Georgia, Atlanta was not dominated by slave labor, Reed claimed. "We were a community of free traders, and it was the general belief that the Southern States would forever remain purely agricultural commonwealths." However, the Civil War revolutionized things. A new Atlanta arose on the site of the old Atlanta, "built by new men with new ideas, new hopes, and new ambitions." The new Atlanta welcomed differences of opinion, encouraged manufacturing and industry, and believed in intersectional harmony—in fusing together the sections of the country that had once been divided between the Confederacy and the Union "in one solid body, knowing no North, South, East, or West, and all pulling together for the common good." Atlanta's progress offered a model for the South's development, Reed believed.[118]

Narratives such as Reed's became essential to the way many southerners learned to think about the aftermath of the Civil War in the South. As a story line emerged about what the South had become and what it could be, civic boosters emphasized the narrative of Atlanta's destruction and rebirth because it fed into their vision of the South's future. Northerners were eager to believe that Atlanta represented a post–Civil War South that differed from the Old South. The assumptions northerners usually had about the South, said one northern observer, did not apply to Atlanta. "Full of life and business activity," he wrote, the city had "already recovered from the desolations of war, and bids fair to outlast Sherman and the memories of his march to the sea." "Enterprise, progress, and a brilliant future" were "stamped upon the face of Atlanta," a city that had become a "jewel of the New South."[119]

Unburdened by economic limitations of the Old South, postwar Atlanta could rebuild and recreate. Yet Atlanta could not completely abandon its past. The war had liberated millions of slaves, and the end of slavery created a new imperative to reconstruct southern society. This imperative confronted whites and blacks, though in different ways. Unspoken in all their talk of economic reconstruction was the compelling assumption, on the part of white Atlantans, that it was necessary to maintain racial supremacy. They encountered a community of ex-slaves deeply skeptical of a message of economic development that excluded them. Though the prevailing narrative, which emphasized the ideal that came to be known as the New South, united whites across different social classes, there remained other—unacknowledged—narratives that could be told about the war and its meaning.

THREE

A Forgetfulness of the Past

Rebuilding the Racial Order

In the summer of 1865, Atlanta offered profoundly contrasting scenes. Felix Salm-Salm, brigadier general in the 68th New York Infantry, had commanded the city's military post for several months. A Prussian nobleman and officer who had served as a Union cavalry officer, Salm-Salm volunteered in 1861, rising to the rank of colonel and, in April 1865, to brevet brigadier general. In July 1865, he arrived with his wife in Atlanta, where they described a "sad sight." One could "scarcely believe," his wife wrote, "that the remaining inhabitants of that country would ever become reconciled to their Northern conquerors."[1] From the perspective of white Atlantans, the sight of freedmen everywhere was jarring. Another inherent incongruity was the fact that a Prussian was in command of the Union occupation of Atlanta. According to Salm-Salm's estimates, "the number of blacks, of all ages, who have flocked into the city from the surrounding region, cannot be less than 10,000." Black people lived in "dense masses," dwelling in "old tents, in huts built of tin and sheet-iron gathered from the ruins, under boards resting, one end on the ground, the other against a ruined wall, in the inside of demolished houses." Everywhere, ex-slaves were "huddled together, where any thing can be found to shelter them, while many sleep without shelter [other] than the sky, and with no hope of the morrow's bread, beyond what the good government affords."[2]

The end of the Civil War made possible the creation of fundamentally antagonistic visions of the future. Most whites, especially civic boosters, believed in Atlanta's unique ability to reconstruct itself and redefine itself as a southern place. Most African Americans, on the other hand, viewed Atlanta's destruction differently—within a context of Union victory and the end of slavery. The city's burning was, in other words, the price that had to be paid for black freedom. A contested question was the establishment of the postwar racial order. African Americans believed that a new racial order must be established in which blacks were liberated from the shackles of white control, but they knew that to achieve this liberation would require economic freedom. Providing unique opportunities as a growing urban area under northern occupation, Atlanta during Reconstruction became a center of African American leadership in the South. Whites, in contrast to blacks, feared a future without black slavery, since emancipation had disrupted the labor and social system. They therefore sought new ways to control former slaves. In these different ways, then, both white and black racial attitudes and experiences were tied up with the realities of economic development.

DURING THE MONTHS AFTER THE CONFEDERATE SURRENDER at Appomattox, whites could see no better evidence of how their world was upended than the presence of armed black men. The sight of uniformed African Americans, who had formed a significant part of the northern occupying force, seemed incongruous. That black soldiers could occupy a position of authority was a "great outrage," complained the *Atlanta Daily Intelligencer* in August 1865.[3] White fears of armed blacks often became sexualized. When a black soldier arrested an Atlanta white in September 1865, a city official commented: "I would rather white men would take me down on the ground and do with me as they pleased than be arrested by a negro soldier."[4] Whites also translated their racial fears into anxieties about crime. In December, the *Intelligencer* asserted that black troops and civilians, encamped for about three-quarters of a mile along Peachtree Road, were responsible for robberies in the neighborhood. "The outrages," said one account, were "of frequent occurrence, and are generally perpetrated by armed squads." "We call attention to the matter," wrote this observer, "in the hope that prompt steps will be taken by the officers in command of said troops to have such practices discontinued."[5]

Black Union soldiers remained in force in Atlanta until early 1866. When they were mustered out with most of the rest of the large Union army, a writer for the *Intelligencer* breathed a deep sigh of relief. The news, he wrote, "will be gratifying intelligence to every one." The community had "suffered as little from their presence as any other—and we believe less—yet it is the universal opinion that the government made an error in sending them among us." Black troops were unnecessary "either to the public welfare or the public safety"; they could easily be replaced by whites. Having African Americans in such a position "seems to look like a disposition to humiliate unnecessarily"; their departure would "exercise a salutary influence and prevent the petty collisions which now take place."[6]

In 1866, freed slaves came in great numbers to the Fourth of July celebration, which they observed by making a festive parade through downtown Atlanta. Before the Civil War, white Atlantans, like other white southerners, celebrated the national holiday with what an observer described as "a respect almost amounting to idolatry." But "how changed things are!" The black parade indicated to whites how much their world had turned upside down. An African American mounted on a white horse led the parade, followed by a marching band, the parade's grand marshal, and members of black voluntary groups. People in the procession clashed with a group of white firemen, also parading, and with celebrating northern troops. The public celebration by Atlanta blacks dismayed the *Intelligencer*'s editor, who commented how painfully the celebration contrasted with past Fourths. Whites expressed a "deep sense of regret" that the celebration had taken place.[7]

Confederate defeat meant, for many Atlanta whites, a loss of power that led to a sense of emasculation. A few miles east of town, in Gwinnett County, white diarist Thomas Maguire recorded in May 1865 that "the times are out of joint . . . I fear we will have bad times, but we must take them as they come." "What a country we have at the present time! We have nothing that we can call our own. The vile Yankees take everything they please and go where they please. We are a powerless people, but by no means a conquered people. I have lost hope of yet gaining our independence."[8] A few days later, however, Maguire expressed his hopelessness. "I look for nothing but hard times for the balance of my life," he wrote, and he had "no heart to do anything." All was "dark and gloomy." He could weep, but it would do no good.[9] The trauma of defeat combined, in his and others' minds, with contradictory impulses and contradictory expectations about what the social and political postwar order would be.

Like other white Georgians, Maguire had little confidence about what the future held in store after the South returned to the Union. While some might think the northerners "kindly," he harbored no such illusions, nor any faith in "their love for us." They had treated Georgians so badly, Maguire believed, that he could "never forget their meanness and dishonesty," and, as a people, he saw them as "rogues and swindlers."[10] Much of Maguire's hostility came from his fears about the end of slavery. In June, he anxiously noted that several of his neighbor's slaves "went off this morning to the Yankees." Going "off to the Yankees" became a fixed expression for slaves' rejection of or escape from their masters. Although in slaveowners' eyes the northern occupiers deserved the brunt of blame, Maguire also described what he believed were the inherent inadequacies of his former slaves. "Nearly all the talk now is of the negroes going to Yankees," he lamented, and though he feared that "some of mine may," he also predicted that his ex-slaves would have a "hard time before long."[11]

In Atlanta and in the counties surrounding it, whites operated under untenable prewar assumptions. When white Atlanta citizens met weeks after the peace, in June 1865, they urged a "speedy restoration of all political and national relations, the restoration of mutual confidence and friendship, the uninterrupted intercourse of trade and commerce with every section." White Atlantans wanted to reestablish "our old position in the list of states, the sovereign and sole conservators of an unbroken and imperishable Union." But restoration meant, for them, the reestablishment of white supremacy. The group claimed that whites did not intend to "deprive the freedman of the results of his labor." Ex-slaves ought to enjoy the "sympathy of all intelligent, Christian, moral Southern men." But the group opposed enfranchising freedmen, on the grounds that they repudiated "every effort to stir up strife among those who had differed upon questions which had produced the late war." They instead recommended "a forgetfulness of the past."[12]

Visitors to postwar Atlanta noted that southern whites held a variety of opinions about the future. Most remained baffled as to what the end of slavery would bring; many feared an insurrection and a repetition of the "scenes of blood and massacre of St. Domingo."[13] When Sherman's army had moved through Georgia, whites were shocked to discover that their previously loyal slaves were deserting their plantations. After emancipation, whites wondered what "our negroes" would do. "I think the excitement of the negroes going to the Yankees is nearly over," Maguire observed hopefully in June 1865. "The poor negroes will be sorry enough after they realize the effects of this, to them, great revolution." Their departure from slaveholder supervision, Maguire thought, would be a "disadvantage to me and a great misfortune to them." Black people, he predicted, would, like Indians, eventually suffer extermination. "They are now of little profit to their owners and they cannot make out by themselves. Work they will not, still they must live. The whites will kill them in self-defense."[14]

During the months after the end of the Civil War, the pages of the *Atlanta Daily Intelligencer* became filled with characterizations of the racial inadequacies of black people. The newspaper described freedpeople as living in "idleness, vice and profligacy"—a self-inflicted condition, the writer believed, brought about because former slaves had deserted the happy homes and the kindness which their masters offered. The freedpeople's "persistent idleness," the *Intelligencer* concluded, meant that "a life of freedom" had become a "curse." "Nothing short of the strong arm of the law," it concluded, could "ameloriate their condition."[15] "Freedman he may be," the *Intelligencer* later said, "but he will still retain the characteristics of the African race. What God has implanted in his *nature*, man may not, cannot remove." The transition to freedom was fraught with difficulties, the *Intelligencer* maintained. "Those who have labored so strenuously to free the slave," wrote a correspondent, "seem to have thought that the change from proprietory to compensated labor would be of easy transition."[16]

Southern whites believed that they understood, better than anyone, the nature and character of the southern black population. They asserted that wage labor would not accomplish for freedpeople "what compensated labor has done for the white man." By nature "indolent and careless," black people would only work under a compulsory labor regime under close supervision, with the threat of physical punishment. According to the prevailing white view, ex-slaves sought to gratify only "temporary wants." They spent all they earned "in extravagant dress, trinkets," claimed the *Intelligencer*, and for the "temporary gratification of any and every caprice" which entered their "fickle" minds. Black people were "proverbially improvident—never taking heed for to-morrow." The *Intelligencer* continued its tirade against former slaves who "straggle over the suburbs, intrude upon private premises, and with characteristic aimlessness of purpose, lounge hither and thither, heedless of the time coming when they must either become a useful member of, or a burthen to society."[17]

White opinion, exemplified in the *Intelligencer*'s columns, saw black "idleness" as a main result of emancipation. Whites focused on imposing new forms of compulsion. The *Intelligencer* favored the vagrancy law enacted by Georgia in early 1866. Atlanta was "seriously suffering by this vagrancy and its results," declared the *Intelligencer*, and "our gardens will next be pillaged." The new law provided that the local government could declare as vagrants anyone who was "idle, immoral, or profligate," able-bodied but not working, with a home but no other property, and who lived by "stealing or by trading in, bartering in, or buying stolen property." Vagrants could be forced to work for the government or bound out to individuals.[18]

White attitudes toward black "idleness" reflected their incomprehension of black freedom. They expected that the racial hierarchy inherent in slavery would survive. Ex-slaves perceived things very differently. From the start of the war, they saw their freedom and an end to slavery as primary objectives. They fully realized the stakes of the war. As one Atlanta slaveholder told his slaves early in the war, "if the South should be whipped freedom would be the result."[19] Enslaved Atlantans were overwhelmingly Unionist. The recollection of one freedman, who described Atlanta's burning in November 1864 as a "grand sight," indicated the extent to which slaves welcomed the destruction of slaveholding society.[20] There is little question that former slaves eagerly greeted emancipation as an apocalyptic event. African Americans were eager to reject most features of the slaveholder regime, govern themselves independently of white control, exercise physical mobility, maintain the integrity of their families, and control their work environments. Freedpeople also rejected the brutal work discipline that was a hallmark of slavery. They believed that they were owed what scholars of emancipation have characterized as uncircumscribed access to "productive resources" of land and property in compensation for their years of uncompensated toil. Along with vital issues defining freedom—access to political power, the integrity of families, the acquisition of literacy—former slaves identified the issue of labor as central to their emancipation.[21]

The post–Civil War history of Atlanta offers fertile ground for examining the formative years following the end of the Civil War, the black transition from slavery to freedom, and the successes and failures of Reconstruction. With clashing perspectives, former masters and ex-slaves sized each other up warily during the months after the war ended. Whites were usually convinced that former slaves could only work under the old regime, under strict regimentation and brutality. The end of slavery and the beginning of black freedom largely redefined the organization of labor, yet major actors—southern whites, northern whites, and freedpeople—triangulated into radically different, though interrelated, points of view.

Northern whites insisted on ending the visible signs of slavery. Military detachments, in the months after Confederate surrender, scoured the South to liberate slaves. The months immediately after the war were chaotic for both whites and blacks. Former slaves' precise status remained murky. "No man in the North can realize the condition of affairs in this region," wrote a northern African American minister visiting Atlanta in August 1865. In some areas, ex-slaves "do not know really that they are free, and if they do, their surroundings are such that they would fear to speak of it, as they would have done in the palmy days of rebellion." Although emancipated slaves often remained with former masters until they found work elsewhere, they were increasingly empowered to "demand that their former masters pay due wages, or share the crop."[22]

Nonetheless, paying black people wages remained an alien concept for most Georgia whites. The "whole fabric of slavery" was now destroyed, wrote a correspondent for the *New York Herald* in 1867, but the institution had "deep and broad foundations in the hearts of the people."[23] Demanding a restoration of the racial norms that were inherent in white dominance, whites expected to maintain control, exercise physical discipline, and enjoy public deference from ex-slaves.[24] "Four millions of a helpless, ignorant, deplorably ignorant, and dependent race, in a twinkling of an eye as it were, turned loose to take care of themselves," observed the *Atlanta Daily Intelligencer* soon after the war's end. "The transition, how sudden!"[25] Freedpeople lived under a "sad delusion" about the meaning of freedom, declared the *Intelligencer*, the city's leading newspaper. Freedom meant that "*labor* must follow his changed condition, else *perish* he must." Ex-slaves must learn that freedom did not mean "idleness" but meant instead the "freedom to labor and to reap such fruits thereof, as, in equity, he may be entitled to; to support and maintain with food and clothing his wife and his children, or, they doing their part, his mother and his sisters."[26]

AGAINST A BACKGROUND OF POSTWAR ECONOMIC and social distress, a political vacuum, and uncertain racial interactions, the Bureau of Refugees, Freedmen, and Abandoned Lands (the Freedmen's Bureau) became the most important governmental force in the emancipated South. In its brief existence, it attempted something unprecedented: to introduce federal power over labor, governance, and law at the community level. Created by Congress in March 1865 and in existence for only four years, the bureau was charged with the daunting task of providing for the transition from slavery to freedom. This "tremendous undertaking"—in the words of W. E. B. Du Bois— gave the federal government responsibility for freedpeople as the "ward[s] of the nation." Since ex-slaves had been "emasculated by a peculiarly complete system of slavery, centuries old," Du Bois wrote, emancipation had brought them "suddenly, violently . . . into a new birthright, at a time of war and passion, in the midst of the stricken, embittered population of their former masters."[27]

Historians have generally judged the bureau to have been a failure, though for various reasons. Early twentieth-century scholars of Reconstruction condemned the agency as the worst example to be found of northern meddling in the South and of the political manipulation of African Americans. The bureau "sought too much for the Negro too soon," said one historian, and thus "fed the flame of race hostility."[28] Using different assumptions, other historians have criticized the agency for having pursued policies hostile to freedpeople. The bureau was overly preoccupied with "stemming migration, establishing order, and restoring the economy," writes historian Tera Hunter, "which led it to force blacks into accepting contracts without sufficient regard for the fairness of the terms."[29] The most recent work about the bureau has acknowledged its significance in the Reconstruction process: the achievements and deficiencies of the Freedmen's Bureau reflected the successes and failures of Reconstruction itself. "If the experience of the Bureau showed the limitations of Republican policy and federal authority," writes Paul Cimbala, "it also suggested their possibilities."[30]

In Georgia and other southern states, an assistant commissioner ran bureau activities statewide and was accountable to headquarters in Washington. The assistant commissioner oversaw eight subordinate field offices, each headed by a subassistant commissioner. Between 1865 and 1868, the bureau's Atlanta subdistrict at various times covered nineteen counties in northwestern Georgia. The Atlanta field office was involved in relief activities, facilitating the reunion of separated slave families, inaugurating schools, and maintaining a rudimentary hospital for blacks in the city. In one of its most important functions, the Atlanta office also worked with local agents to negotiate and oversee wage labor contracts, protect freedpeople against white depredations, and serve as an agency of last recourse for ex-slaves. The bureau faced immense challenges in that it lacked funds—it received no appropriation until 1866—and in the fact that its intervention represented an unprecedented federal involvement in local affairs.[31]

As shown by the editors of the volumes published in the *Freedom* project, which documents emancipation in rich detail, the Freedmen's Bureau sought to make former slaveholders and ex-slaves "into employers and employees."[32] Northern free-labor ideology, wrote bureau commissioner O. O. Howard, would be transformative. "Until the system of free labor shall be practically understood in the south," Howard said in November 1866, "some agency like this bureau seems vital to the success of all those agricultural enterprises which depend upon the labor of the freed people." Ex-slaves were "willing and anxious" to work, but they needed federal protection from cruel ex-masters and from an unjust legal system.[33]

All bureau agents, no matter their racial attitudes, insisted on an end to overt indications of slavery. In February 1866 a bureau agent ruled that a young male ex-slave who had been hired outside of Atlanta under the "previous existing laws of Slavery" was now free of any further obligation. These laws were now "*null and void*," the Atlanta agent declared, and "you can therefore no longer hold him under your former article of contract or agreement."[34] When the bureau was first established in Atlanta in October 1865, it

Harper's Weekly interprets the Freedmen's Bureau

functioned with local agents, without a subassistant commissioner. Although four army officers were later appointed as federal officials to run the bureau's office in Atlanta, not until 1867 were sufficient resources made available to them through the creation of a larger field office. Fred Mosebach, the most energetic of these federal officials, was a New York army veteran. By the time he arrived in Atlanta in 1867, Mosebach had achieved the rank of brevet major and was serving in the Veteran Reserve Corps—the so-called Invalid Corps, composed of disabled soldiers—a group that tended to be heavily represented among bureau officials. Mosebach already had bureau experience in Georgia, having headed field offices in Albany and Columbus.[35]

Despite the bureau's presence, a sizeable portion of white troops in Atlanta remained unsympathetic toward freedpeople. During the early weeks of the northern occupation, the army ordered all black people to register with the provost marshal in order to receive passes to live in the city. The order threatened arrest for transients who could not document their addresses. Occupying authorities only sporadically enforced the order, however, despite urging from local whites.[36] On Christmas Day, 1865, John Richard Dennett, visiting Atlanta and reporting for *The Nation*, described an encounter with a Union officer in Atlanta. The officer told Dennett that he was going to "punch every d——d nigger I see." He then randomly assaulted two blacks walking on the street; the men "seemed too much astonished to retaliate." That same day, a fight occurred in which two freedmen were shot by soldiers. No arrests were made.[37]

Clashes between freedpeople and northern troops were not unusual. In July 1866, after two white soldiers started shoving black women on the sidewalk, several black men intervened. A fracas ensued, and one of the black men was shot in the head. But in the meantime, more troops poured out of the barracks with bayonets fixed in defense of their comrades. White officers regained control over their men only after considerable effort.[38] In September 1867, soldiers from a New Jersey regiment robbed and severely injured some freedmen. Despite an investigation, there were no prosecutions.[39] In what became known as the Fourth Ward Riot, in October 1868 troops from the McPherson Barracks knocked down chicken coops, pulled down the fences of the freedpeople, and rioted. According to the *Atlanta Constitution*, they "came to the very natural conclusion that the city belonged to them, and that they had a right to do just what they pleased, the prerogatives of municipal authority to the contrary notwithstanding." The riot only ended when local police opened fire, wounding some of the troops. Mockingly, the *Atlanta Constitution* concluded its account by quoting Ulysses S. Grant's presidential campaign slogan of 1868, "Let Us Have Peace."[40]

For whites, the Freedmen's Bureau replaced Sherman as the chief villain and scapegoat and served as a symbol of the uncertainty of the postwar world. Southern whites suspected that the bureau was seeking to undermine the racial order by promoting black equality. Their critique of the bureau folded into their critique of black freedom. They believed that ex-slaves were unprepared for emancipation, that they had left the guiding hand of slavery too quickly, and that northern outsiders were upsetting the racial equilibrium. In most respects, the bureau was a "miserable failure," wrote the *Intelligencer* in June 1866, in that it fostered "idleness and vagrancy" and alienated the "affections of the freed population from their former owners, and from their natural protectors." The bureau, according to this point of view, had "sown seeds of discord where breaches should have been healed, and had done an incalculable amount of injury to the very people for whose good it was intended."[41]

The most immediate task facing the bureau was the reunification of black families who had been separated during slavery or because of wartime dislocation. During much of its existence, the Freedmen's Bureau insisted that black parents had the right to control their children and their labor.[42] In

April 1866, Phillis, a sixty-year-old Atlanta freedwoman, sought to return to her family in South Carolina. Before the war, she had been sold to new owners in Mississippi. The bureau paid for her transportation home.[43] In November 1867, Willis Love, a freedman living in Atlanta, was searching for his daughter, Maria Jane Bunch, who had been sold to a white resident of Perryville, Tennessee, sometime in the late 1850s. Since his emancipation, he had "spared no trouble nor expense to find her out," but the trail went cold after he learned that his daughter's Perryville master, taking his slaves with him, had become a refugee during the war. Love requested the bureau's assistance in locating Maria. The record, in this case and in many others, remains silent about whether they succeeded.[44] Having used its resources to locate separated families, the bureau often paid for transportation to reunite them. In October 1867, Julia Gibbs, a freedwoman in Atlanta, requested transportation from Savannah for her son, and she pressed the Atlanta bureau office daily with "great solicitude in regard to the restoration of her boy."[45] Angeline Ellis, another freedwoman who lived in Atlanta in 1868, reported that her daughter, Mary, "a bright freed girl fourteen years of age," was being held against her will by her former master in Virginia. Having failed in her earlier efforts to get her daughter back, Ellis appealed to the bureau for help.[46]

SOON AFTER THE CONFEDERATE SURRENDER, Atlanta was overwhelmed by an impoverished population of migrants and refugees. In May 1865, an officer of the occupying army reported that as many as fifty thousand people in northern Georgia were "utterly destitute of bread or any kind of food." Women and children walked from ten to forty miles for food, to receive "only a moiety, frequently not any."[47] "There is much destitution in and about this city, among both white and colored," wrote a *New York Tribune* reporter in December 1866, adding that there was "perhaps no place in the South where there is so much suffering as here." Among the sufferers were women and children "with nothing but an old and tattered piece of canvas, picked up in the wake of Sherman's army, to shelter them from the wind and rain of winter, and no bedding fit for a dog, and who are really on the verge of starvation."[48] Over time, the destitute declined in number but did not disappear. In the spring of 1867, Subassistant Commissioner John Leonard described the "great destitution and suffering for want of the necessaries of life in each of the counties comprising the district of Atlanta." According to a count made in April 1867, 2,200 whites and 1,200 blacks were destitute in Atlanta, while the number for the surrounding counties was nearly 16,000 people.

The military provided rations to the returning white refugees, freedpeople, and demobilized Confederate veterans. During June 1865, military authorities in Atlanta issued rations to about 15,000 people, including 95,000 pounds of breadstuffs and the same amount of meat. Atlantans also received salt, coffee, sugar, soap, candles, and other articles.[49] In October 1865, the bureau's agent in Atlanta reported that about 300 white women and children had been "left entirely destitute by the fortunes of war," and he reported almost 700 blacks in the same condition.[50] A bureau official visiting from Washington at about the same time reported that there was in Atlanta "more of an accumulation of destitute freed people than I had seen elsewhere." The countryside surrounding Atlanta was "completely devastated."[51] As late as December 1866, a bureau official warned that there was a danger of widespread starvation if rations did not soon reach freedpeople.[52]

The logistical planning required to maintain the distribution of rations was daunting.[53] The management of rations and of the mules and wagons to transport them was "a subject of more annoyance to me, lately," reported one subassistant commissioner, "than all the business legitimately connected with the bureau in this district."[54] There were reports, as well, of "bushwhackers" raiding the supply wagons as they made their way to the camps; these bandit attacks necessitated still more military resources.[55]

The army maintained housing—a so-called contraband camp—for ex-slave refugees who had fled their masters, followed Sherman's army, and then received temporary housing in Savannah, Albany, Macon, and, finally, Atlanta.[56] In February 1866, Subassistant Commissioner George R. Waldridge complained about the freedpeople who "are now and have been for some time at the contraband camp at this post" and were being "furnished with quarters & rations at Govt expense."[57] The Atlanta "contraband camp" fanned white fears about the "idle" population of blacks who seemed to be overwhelming the city. "On the outskirts of the city, in hovels, tents, and without shelter," observed the *Intelligencer*, "these poor creatures pass from earth with no sympathizing hand." The "sympathizing hand," the writer believed, should be white—and a societal structure should be imposed that required blacks to work under white supervision. From the writer's perspective, ex-slaves "believe that a state of freedom is to serve as an exemption from labor."[58] "Atlanta is more or less round, and about three miles in diameter," wrote a white schoolteacher. "Taking the thickness of ¾ of a mile in circle all around, this circle, or ribbon if you will, is crowded with poor people piled the one upon the other, perfect heathen[s] in a civilized country, with the most savage tastes, fighting, murdering, stealing, quarreling, begging, swearing, drinking, and possessing the most abject ideas of life—they are beasts with a soul. They know not here exactly how to manage them."[59]

Whites misread the motives of black women, confusing their desire for a stable domestic life with idleness. In the aftermath of the war, black women redefined their womanhood by leaving their former masters, asserting freedom in their work, and, in some instances, choosing to remain in their homes to raise their families rather than work outside the home. Whites saw matters according to their own, racially based notions. Black women, complained an Atlanta newspaper, would rather "sleep and shiver at home in any sort of hovel or hut that offers an apology for a shelter" than go to work. Because most white women had "frequently to go into the kitchen and prepare their own meals," they needed domestics. Only when black women became "very hungry and ragged" were they prepared to work.[60]

White Atlantans perceived the contraband camp as a source of crime and disorder, an attitude to some extent shared by northern white bureau officials. "Horse thieves in this vicinity," complained the *Intelligencer* in September 1865, were "pursuing their avocation with a zeal greater than ever was known." "Not a day but what we hear of some new operation." Samuel Richards reported the prevalence of theft. In October 1865, he and his father discovered that two blacks had taken down a chimney in order to haul off the bricks. About a month later, some of his horses disappeared and were later recovered from a gang of white and black horse thieves. Scavenger wood haulers looking for fuel cut down trees and sold the wood from wheelbarrows. Atlanta's antebellum forest, according to a local historian, was "sadly decimated."[61]

During 1865 and 1866, the bureau and the U.S. Army provost marshal served as the police force in Atlanta. Its main targets were black people. As early as August 1865, the army indicated that it would police the transient population, and it required that temporary huts and tents be moved to outside the city limits.[62] The provost marshal's record included cases in which freedpeople had been jailed for petty crime, and these people occupied an increasing share of the space in the military guardhouse.[63] After the transition to civilian policing, local whites still complained about "great disorder and distress" and even maintained that a "reign of terror" was evident from rising black crime.[64] The bureau's policies toward the urban ex-slaves combined relief and forced labor. From the outset, the bureau was willing to coerce freedpeople into work. Those at the contraband camp who were unwilling to work "ought to be made to," wrote Lt. Col. George Curkendall, who commanded the military post and ran the Atlanta bureau in late 1865.

He believed that a number of freedpeople could be put to work with a *"little compulsion."*[65]

The bureau's concerns about crime also affected their attitude toward freedmen's labor: vagrancy became criminalized. George Waldridge, in charge of the Atlanta bureau in early 1866, complained that there was a "worthless set" of men who were imprisoned, obtained a "few days rest rations & quarters," and were "turned loose to again violate the laws and commit further depredations." When it was reported to Waldridge that two freedmen, Elijah Whitaker and Alfred Liquir, were guilty of horse theft, he threw them into a military jail.[66] Waldridge, in alliance with local whites, was aggressive in rooting out black crime. In March 1866, he informed Atlanta mayor James E. Williams that the bureau would send out military details to round up and arrest "all the idle, loafing and vagrant negroes, who now infest the public thoroughfare; until they signify a willingness to enter into a permanent contract for their future support."[67] Waldridge's roundup of unemployed freedpeople was problematic; the question remained what to do with the internees. He proposed sending them to other states as contract laborers. "They will not Enter into Contract voluntarily (and *no person here* would have them)," he complained. Could he "compel them to contract with parties *who will receive them*?" He sought to contract freedpeople forcibly to employers as far away as Mississippi.[68]

Increasingly, local whites called on the Freedmen's Bureau to adopt compulsory labor measures to deal with black transients. The cotton crop, warned the *Intelligencer*, was imperiled if ex-slaves refused to work in the fields. "Shall either a mistaken philanthropy, or misdirected judgment," it asked, "prevent what is so absolutely necessary to the maintenance of the nation's credit?" It would be necessary to sponsor a new, revised labor system in which a freedman could be "induced, and where he cannot be induced, by his being compelled, to labor, in his cultivation of the cotton fields of the South." The *Intelligencer* proposed an intersectional alliance. "Let the Southern States be received in the Union, and let them regulate the labor of the freedman, as they would do in a manner both liberal and just to those of them who will labor."[69]

In August 1866, an Atlanta deputy sheriff attempted to evict the residents of the contraband camp, an action that bureau officials reversed. But throughout 1865–66 the bureau at least partly accepted the views of many Atlanta whites about black "idleness."[70] In October 1865, Georgia state commissioner Davis Tillson prohibited the distribution of rations to freedmen who were able-bodied but unwilling to work. In late December 1865, Tillson issued orders specifying new wage rates and compelling freedpeople to work under the bureau-supervised contracts. Moreover, Tillson further ordered that only working freedpeople could remain in cities, the remaining unemployed being compelled, if necessary, to work in labor arranged by contract. Tillson's policies had reduced the distribution of rations substantially by 1866.[71]

The dominant northern ideology of free labor shaped many of these policies. Northern whites, especially those associated with the bureau, expected that freedpeople would willingly work and would embrace a free-labor ethos. With the abolition of slavery, as Heather Cox Richardson has shown, northern Republicans began to insist that ex-slaves discover their freedom through work. "The idea that freedmen must work out their own fate in American society," Richardson writes, "appealed to those who expected them to fail as well as those who believed in African-American equality." Bureau officials fully subscribed to a northern work ethic, and, as Susan O'Donovan puts it when she describes white attitudes in southwest Georgia, they believed without question that relief and philanthropy would reinforce habits of "indolence, intemperance, and immorality that supposedly were learned under slavery when whips drove black people to work." When a free-labor ideology did not appear to take root, disillusioned northerners showed that there was no shortage of racism in their assumptions.[72]

The bureau strongly believed that freedpeople should work. As a result, while on the one hand attempting to root out the vestiges of slave labor, the bureau sought to inculcate a northern free-labor ideology among freedpeople. Meeting both these goals at once was a challenge for the bureau, but the most daunting obstacle it had to contend with was the wall of white racism that encircled the freedpeople. Only a minority of planters were "disposed to treat their laborers kindly and justly," according to Dennett, while a majority were "indisposed to give adequate wages and to recognize in practice that the negroes are free; that the negroes evinced an unwillingness to make contracts unless in cases where the person wishing to employ them was a Northern man."[73]

Overseeing labor contracts occupied much of the time of bureau officials, and it was through these contracts that the agency attempted to guide the transition to a free-labor society. In its attempt to use contracts as a new basis of free labor, the bureau made a better effort to be an honest broker. In July 1865, bureau commissioner Howard specified that the cornerstone of the attempt to institute free labor in the South would be contracts. Bureau agents were furnished with blank contracts, and they were expected to sign up ex-slaves and ex-masters according to a standard of "regular fair wages," which could be secured against a lien on crops or land. In practice, the contracts recognized arrangements by which ex-slaves could receive a share of the crop.[74] Bureau agents were instructed to consider "the entire change of circumstances, and be sure the laborer has due protection against avarice or extortion." No agent should tolerate "compulsory unpaid labor, except for the legal punishment of crime." Although Howard recognized that the bureau's policies might contribute to freedmen's suffering, he declared that their suffering was "preferable to slavery, and is to some extent the necessary consequence of events."[75] Bureau agents were to require employers to inform workers that they were free and "to recognize them as free men to make suitable agreements with them, whereby a just and equitable compensation will be accrued to them for their labor."[76] Typically lasting a year, the contracts specified wages and working conditions. In its insistence that freedpeople subscribe to a doctrine of free labor, bureau officials also attempted to use the labor contracts to transform the habits of southern white employers. After his arrival in October 1865, Curkendall was besieged by complaints from freedpeople of the abuse and cruelty they experienced from their white employers. In late 1865, he received an average of twelve applications per day for redress from freedpeople.[77]

Former slaveholders, especially during the early years of emancipation, contested the social and economic status of black people. Many, perhaps most, resented bureau interference in labor relations. Some planters refused to sign written contracts and insisted on verbal agreements, despite regulations that "persons employing Freedmen to labor for them," as an Atlanta bureau official put it in February 1866, "*must* have a written contract to that effect, said contract to be approved by an officer or agent of this Bureau."[78] Complaints about white planters violating their contracts and refusing to pay wages became common. In Cherokee County, freedman Columbus Allen testified that in the latter half of 1865 he lived on LaFayette Allen's plantation and helped him to harvest his corn crop. Once the corn was in the crib, Allen complained, the white planter made "threats of personal violence" and encouraged local whites to whip Columbus and drive him from the farm.[79] A few months later, a white employer in Campbellton, complaining that his workers were "saucey," refused to pay their wages.[80] When black workers insisted that their contracts be honored, they violated white expectations of black deference. In May 1867, freedman E. Tolfson claimed that he was shot by a white man, Bird Croel, after he demanded his wages.[81]

The bureau intervened in some instances of white brutality. In November 1866, H. F. Barrence, sheriff of Gwinnett County, was accused of "forceably" keeping freedwoman Lewisa Beats "without any compensation for her labour" and using "violence towards this woman for the purpose of retaining her contrary to the laws of this State or the United States." The bureau ordered Barrence to free Beats.[82] Many planters used the excuse of emancipation to cut ties with freedpeople when it suited them, and to evict aged, infirm, and inefficient workers. The bureau in Georgia specifically forbade former masters from turning away the young or the infirm—to force out "from their plantations faithful hands, who have helped to make the crops, when the crops are saved without paying for the labor already performed."[83] A frequent point of contention was whether the contracts between black workers and white planters implicitly covered their food and housing. Jane Harris and her husband George contracted with white planter John P. Harrington to work for him for a year in Palmetto, twenty-eight miles southeast of Atlanta. When he charged them for their room and board, they objected. The Harrises left over the dispute in March 1866, and Harrington followed them, beat George with a club, and threatened to "blow his brains out, if he did not return, which he did." Waldridge, in charge of the Atlanta bureau, ordered a local official to arrest Harrington.[84] In June 1867, Clayton County freedman York Hunter complained to the bureau that he had contracted himself to John Maddock. The contract specified six dollars a month in wages, plus three suits of clothes, three pairs of shoes, and rations for the year. But midway through the contract, Maddock assaulted Hunter and drove him off his farm. The local agent forced Maddock to make restitution.[85]

Fearing that northern officials were inciting freedpeople, whites regarded members of the bureau as invaders and occupiers. Although Atlanta was a city that already had a significant number of northern immigrants in the 1850s and 1860s, rumors about the behavior of these outsiders swirled through the community. An example of the paranoia about outsiders occurred in February 1866, when reports circulated that some "Yankee speculators" had carried off a "large gang of negroes" and left their wives and children on the street to starve. David S. Poole, then in charge of the Atlanta bureau, investigated the rumor, concluding that no such event had occurred. Having met with the mayor and city council to reassure fears, he also conferred with the military superintendent of the railroad. Poole discovered that a group of women and children had been stranded en route to western Tennessee because of the sickness of the children. The railroad superintendent confirmed that the rumors about northern kidnappers had no basis.

Although federal officials enforced the labor contracts only sporadically, the contracts afforded some isolated protection. When freedman Charles

Gaines claimed that his employer owed him ten dollars, Fred Mosebach, the subassistant commissioner, ordered the white employer to "pay that money without further delay if possibly due him otherwise I shall be compelled to enforce settlement [of] the case at this office."[86] On a farm outside of Newnan, ex-slave Cris Vinyard worked under a contract in which he was to receive an eighth of the fodder, half the cotton, half the oats, and half the potatoes of his white employer. But after harvest, the employer paid him only seventy-two pounds of pork and then ran him off the farm. The bureau allowed Vinyard to return to the farm under the terms of the contract, though the white farmer again ran him off in October 1867. With only a single agent in the county reporting to the Atlanta office, there was little that the bureau could do in reaction to such cases. White employers simply bided their time until they could secure the upper hand.[87] These cases continued to come before the desk of Subassistant Commissioner Mosebach, who took over the Atlanta office in early 1867 and served until the disbanding of the bureau in late 1868. Mosebach became known as sympathetic to freedmen and, in Atlanta, succeeded in using federal power to intervene on their behalf in the legal and economic system in the interests of justice. However, Mosebach's reach was weak in the surrounding north Georgia counties.[88]

THE BUREAU EXERCISED what can best be described as spasmodic influence in northern Georgia, and their record, from the freedpeople's perspective, remains mixed. Because federal presence in northern Georgia was isolated and regarded with hostility, management of the bureau enjoyed little continuity. During the six months after the Confederate surrender at Appomattox, the bureau operated in Atlanta with one subassistant commissioner, George Curkendall, who arrived in October 1865 and remained only two months. He was succeeded by three other subassistant commissioners during the next year. They supervised nineteen counties, relying on local agents who were paid by fees from freedpeople and their former masters. Only after early 1867 did the bureau actually pay salaries to agents. Perhaps equally important, federal authority lacked military force. The bureau's activities were "crippled by the want of cavalry," wrote Dennett in late 1865, and outside of Atlanta, federal authority often went unenforced. Instances of white fraud and cruelty, according to Dennett, "occurring at a distance from the town and from railroads necessarily go unpunished."[89]

The northern whites of the bureau often regarded African Americans suspiciously and condescendingly. Many of the officials found the southern white narrative about black indolence compelling, and they sometimes allied themselves with former slaveholders. On the other hand, the bureau, and, more generally, the federal military power, represented African Americans' best chance of protection against white oppression. The bureau's protective umbrella, however limited, offered some prospect for enforcing black freedom. Certainly, freedpeople invested great hope in federal authority. With the end of slavery, freedpeople flocked to urban areas to escape their ex-masters and the repressive atmosphere of the plantation South. Atlanta, like other towns and cities, became a mecca for the migrants, who lived in huts, tents, lean-tos, and dilapidated housing.[90] Freedpeople, Tera Hunter has noted, "eagerly rushed into Atlanta in even greater numbers than before," as their population grew from 1,900 to 10,000, out of a total city population of nearly 22,000.[91] The presence of the bureau and the northern army, which made Atlanta the headquarters of the Northwestern District of the Department of Georgia—one of four divisions in the state—offered protection for the black community.[92]

Before 1867, none of the bureau officials in Atlanta had expressed much sympathy with freedpeople. The bureau's approach in Atlanta changed radically in May 1867, with the arrival of Fred Mosebach as subassistant commissioner.[93] Mosebach's energetic administration of the bureau reflected the advent of Radical Reconstruction in Georgia—with its military government and the imposition of theoretically equal civil rights for freedpeople, along with their full enfranchisement. In the spring of 1867, Congress had adopted the Reconstruction Acts, which swept away civilian postwar governments in those southern states, including Georgia, which had refused to ratify the Fourteenth Amendment. Organized in March 1867, the Third Military District—including Georgia, Alabama, and Florida—was headquartered in Atlanta under the control of Maj. Gen. John Pope. Succeeded by Gen. George Meade in January 1868, Pope supervised the election of representatives to a constitutional convention that would meet starting in December 1867. Following the requirements of the Reconstruction Acts, the convention adopted a new constitution incorporating black suffrage.

Georgia Republicans—a coalition of conservative whites, former Unionists, and nearly all of the state's black voters—dominated the convention of 1868. Conservative whites, such as former governor Joseph E. Brown, became Republicans for pragmatic reasons. They had little confidence in the wisdom of enfranchising ex-slaves, but they favored a "New Era" that acknowledged the Yankee victory in exchange for a quick end to occupation. White Republicans included the small number of wartime Unionists in Georgia, mostly in middle and north Georgia. The coalition that they forged with their black allies was tense and fragile, and the enemies of Reconstruction sought to drive a wedge into the party by racially polarizing the political scene. After 1867, the military government of the Third Military District located itself in Atlanta, with Gen. Meade in charge. He remained in command until July 30, 1868, when civil authority was restored. The military unit was posted in a new fifty-three-acre base, the McPherson Barracks, that was completed in southwest Atlanta in late 1867. Even after Meade had relinquished control to the new civilian government, a small military presence remained for much of the nineteenth century.[94]

With the mandate of military rule, Mosebach, unlike his predecessors, was more likely to suspect white oppression than to blame freedpeople's inadequacies. The local Atlanta police, previously allied with the bureau, came under closer scrutiny, as did local government in the counties surrounding the city. Mosebach intervened more frequently than had his predecessors with his field agents, and he encouraged those blacks who were willing to risk antagonizing local whites by championing the freedpeople's cause. Unlike his predecessors, he spent less time with issues related to labor contracts, and more time focused on providing some justice for freedpeople.

The differences between Mosebach's and Waldridge's dealings with the Atlanta authorities can be illustrated by two events that took place a year apart from each other, in May 1866 and May 1867. In May 1866, police arrested Sally Ann Donohoe, a freedwoman, at the railroad depot on a charge of "indecency & vulgar conversation & abuse to passengers." It is difficult to evaluate the charges, but it is likely that the arrest reflected a perception of insubordinate, arrogant public behavior on the part of Donohoe, behavior which was perceived as a serious transgression of the racial code. Donohoe was arrested, released, and then arrested again. Waldridge reported that she had now become so "uncontrollable and unmanageable that she has to be kept in close confinement to prevent her from injuring herself and those in the camp." Atlanta police arrested another black woman, Mary Price, a year later, charging her with using "profane language." Mosebach questioned the arrest. "It is evident to me," he wrote to the mayor of the city, "that there was no necessity whatsoever for making the arrest, if the woman had violated any city ordinance a summons to appear before the proper court and answer to the charge would have been sufficient." The policeman had revealed by his behavior, Mosebach said, "that he has no respect for the rights of the free people, that instead of protecting them in their rights he uses his position to impose upon them, and therefore he is in my opinion not fit for the position."[95]

In April 1866, the U.S. Supreme Court, in *Ex parte Milligan*, prohibited the exercise of military authority over civilian courts—a decision that limited bureau authority.[96] Nonetheless Mosebach, who remained convinced that Atlanta's justice system worked to oppress freedpeople, refused to abandon his effort to counter the injustices he perceived. In August 1867, he complained that a city policeman had exercised "wanton cruelty towards the colored people of this city." Black citizens were treated "very roughly."[97] The problem went beyond the Atlanta police, as local magistrates also worked against black citizens. In January 1868, Mosebach wrote to Assistant Commissioner Caleb Sibley, describing A. G. Gaulding and William M. Butts as magistrates who handled legal cases involving African Americans in a way that was "arbitrary unjust and partial." Gaulding was an "unprincipled, corrupt, and worthless man," Mosebach said, who used his office "for the sole purpose of obtaining the fees thereof, without much regard for justice, law or duty."[98] In August 1868, Mosebach urged the newly elected civilian governor of Georgia, Rufus Bullock, to remove the Atlanta magistrates and replace them with more competent, and evenhanded, officers.[99]

Despite the restrictions on his power that had been imposed by *Ex parte Milligan*, Mosebach continued to intervene to protect freedpeople. After John Blake, a freedman, complained that an Atlanta magistrate had unlawfully seized his cow, Mosebach ordered the magistrate to return the property "immediately, or appear at this office and exhibit legal grounds and authority for the above mentioned seizure."[100] In early 1868, freedman Richmond Nutting was convicted of simple larceny in Atlanta Superior Court. Though only a small amount of property was involved, Nutting was nonetheless sentenced to nine months in the penitentiary. Stating that Nutting had a wife and five children "who need his support and pray that you may pardon him and remit the remainder of the sentence," Mosebach endorsed a petition to Georgia's military governor, Thomas H. Ruger.[101] Mosebach took the same aggressive approach with local officials outside of Atlanta under his jurisdiction. After a white man refused to pay a black worker with whom he had contracted in Carroll County, Mosebach encouraged a bureau agent, Edwin Belcher, to seize his wagon and oxen.[102]

Freedpeople were unquestionably sometimes committing crimes; not all accusations of lawbreaking reflected white racial prejudice, and untangling white injustice from black criminal conduct remains difficult. The maze of disrupted family relations among slaves that existed by virtue of slavery's very nature—with the constant separation of families that was occasioned by the slave trade—meant that it often proved difficult to reconstitute black families after the war. We can point to plenty of instances of blacks criminally exploiting each other in the chaotic postwar years and after. Furthermore, there were sometimes complications in determining the lines of familial authority.

An Atlanta freedwoman, Mahaley Wright, apprenticed her son to learn plastering and painting from a black artisan in Ringold, north of Atlanta, only to learn that the artisan had unlawfully subcontracted him and was collecting his earnings.[103] In February 1868, Mosebach investigated a case of ex-slave children who had been separated from their family and indentured to a white family. But he discovered that the children's mother was dead, the person making the claim was unrelated to the children and had uncertain motives, and the children were reportedly well treated. The matter had assumed a "different aspect," Mosebach wrote, from what had first appeared to be the case, and he found it difficult to advise a local agent with "definite instructions in regard to cases of similar character." If no law was broken, he was cautious about interfering in family matters. Early orders from the bureau in Georgia specified that common law, which gave parents authority over children, applied to former slaves.[104] Although parents were entitled to keep their children, other relatives had less certain claims, unless demonstrable instances of "cruel treatment or neglect of the apprentice can be established, or the law gives the right." "In all these cases we must proceed with caution and carefully examine the claims of the applicant," Mosebach advised, ordering the agent "not to make any decision yourself, but collect all facts connected with a case and submit them with your own opinion thereon to the Asst. Comr and let him cancel the indenture or reject the application."[105]

In the postwar chaos, many former slaveholders, especially in the first two years after emancipation, continued to treat black people as if they were slaves. These practices appeared more pronounced in the counties outside Atlanta that were under the bureau field office's jurisdiction. Shortly after the war, in the summer of 1865, German-born Union general Carl Schurz had toured the South to report to Congress on postwar conditions. Although most Georgians might eventually be reconciled to the end of slavery "in the old form," he discovered, "many attempts were made to introduce into that new system the element of physical compulsion, which, as above stated, is so generally considered indispensable." The brutalization of blacks that was common when they were slaves still prevailed, and the practice of whipping continued "to a great extent, although, perhaps, not in so regular a manner as it was practiced in times gone by." The habit of violence remained "so inveterate with a great many persons as to render, on the least provocation, the impulse to whip a negro almost irresistible."[106]

The bureau became an object of southern white resentment against federal intervention in their affairs. According to one account, the idea of a "strong Federal agency placed in the midst is naturally repulsive to the [white] masses."[107] Violence became increasingly commonplace. Educators in the newly established black schools became targets. White teachers were accused of "sowing ill feeling and hatred among the colored people" and convening "secret meetings" to mobilize African Americans politically, and many were run out by local vigilantes.[108] Federal officials, a northern white observed in 1868, had a limited ability to control this violence, as a majority of Georgians seldom saw federal officials.[109]

Outside Atlanta, racial violence accompanied emancipation and accelerated during the Yankee occupation. The bureau required its subassistant commissioners and their agents to document "outrages" against freedpeople, and it reported them dutifully. Though these numbers were probably underreported, they suggest a rising level of terror and intimidation against freedpeople in the counties surrounding Atlanta. John Leonard in September 1866 wrote of the "bushwhackers and Regulators who reside in Heard & Coweta counties these men are reported to me as having been engaging in all of the recent murders and outrages committed on freed people."[110]

In 1868, violence against African Americans peaked in portions of the state, and outside of Atlanta vigilantes freely beat, abducted, and murdered them. Thus in May 1868, in Forsyth County, John Lambert, a black man, was attacked by a party of white men, who broke into his home at night and shot up his house. No charges were filed. The following October, also in Forsyth, freedman Adam Holbrook was shot and severely beaten by a party of white men. Local authorities refused to issue any arrest warrants. In Henry County, Peter Turner was shot by "unknown parties, all disguised," and he died two days later. The murderers went unpursued. In nearby Cherokee County in October 1868, a party of disguised white men burst into the home of Jerry Garrison, a black man, and shot him and his sons. In this wave of violence in 1868 in the Atlanta bureau district, white men assaulted nine freedmen with intent to kill, while six more freedmen were assaulted and murdered.[111]

Near the end of the bureau's existence, there were four cases of murder and four of assault reported in Fulton County.[112] Outside the city, in Campbell County, in October 1868, William Latham, a black man, was stabbed and killed by his white employer, Thomas Latham. After a coroner's inquest dismissed the case, the bureau agent intervened and arrested Thomas Latham. But, since no legal mechanism was in place to try him in civilian courts, he went free.[113] Bureau agents found themselves overwhelmed outside of Atlanta with too few resources and insufficient military force and police power. In all the surviving records of murder or assault by whites of blacks, there is no record of prosecution, let alone any conviction. Whites realized that they could attack ex-slaves with impunity because federal authorities lacked the wherewithal to act, even if they wanted to act. In February 1868, Mosebach investigated the case in Heard County, near Franklin, of Matthew A. Straighorn, accused of assaulting James Moore, a Coweta County freedman, with intent to kill. Mosebach traveled to Newnan, Georgia, where he discovered Straighorn's address. Arriving at his house, he found it unoccupied. A local black farmer informed Mosebach that Straighorn had sold his property and left for Alabama three weeks earlier. Using "due precaution" with local whites, Mosebach discovered Straighorn's new address, but, without a way to travel there, he returned to Atlanta. Mosebach then requested that assistant commissioner Sibley dispatch a squad of cavalry to arrest Straighorn. There is no evidence that Sibley pursued the case.[114]

In March 1866, when Mosebach ran the bureau in Augusta, he reported to his superiors that ill-treatment of freedpeople in rural areas was growing "worse from day to day." African Americans were moving to urban areas because "here they are protected, but beyond 10 miles from town they must live in continual fear of their lives and property." He found it nearly impossible to provide protection in rural areas without enough military force.[115] Mosebach expressed his frustrations again two years later in Atlanta.[116] Requesting additional staff in his district, he wrote Sibley that the "great number of complaints made by freedpeople" were impossible to address because of his inability to enforce the law. Cases involving ex-slaves required "regular judicial proceedings to investigate and determine, which takes time and patience, neither of which I have at the present time." Consulting "eight of the best colored citizens of this City," Mosebach recommended Bluford Smith, a judge of the Fulton County Court, as a "suitable and proper person for the office." Smith enjoyed a good reputation among ex-slaves as a judge who worked with "impartiality and justice, doing right without making any distinction of race or color."[117]

Mosebach's frustrations suggest that the legacy of the Freedmen's Bureau in Atlanta was mixed. As a single sympathetic official, he could go only so far to protect African Americans in the face of unrelenting white hostility. For southern whites, the bureau was a potent symbol of northern interference. Whites still regarded the northerners as an invading, occupying force in the late 1860s, and that feeling became, if anything, even more pronounced in Reconstruction Georgia. For ex-slaves, the meaning of freedom remained ambiguous; white violence had reinstalled white dominance throughout Georgia. But, in Georgia as elsewhere, enclaves of exceptionalism could be found. Atlanta provided a distinctive environment in which northern whites, ex-slaves, and white Atlantans could interact with each other. White dominance reigned supreme in the city, yet African Americans migrated there in large numbers, seeking jobs and refuge. In the antebellum period, Atlanta had been a fortress of white solidarity. In the postwar period, freedpeople gained a toehold in what would subsequently become a center of black cultural, economic, and political power. That development found its roots in postwar Atlanta, and the bureau played a role, unwitting or not, in its evolution.

FOUR

Every Contrivance of Cruelty

Violence and White Supremacy in the New South

On March 31, 1868, in a spectacular act of Reconstruction-era political terror, a group of about thirty masked white men assassinated George W. Ashburn, a white Republican leader in Columbus, Georgia. The killing of Ashburn, a Unionist who became a Republican during Reconstruction, laid bare the realities of white supremacy in the aftermath of the Civil War. His murder, and the controversial efforts to prosecute his killers, brought to public attention and exposed southern notions about the Yankee invasion, the role of African Americans in postwar southern society, and the characteristics of southern white resistance. Violence and intimidation served as the primary tools used by whites to fight Reconstruction. White allies of ex-slaves were especially loathsome and treacherous, according to whites who opposed Reconstruction. In attempting to justify the suppression of white and black Republicanism, opponents of Reconstruction developed their own version of history, which existed side by side with their narrative of rebirth and rejuvenation in the South.

For the anti-Reconstructionists, even economic development was subordinate to the necessities of power and the reestablishment of racial control. Although Ashburn's murder occurred in Columbus, the trial of his accused murderers took place in Atlanta. The city, at once a safe haven for African Americans and the scene of white supremacy's triumph, provided a setting for one of the most important moments in the history of Reconstruction Georgia. In highlighting the political, social, and legal consequences of the federal occupation, as well as the significance of race, this instance of vigilante violence reverberated throughout the state.

WITH THE ESTABLISHMENT of the congressionally imposed military government in the spring of 1867, men like George Ashburn reasserted their Unionist principles. In pockets of north Georgia, the spirit of Unionism was celebrated in the postwar years with the formation of units of the fraternal organization, the Grand Army of the Republic (GAR).[1] Having been a vital cog in the Confederate war machine, Atlanta remained a hostile environment for those who had been antebellum Unionists. After the arrival of Gen. John Pope as military governor, Atlanta Unionists organized an effort to establish a monument honoring the martyred president Abraham Lincoln. In the summer of 1867, the group distributed a circular urging the establishment of a Lincoln monument. Atlanta, a "keystone and central prop of the Slave Confederacy which Mr. Lincoln led the nation to destroy," offered a "ground made sacred by the dust of the victor and the vanquished, the Unionist and the Seceder." The group proposed creating a monument "around which the living may gather and forget the bitter past" as "imperishable proof of our reconciliation, no less than an everlasting record to future generations of National Union and National Glory."[2]

As president of the Lincoln National Monument Association, James L. Dunning led the effort. A Connecticut native who had immigrated to Atlanta in the late 1840s, Dunning became a successful entrepreneur. Remaining an ardent Unionist during the war, he refused to conduct business with Confederates. In 1864, Atlanta authorities imprisoned Dunning. Subsequently becoming a Republican activist, Dunning was elected to the 1868 state constitutional convention and was appointed Atlanta's U.S. postmaster.

As a southern white loyalist, Dunning expressed a view of the war starkly different from that of the mainstream.[3] In September 1867, he petitioned the Atlanta City Council for permission to erect the monument. A special committee of the council recommended providing ten acres of land for a park to house the monument if Dunning's Lincoln Association could raise at least $750,000. The council adopted the resolution by a vote of 6–4, but with no expectation that the money could ever be raised to establish such a monument. Council members wanted to assuage Republican opinion but also to subvert the proposal.[4]

The issue of the Lincoln monument immediately became a flashpoint. "Let them send out and gather the bones of the brave and patriotic Southerners who fell by the bullets of Lincoln's hirelings while fighting for their country's rights, and which lie bleaching upon the hills and valleys of every Southern State," the *Augusta Chronicle and Sentinel* announced in August 1867. "Let them collect the crimson gore of their noble hearts which stained the fields and reddened the grass of a thousand farms in Virginia and Georgia, Mississippi and Tennessee."[5] The *Atlanta Daily Intelligencer* agreed. If there was to be a national Lincoln monument, why should southern taxpayers' funds be used? it asked. The people of Atlanta did not "owe such a monument to his memory."[6] The city lacked even the money to build a fence around the cemetery where fallen Confederates were laid to rest. "If the friends and admirers of the late Mr. Lincoln want a monument," it declared, "let them build it." But Republicans should not ask the people of Atlanta to pay for a monument "commemorated to their own degradation."[7]

The dialogue continued when two Republican newspapers in Atlanta, the *Daily Opinion* and the *Daily New Era*, both endorsed construction of the monument. The *Daily New Era*, which was allied with former Civil War governor and Republican Joseph E. Brown, supported building the monument as a way to promote Atlanta's development and to spur outside investment by helping to transcend the war's immediate and painful memories. The *Daily Intelligencer* responded sharply, accusing the *New Era* of engaging in the "traffic of *a dead man's memory*, and making a *merchantable commodity* of the remains of an ex-President of the United States." At the head of a "merciless horde sent hither at *his* bidding," Lincoln had led a "holy crusade" against the South. He "burnt our cities, towns and villages—despoiled us of our property—made us a nation of paupers." This was a "monstrous" bargain indeed. Building a Lincoln memorial would show "duplicity and hyprocrisy."[8] The *Intelligencer* censured the six city councilmen voting in favor of the monument.[9]

The idea of erecting a Lincoln monument alarmed other residents. "Is Atlanta a Southern city or a Yankee metropolis?" asked an Atlantan. "If building monuments to Lincoln is to draw Yankees, don't you suppose it will drive away Southern gentlemen?"[10] A Lincoln monument would cast a shadow across the hallowed ground where twenty thousand Confederates had fallen.[11] "A Lincoln monument at Atlanta! Great God, what an insult!" Having suffered from the "brutal Sherman" under Lincoln's command, Atlanta had been left a "heap of ashes and smouldering, blackened ruins." A monument to Lincoln would remind residents "how completely subjugated and humbled were the Southern people."[12] Another resident suggested that a "Lincoln-Sherman" monument should be erected in the middle of the downtown district, where it could commemorate Lincoln's decision to send "his legions here with torch in one hand and sword in the other, to burn, pillage, and destroy, and to wage war upon helpless women and children." The monument would rest on the "mouldering *debris*" that told a "silent tale of horror and cruelty" and reminded southerners of "one who drenched our own Sunny South in blood!"[13] Lincoln's monument already existed, said the *Daily Intelligencer*, in "ghastly cemeteries and battlegrounds" and in the "armless, legless, mutilated epitaphs to his memory." Lincoln was memorialized in "a broken Union, a violated Constitution, a debt of three thousand millions, reared upon the labor of every working man." His memory lived on "without a monument."[14]

Twenty years after the failed attempt to establish a Lincoln monument, a newspaper commentator calling himself "The Old Colonel" recalled Dunning's efforts as part of a larger failure to impose Yankee rule on Atlanta. The Old Colonel wrote in the summer of 1888 about the Civil War siege of Atlanta, recalling the hardships endured by the city's civilian population. Recalling the immediate postwar era, he described the efforts of Union commander Pope to control city affairs. "Negro soldiers swarmed everywhere," he wrote, and they were "brutal and insolent, with a musket in one hand and a dirty spelling book in the other." According to this account, the city council only went along with the resolution allowing a Lincoln monument to be established because it did not want to offend the "Dictator Pope." The members of the council had been able to persuade Pope not to appoint black members, thus making Atlanta the "only city in the south so fortunate as to escape negro domination." These had been "dark days" that belonged to the "dead past" in which the "indomitable spirit of a free people asserted itself, and the dictator with his bayonets sullenly departed, leaving the historic city to rise again in more than her former beauty and power."[15]

This narrative of Yankee occupation, "negro rule," and economic redemption came to dominate the popular southern understanding of the Reconstruction era. And this narrative was woven into Atlanta whites' memories of how the war and its aftermath had physically and emotionally damaged the social structure. Left out of this narrative, of course, was the role that white violence and oppression played in undermining Reconstruction, Republicanism, and African American political empowerment. Although Atlanta largely escaped the political violence that prevailed over much of the rest of Georgia, the city's white residents embraced racial repression as a necessary instrument to urban rebirth.

DURING THE LATE 1860s, rising white violence elsewhere in Georgia sought to limit black political power, cripple the Republican party, and end Reconstruction. The best-known vigilante organization, the Ku Klux Klan, worked closely with the state's anti-Reconstruction Democratic party. During the spring and summer of 1868, the secret organization spread quickly throughout the South, employing networks of ex-Confederates in loosely structured and decentralized cells. In March 1868, according to a widely held view, the arrival of Grand Wizard Nathan Bedford Forrest to Atlanta led to the formation of a Georgia Klan. The Klan's purposes were to terrorize freedpeople, intimidate white Republicans, and turn public opinion against Reconstruction by provoking a military crackdown.[16]

As elsewhere in the South, racial violence erupted in Georgia in areas where white majorities prevailed. The two important centers of Klan violence in Georgia were located near Atlanta, in eight or nine counties northwest and in the seventeen counties east of the city on the South Carolina border.[17] Reputedly, during the late 1860s the Georgia Klan claimed ten to twelve thousand members and was headquartered in Atlanta. Its avowed purpose was "to control the negro vote, and to defeat the republican party in obtaining offices."[18] Yet, because of the McPherson Barracks garrison and the presence of several thousand soldiers, the city remained relatively tranquil in one of the most Klan-infested areas of the upcountry South.

Atlanta thus became, paradoxically, a bastion of both white supremacy and black autonomy, a locale in which competing visions of the postemancipation world emerged. After the presidential election of 1868, a white Republican recalled that Atlanta escaped the political terror gripping much of the state. "There could not have been a fairer election than there was there," he testified.[19] The Republican members of the legislature, who were harassed by death threats and political violence, reported that they "refugeed to this city . . . for the purpose of escaping personal injuries at the hands of white men in our respective counties."[20] When Pennsylvania editor and politician John W. Forney visited Atlanta in May 1869, he reported that hotels were packed; the "whole population, white and black, was out." Atlanta had assumed a "metropolitan appearance" and had become a "city for live men." The city, according to Forney, had become a "place of refuge for the Republicans who are driven away from those quarters in the interior where the white Unionists are still persecuted, and where the blacks are intimidated or subsidized." In Atlanta, there was little evidence of the terror that prevailed in surrounding counties. As another white Republican noted, "nothing has occurred that would cause any great excitement."[21]

The city's communities of former Unionists and of black refugees from rural areas continued to grow. Forty-one-year-old ex-slave Columbus Jeter was teaching night school for African Americans in Douglas County, about twenty miles west of Atlanta, when he was visited by white vigilantes in April 1871. One evening, he and his wife heard a "terrible howling" outside his door, the "most curious howling of dogs I ever heard." Realizing that it was the Klan, Jeter hid in his chimney just before they burst through the door. When they realized where he was, the Klansmen said: "God damn him, here he is in the chimney. Fire up the chimney." Jeter, agreeing to come out, faced the vigilantes, several of whom he recognized. Jerking him down and holding him by his hair, the whites tied an apron over his face and took him outside. "Now, Columbus," one said, "do you think a colored man is as good as a white-man?" While beating him, they also said: "This is for saying that a nigger is as good as a white man, and for drawing a stick on a white man." Jeter somehow escaped, but was shot in the shoulder. Managing to recover from his wounds, Jeter went to a local justice of the peace, demanding justice. "Can you give me justice here?" Jeter asked the magistrate, who responded: "I can't, for if I do my house will be burnt up before four-and-twenty hours." Jeter fled to Atlanta.[22]

Other instances of political violence drove refugees to Atlanta. Alfred Richardson, an ex-slave and house carpenter, participated in Republican politics in Walton County, about fifty miles east of Atlanta. Advised by a sympathetic white that he was "making too much money" and that the Klan would not permit "any nigger to rise that way," Richardson was targeted because he was thought to control "all the colored votes." In December 1870, Klansmen attacked and slightly wounded Richardson in a gun battle. Although a marked man, he remained in Walton County. Sometime around midnight in January 1871, a group of twenty-five to thirty men wearing black cambric masks and long white gowns visited him. When Richardson barred the door, eight men unsuccessfully tried to break it down with an axe. Richardson retreated to the second floor of his house, firing shots at his attackers. His willingness to use firearms against white men—an unusual thing in post–Civil War Georgia—saved his life. Like other victims of Klan violence, he left for Atlanta.[23]

African Americans who succeeded in accumulating property or in exercising political power became exposed to Klan violence. In Morgan and Greene counties, about sixty miles east of Atlanta, Monday Floyd, an African American who had been elected to the state House of Representatives in 1868, was abducted in December 1870. Although the perpetrators released him, a few days later he was again attacked. Floyd fled to the woods and hid out until he made his way to Atlanta, where he remained permanently. Only occasionally did he return to Morgan County for short, surreptitious visits.[24]

ATLANTA BECAME A SOCIAL AND POLITICAL refuge for African Americans primarily because of the small contingent of federal troops posted at McPherson Barracks. These troops were often unsympathetic to black people, but their presence restrained white violence. During elections held in

Atlanta in December 1870, for example, local constables, working against Republican voters, shoved back African Americans from the polls, barring them from the franchise. After two days of disrupted elections, federal marshals and a detachment of forty soldiers appeared on the scene. Shouts went up. In defiance of the soldiers, the constables called out "Three cheers for Bull Run" and "Hurrah for Manassas." But the marshal organized a line of about three hundred to four hundred Republican voters, in ranks of two, and the voting resumed. Although Democrats continued to harass Republicans, this was a rare instance of federal intervention in local elections. Similar supervision of elections never took place elsewhere in Georgia.[25]

African Americans within a hundred miles of Atlanta saw the city as a last resort. Abram Colby, who was born in 1820 in Greene County to a slave mother and her white master, was freed by his father and inherited property from him. A minister and barber, he became one of the county's most important Republican leaders.[26] Elected to the legislature in 1868, Colby confronted white intimidation, refusing to join the Democrats. On October 29, 1869, vigilantes abducted Colby and savagely beat him for three hours. Despite continuing to resist Klan pressure, Colby found it impossible to mount a campaign in the elections of December 1870. "No man can make a free speech in my county," he declared, adding that he did not believe "it can be done anywhere in Georgia."

Sometime in late 1870, Colby fled to Atlanta. Asked why he did not return to Greene County, Colby responded, "Because they Ku-Klux my house every time I go home. Any day that I am home I may expect the Ku-Klux at my house. I have not staid there more than one night this year; I had to stay in the woods." Atlanta, he declared, became a refuge "for protection" of the black population. Because of the presence of the U.S. Army, "nobody interferes with us here." "For that reason we have come here for protection; we cannot stop anywhere else so safely, and that is the reason I came here." Lacking federal protection meant "death at once," according to Colby. He had little faith in the ability of Georgia courts to protect African Americans from white assault. Black people were assaulted for any sign of political and economic independence. "I have had my case for two years," he told congressional investigators in 1871, "and I have never carried it before one of them, because I believed I could not get justice."[27]

Flight to Atlanta also provided black people with some leverage. Greene Westmoreland, an ex-slave from Spalding County, visited his wife and children regularly after he moved to work in Atlanta. His wife owed two dollars to a local white doctor, Jim Nunnally. When Westmoreland passed through a rural grocery store, he encountered Nunnally, who demanded immediate payment. Nunnally's main grievance was Westmoreland's physical independence. "Are you going back to Atlanta?" Nunnally demanded. Westmoreland said that he was, and Nunnally accused him of becoming an "Atlanta gentleman" and "above working on a farm." When Westmoreland admitted that he could "make more money at Atlanta than down here," Nunnally took this as an affront and attacked him with a knife, rocks, and an iron poker. Westmoreland did not resist the assault, though he used his arms to try to ward off the blows, as twenty or thirty whites watched. After Westmoreland informed local authorities, they told him: "We aint agoing to do anything for you." Returning to Atlanta, Westmoreland had "staid here ever since" and sent for his wife and family.[28]

EVENTS OCCURRING IN 1868 punctuated Atlanta's increasingly central role in the state, reminding Atlantan residents that developments elsewhere in Georgia shaped their fate also. An act of political violence that occurred in Columbus, Georgia, more than a hundred miles to the south, illustrates Atlanta's stake in state affairs. Founded in 1827, at the falls of the Chattahoochee River, Columbus became a trade, transportation, and financial center, with railroads, banks, steamboats, and a steadily increasing population. Water power from the river facilitated textile manufacturing; antebellum Columbus called itself the "Lowell [Massachusetts] of the South." Local capitalists continued to found new enterprises, such as paper manufacturing and grain milling. Like Atlanta, Columbus served as an industrial and transportation center for the Confederacy. The city produced uniforms, arms, and war matériel. Three railroad lines ran out of town.[29]

In the years after the Civil War, George Ashburn was one of a group of people Columbus whites disdainfully referred to as "scalawags"—white southerners who supported the Republican party. His origins remain murky. Wallace Reed, an early historian of Atlanta, wrote that he was from North Carolina but had lived in Georgia for thirty years. Another source claimed that he migrated to Columbus in 1867.[30] In reality, the popular image of Ashburn represented a combination of fictions. He always asserted that he was born in Georgia, an assertion that appears to be correct.[31] He first appears in the documentary record in January 1848, when the local government of Upson County, northeast of Columbus, hired him to teach the "poor schools" of the county.[32] During the next decade, Ashburn operated hotels in Columbus and Macon and in Lookout Mountain, Tennessee.[33] In 1860, the federal census recorded that he lived in Columbus, was forty-eight years old, had a wife and three sons, worked as a cotton broker, and possessed about $300 in property.[34]

Ashburn's adamantly Unionist views alienated him from most Georgia whites. In June 1861, Columbus secessionists demanded that he refrain from "derogatory" statements about the Confederacy and sign an oath of allegiance, or leave the state. Ashburn fled Georgia to his hotel in Lookout Mountain, and then moved behind Union lines in Murfreesboro, Tennessee. During the war, he raised a regiment of southern loyalists and worked as a scout and teamster for Union forces.[35] In October 1862, Ashburn turned in a British trader who was attempting to supply the Confederate army in Tennessee.[36] He emerged from the war with a deep hatred for the Confederacy. Days after Lincoln's assassination, Ashburn wrote to President Andrew Johnson. The "hand of God is in the assassination," he said. The nation needed "a more vigorous administration." The southern rebels were "all assassins, and ought to meet their inevitable fate."[37]

In the fall of 1865, Ashburn returned to Columbus, where he became one of the state's leading Radicals. When Georgia seceded, Ashburn wrote in October 1865, he refused to participate in its "hellish crusade against the best government man ever lived under." He later opposed conciliating ex-Confederates: "Such by-gones," he wrote, "we have not consented to let be by-gones, but hold each individual responsible before the laws of the country." "Few in number, poor in purse, and less in influence," Union men such as Ashburn continued to argue against the principles that had led to secession.[38]

Ashburn quickly became a Republican activist. Serving as a member of the 1868 constitutional convention, he wrote the civil rights sections of the state constitution. He opposed efforts to limit the black franchise, and was described in February 1868 as having been "pale with rage" during a contentious debate about the African American right to vote. He was known for his intemperate political behavior: a fellow white Republican called him unbalanced, "flighty, and enthusiastic."[39] In 1868, Ashburn assembled an organization to support his election to the U.S. Senate after Georgia had been readmitted to the Union. As one of Georgia's most prominent white allies of African Americans, Ashburn became an obvious target for white hatred.[40]

On the evening of March 30, 1868, Ashburn participated in a meeting of eight hundred Republicans at Columbus's Temperance Hall.[41] He shared the stage with Henry McNeal Turner, an African Methodist Episcopal bishop, Civil War chaplain, and Republican organizer. Addressing the crowd for over two hours, Turner was frequently interrupted by applause. "I have never known a meeting in this place," said a reporter from the *Washington Chronicle*, "to break up in a better spirit than this did." The white press told a different story. It described how Ashburn marshaled his "black clans," including a "few hundred idle vagabonds of the worst class." The "immense assemblage of negroes," according to this account, had listened to a "violent and incendiary" address by Turner. After the meeting, Ashburn returned to his room in a local boardinghouse, which he rented from Hannah Flournoy, an African American woman.[42] The white press, foes of Reconstruction, described Flournoy as a "yellow negress" and her house a "colored bawdy-house." Ashburn had been driven into these living arrangements "on account of his immoral character, not political principles." But Ashburn lived at Flournoy's boardinghouse because white Columbus had shunned him.[43] A one-story structure, Flournoy's house contained three bedrooms arranged in shotgun style, with one room behind another. Ashburn occupied a low-pitched rear room, described in newspaper accounts as dirty, with doors on three sides and a wooden shutter.[44]

After midnight on March 31, a band of well-dressed masked men, their faces blackened—men who were subsequently described as "nice, dandy, young gentlemen"—approached the boardinghouse.[45] Alexander Gordon Bennett, a Columbus machinist and fellow white Republican, rushed to warn Ashburn. Convinced that the men meant no harm, Ashburn calmly lighted a candle and put on his coat. Amanda Patterson, a white woman who occupied Flournoy's front bedroom, then watched in horror as the men battered down the door. A mask slipped off the face of one of the perpetrators, and he warned Patterson, "Damn you, if you tell on me, I'll kill you." When the assailants burst into Ashburn's room, some witnesses claimed that he drew a pistol; others said that he was unarmed. At some point, someone shouted, "There's the damn shit," a shout that was followed by, "Shoot the damned rascal." At least five men, entering from the middle room and an outside door, opened fire. Ashburn fell immediately, mortally wounded, struck by three bullets.

Two Columbus policemen heard the shots and, arriving in the neighborhood, saw men fleeing. Local police, almost certainly complicit in the murder, unenthusiastically pursued the perpetrators. Hearing a woman's screaming, they turned their attention to Flournoy's house. The coroner's inquest, which was held on April 3, determined that Ashburn had been hit in the buttocks and his left leg, with the third and fatal shot a bullet striking him between the eyes. Unable to determine the assassins' identities, the coroner concluded that Ashburn had died at the hands of "persons unknown."[46]

The murder of George Ashburn, *Frank Leslie's Illustrated Newspaper*

ASHBURN'S MURDER coincided with a surge in political terrorism throughout Georgia. Much of this violence was attributed, in a general but vague way,
to "the Klan." Allen W. Trelease, a historian of the Klan during Reconstruction, describes Ashburn's murder as the "first Ku Klux outrage to be reported
outside of Tennessee."[47] A number of contemporaries confirm Trelease's assessment that the conspiracy to murder Ashburn followed the Klan's arrival
in Columbus, Georgia. The *Columbus Sun*, serving as an unofficial vigilante
mouthpiece, published notices of KKK activity during late March 1868. Three
days before Ashburn's murder, the *Sun* had published an editorial warning
"Radicals" and "Scalawags." "Let traitors beware!" it declared. During the last
week of March 1868, Klan signs and markings were posted on the house
walls and doors of Republicans and Union men. These signs included images
of skulls, coffins, skeletons, and crossbones. One sign portrayed a coffin with
a skeleton inside it and with Ashburn's name written on it. "Their time was
short," the signs reportedly said, and "their days were numbered"; Republicans should "prepare for sudden and awful death." The time was coming
when the "blood of the Confederate dead" would be avenged.[48]

Nonetheless, it remains uncertain whether, and perhaps unlikely that, Ashburn's murderers belonged to the Klan, at least in a formal sense. The murder did not follow the Klan's modus operandi or occur in the kind of locale usually chosen for Klan activity. Ashburn was killed in an urban-industrial community; Klan violence rarely occurred in cities. The descriptions of the perpetrators of the Ashburn murder reported men with blackened faces and masks, but with none of the costumery normally associated with the Klan. The conspirators were more likely local vigilantes who were perhaps inspired by the success of white violence elsewhere. The Columbus perpetrators were opportunistic and adaptive, precise and determined in their methods, and ruthlessly violent. Although this killing was probably, at the most, only loosely associated with statewide Klan organization and activities, both supporters and opponents of Reconstruction embraced the case as an example of KKK violence.

Whether the killers were Klan or not, the occupying military forces immediately recognized the threat that Ashburn's assassination exemplified. The brazen murder of a leading white Republican challenged northern authority and the very legitimacy of Reconstruction, while it undermined the viability of the coalition between former Unionists and African Americans. The force that could most powerfully counter the white terrorism was in Atlanta, in Gen. George Meade's Third Military District. Meade condemned the actions of the "apparently . . . secret organization . . . which seems to be rapidly spreading through these States" and to which he attributed the murder. From Atlanta, Meade ordered military commanders in Columbus to arrest the perpetrators and to compel local authorities to bring them to justice.[49]

Northern newspaper correspondents portrayed Ashburn as a martyr who was the victim of vigilantism. His murder, according to the *Washington Chronicle*, was "one of the most brutal and inhuman events ever recorded by mortal pen." His only fault was "his loyalty to his country, and the belief that Congress was right in its plan of reconstructing the South." Northern observers saw the killing as the sign of a conspiracy, a "concerted thing between the parties themselves and the police."[50] The motive behind Ashburn's murder was purely political, said the *New York Times*. The assassination of an "active and influential" Radical and organizer of African Americans sent a message to white Republicans across the South. Ashburn's killing was "deliberate and concerted," part of "secret conspiracies" seeking to subvert Reconstruction. The *Times* favored military intervention as a response, along with suspension of habeas corpus and a wholesale effort to crush the uprising.[51]

Ashburn had been killed in a deliberate act of political terror, said the *Chicago Tribune*. A Unionist advocate of black political and civil rights, Ashburn had earned former Confederates' "bitter hatred" because of his "uncompromising detestation of the institution which produced secession and now produces the Kuklux-Klan."[52]

Commanding the only significant military force in the Deep South, Meade agreed with this assessment. The murder, he declared, was "in great measure political as well as social." The event electrified southern white opposition to Reconstruction, revealing a pattern of disorder and violence—a sort of insurrection—that was tied to vigilantism and political violence. Local government made little attempt "to ferret out the guilty." Meade was ill-equipped to deal with the situation. His authority, Meade realized, was dependent on the moral authority that the government seemed to have in people's eyes rather than on physical force alone.

Meade ordered his commander in Columbus, Capt. William Mills, to take charge of the investigation. Mills had little confidence in the ability of whites to administer justice, and he had already concluded that Columbus's "better class of citizens," including its government and police, were behind the murder.[53] Indeed, a Columbus policeman later participated in an unsuccessful assassination attempt of another white Republican, A. G. Bennett. When Ashburn was gunned down, four policemen were near enough to the assailants "to hear the cocking of their pistols." But rather than pursue the murderers, they turned off in the opposite direction. During the evening of Ashburn's killing, a black woman saw the Columbus chief of police wearing a mask identical to the masks worn by the killers. Police collusion and the "very great indifference of the people generally" had intimidated white Republicans and their African American allies.

Concluding that the Columbus police's efforts were "all show and merely assumed," Meade dissolved the local government and appointed Mills mayor. On April 6, 1868, about a week after Ashburn's assassination, Mills arrested nine Columbus whites and one African American blacksmith, John Wells.[54] Four days later, Mills detained another group of citizens, including two additional African Americans. On April 18, the War Department dispatched an investigator, William H. Reed, to Columbus and, on May 1, Internal Revenue Service detective Maj. H. C. Whitely joined him. Reed and Whitely transferred the detainees held by Mills from Columbus to Fort Pulaski, at the mouth of the Savannah River. More arrests followed in June, and the prisoners were transferred to the military barracks in Atlanta. On June 19, 1868, because Georgia had not yet been readmitted to the Union and remained under military rule, Meade ordered that the prisoners be tried by a military commission in Atlanta.[55]

Public attention shifted away from the drama of Ashburn's murder in Columbus, to Atlanta and to the trial of the "Columbus Prisoners" itself. Trials of civilians by military commissions had been common during the northern occupation of the South in the Civil War. In the early years of occupation, at least ten civilians had been tried in military courts in Atlanta for various infractions. The Supreme Court's *Milligan* decision had limited the authority of military commissions, yet these courts continued to exist in the occupied South. Meade asserted his authority under the Reconstruction Acts of 1867, which imposed military government on the unreconstructed South and authorized military measures to subdue insurrection. In the circumstances of the spectacular Ashburn case, Meade realized that he possessed limited options. No civilian court would even try, let alone convict, the murderers; military trial became the only feasible setting for a prosecution. But by bringing the trial to Atlanta, Meade elevated the political stakes significantly.

THE TRIAL OF THE COLUMBUS PRISONERS effectively transformed the meaning of a sordid political killing. Rather than an act of terrorism, Ashburn's murder became to southern whites a story of northern oppression and racial insubordination, themes that the Democratic press exploited statewide in what Meade later called "numerous malicious and false statements."[56] Contention over the meaning of the Civil War remained a burning and very real issue. The *Columbus Sun* issued attacks, republished statewide, about Ashburn, who, it claimed, had collaborated with the northern occupiers. His purpose, said the *Sun*, had been to "commence an active crusade against the white people of the State of Georgia" and to cause a "breach of the peace" that would promote strife.[57] Ashburn's most serious transgression, to many Georgia whites, was his alliance with African Americans. Describing him as "the chief organizer of the black Radical Party in Georgia" and as a man whose "influence over the negroes was great,"[58] the white press demonized him. Ashburn was a "notorious racial adventurer," claimed the *Sun*, an adventurer who depended on scalawag and black support. Columbus whites "thoroughly detested" Ashburn and had a "most profound contempt for him, socially and politically."[59] Anti-Reconstruction newspapers often charged that Ashburn was involved sexually with black women. The *Atlanta Constitution* claimed that he had been "exceedingly intimate" with Hannah Flournoy, the black woman who owned the boardinghouse where he was murdered, describing her as Ashburn's "concubine" and "paramour."[60]

Ashburn's white critics blamed the victim rather than the perpetrators. His murder had been nothing more than a "horrid blunder," the *Weekly Georgia Telegraph* suggested. A mob had intended only to intimidate Ashburn, perhaps by subjecting him to a tarring and feathering, or by riding him on a rail. When Ashburn fired his gun, the *Telegraph* contended, the mob had responded in "quasi self defence." Although a murder had occurred, "the intent to murder did not exist." Somehow, the *Telegraph* excused the mob's actions through this contorted and inconsistent logic.[61] The anti-Reconstruction press threw scorn on Ashburn's political allies and the northern occupiers. The *Columbus Sun* predicted that Ashburn would be "canonized with John Brown among the Radical saints, and his murder will be charged to the unprovoked and savage malignity of Southern rebels." The reality, it believed, was far different. Ashburn had been "a most dangerous character, ignorant, energetic, vain, and unscrupulous, cruel, malignant and vindictive." He was "abusive and insulting" to whites and "arbitrary and overbearing" to blacks. Whether this "miserable man" had fallen victim to his political enemies or to "his own vile partizans" remained murky. The moral guilt lay upon the North, where for many years men had promoted "lawless, violent, revolutionary and incendiary doctrines" that caused the breakup of the Union and resulted in civil war. These northerners were "now rolling up the whites of their eyes and groaning over the moral depravity of the barbarious South."[62]

The military crackdown and the trial of the Columbus Prisoners provided fodder for the anti-Reconstruction critique. In the broadside *Radical Rule: Military Outrage in Georgia: Arrest of Columbus Prisoners*, published in 1868, anti-Reconstruction forces condemned the northern occupation.[63] No citizen could feel exempt from arbitrary arrest and imprisonment, they said.[64] The Columbus Prisoners were suffering from a "stupendous scheme of Radical villany," the *Atlanta Constitution* asserted.[65] The true facts about the case, predicted a correspondent for the *Cincinnati Enquirer*, would "shock the moral sense of the country." The opponents of Reconstruction heightened the stakes by suggesting that radicals such as Ashburn engaged in interracial sex. He was nothing more than a "wretched outcast," they claimed, who was "forced to seek a home in a negro brothel." The murder trial was serving the political purposes of Washington Republicans, who wanted to "manufacture political capital, and to prove Southern tyranny." A Washington Directory had dispatched detectives who were engaged in the "manufacturing of witnesses" and had concocted a plan for "political effect."[66]

The *Columbus Sun* played a leading role in promoting the idea that the military investigation had trammeled personal liberties and encouraged false statements through bribery. Although these charges had little if any basis in fact, the *Sun* suggested that the military's reward money was a "big sum of money to place before the eyes of a bad negro as an inducement to bear false witness."[67] A narrative began to emerge about the treatment of the Columbus Prisoners. Their arrest "should make boil the blood of every freeman," the authors of *Radical Rule* declared. Further, the *Sun* claimed that the prisoners' treatment was "barbarous in the extreme," involving confinement in small cells lacking ventilation or lighting, inadequate bedding, and small rations. *Radical Rule* repeated this claim, maintaining the use of torture and bribery.

This critique thus highlighted the anti-Reconstruction sentiment that the northern occupation was unlawful. "How long are the denizens of our Southern States to be made the victims of military misrule?" asserted the authors of *Radical Rule*. "Must the people of that region forever be made the shuttlecocks of military power? Will not the people enforce some rule whereby peaceable, industrious, order loving citizens can prosecute their business without momentary dread of being incarcerated upon charges trumped up by political or personal foes?" Military rule had become "an engine of oppression."[68]

Unpacking fact from fiction in the Ashburn assassination remains difficult. The charge, often made by Columbus newspapers, that Ashburn was murdered by fellow Republicans is ludicrous. Bennett, a white Republican associate of Ashburn's, was present at the assassination, but he was the only person there who was not masked. That Republicans did not rally around Ashburn as a martyr is more indicative of the success of the political terrorism than it is of the possible implication of Republicans in his murder. Anti-Reconstruction activists grossly exaggerated divisions among Republicans in order to drive a wedge into the party. The charge of mistreatment of the Columbus Prisoners also reflected overblown rhetoric. In late June 1868, Detective Whitely, in response to charges that he had tortured and mistreated prisoners, admitted having committed only one case of prisoner abuse, when he harshly interrogated two black prisoners, John Stapler and John Wells, at Fort Pulaski. Interrogators had soaped Wells's and Stapler's heads and threatened to shave them. Wells and Stapler were witnesses rather than suspects, and Whitely justified the abuse by claiming that he knew the "negro character well," and that the black witnesses were "naturally more easily frightened into measures than white men." None of the white prisoners was tortured or abused.[69]

In June 1868, a correspondent for the *Chicago Tribune* visited Atlanta. The correspondent interviewed the prisoners, inquiring about conditions.

All reported that they were treated "as well as prisoners could expect to be" treated. Other military prisoners in the Atlanta barracks—soldiers accused of crimes—were held in conditions that were probably worse than those. "Upon the whole," the correspondent concluded, "I cannot find from the testimony of the prisoners themselves that any of them have been treated with the slightest degree of cruelty." Most of them, indeed, were living in conditions that were "more comfortable and luxurious than three-fourths of the citizens of Illinois."[70]

TWELVE COLUMBUS WHITES—James W. Barber, Columbus C. Bedell, Herbert Blair, William D. Chipley, William A. Duke, Henry Hennis, Robert Hudson, Elisha J. Kirksey, Milton Malone, Alva C. Roper, James L. Wiggins, and Robert A. Wood—faced murder charges in a trial by military commission. They achieved celebrity as heroes of the resistance to northern military occupation. Among the seven defense attorneys were Alexander H. Stephens, the longtime U.S. congressman and vice-president of the Confederacy; former Georgia Supreme Court justice H. L. Benning; and future governor James Smith. The prosecution had its own celebrity: Joseph E. Brown, the controversial Civil War governor of Georgia who, after the war, became a Republican.[71] When approached to join the prosecution, Brown was already a political outcast. By supporting Reconstruction, he explained in March 1868, he made "bitter enemies of a host of old friends personal and political." His position on Reconstruction represented both pragmatism and opportunism. Unenthusiastic about black suffrage and civil rights, he favored appeasing northern interests in order to end Georgia's military occupation. His primary motivation, he wrote, was to see the state "restored to peace and prosperity upon the best terms that we could obtain."[72]

The military commission convened on June 29, 1868, in the McPherson Barracks in Atlanta, and met until July 24.[73] Chairing the seven-member commission was Gen. Caleb C. Sibley, the head of the Freedmen's Bureau in Georgia. The prosecution's case, which was mounted by Assistant Judge Advocate General William McKee Dunn, rested on the testimony of eight witnesses, three of them eyewitnesses to the murder. One witness, Charles Marshall, was a U.S. Army sergeant who had participated in the murder and then testified against the conspirators. Marshall, who had come to sympathize with local whites, enjoyed their financial sponsorship. He described Ashburn's assassination as the result of a conspiracy organized by Kirksey. On March 30, a black boy delivered a pasteboard mask to Marshall, with the message "meet to-night at twelve o'clock." Sometime between 11:30 P.M.

and midnight, Marshall met with the conspirators in a vacant lot across the street from Ashburn's boardinghouse, where he was handed a long, grayish English walking coat that could be used to cover his uniform. According to his testimony, he was joined by six others—Hudson, Duke, Barber, Bedell, Kirksey, and Malone—and they then led a crowd of about thirty masked men to Ashburn's residence. Marshall testified that the shooters included Duke, Barber, Hudson, and himself. After Ashburn's killing, Kirksey and Bedell entered the room to make sure that he was dead.

Marshall's role in the conspiracy remains murky. With ties to Columbus whites, he participated in anti-Reconstruction political organizing. A Savannah newspaper described him after the murder as "highly thought of by our citizens."[74] Marshall's role in anti-Reconstruction activities became so prominent that he was demoted in rank from First Duty Sergeant to Duty Sergeant. He also harbored a grievance against Ashburn. On the afternoon of his murder, Marshall and his soldiers, who were drunk, scuffled with a group of blacks. Ashburn intervened, claiming that the blacks had been roughly and unjustly treated. After Ashburn threatened to report Marshall for his political activities, Marshall slapped him and spat in his face. By the time of the trial, however, Marshall had made a deal with the prosecution. Testifying against the Columbus Prisoners, he became the prosecution's most important witness.[75]

Stephens, on cross-examination, pounded away at Marshall's credibility as a witness, contending that the prosecution had suborned his testimony by offering him immunity. However, according to one account, Stephens's cross-examination "failed to shake his testimony."[76] George F. Betz, another conspirator, also testified in exchange for immunity. A railroad fireman, Betz told how Kirksey had recruited him, offering $100 if he participated in the assassination. Betz admitted that he was one of the shooters; his testimony confirmed Marshall's version of events. Testimony by Bennett, another eyewitness, corroborated the prosecution's case, though Bennett admitted that he came forward later because he feared retaliation. The "Ku-klux Klan would have put an end to me," Bennett said, and he would have been "cutting . . . [his] own throat" had he told the truth.[77]

Other testimony reinforced a strong case for criminal conspiracy.[78] Amanda Patterson, the white woman who lived with Ashburn in the boardinghouse, testified that the accused men had burst into Ashburn's room and shot him. She identified Columbus Bedell as the attacker who had lost his mask when he came through the front door. Patterson recounted that, before the crime, some of the conspirators had confided their plans to her. Barber and Chipley reputedly told her that they were "going to kill old Ashburn the night of the day he speaks." Later that week, she heard Barber tell Bedell about their plans. Based on her previous associations with the conspirators, Patterson was able to identify the killers. Like Bennett, she had feared retribution and kept quiet.

Another prosecution witness, Wade H. Stephens, supported Patterson's testimony. About three weeks before Ashburn's killing, he remembered, he had met Kirksey near the courthouse. Stopping his buggy, Kirksey had asked Stephens if he could "keep a secret." Kirksey had offered Stephens fifty dollars to join the conspiracy. When he refused, Kirksey had told him not "to expose what he said to me." Another witness, a liveryman, told the court that, the day of the murder, James Barber, while drunk, had boasted that "Ashburn will be dead shorter than any of you have any knowledge of."

The defense's case rested on the provision of alibis for all of the defendants. Witnesses testified that William Duke was at home when the murder occurred. Defense attorneys spent three days examining witnesses for Kirksey, mostly family members, who swore that he was home the night of the murder. But on cross-examination, one of the witnesses, Kirksey's sister-in-law, admitted that, regarding Ashburn, "we was glad he was dead." The entire Kirksey family, she said, agreed with the sentiment. "I recollect the female members of the family delighting in his death—being glad to hear of it," she said. Joseph Brown asked her if all the female members of the family wanted to see "all the Radicals" dead. Before the defense could object, she answered: "We do." Brown's cross-examination, according to one account, was administered with "unremitting vigilance." But his aggressive questioning of female witnesses would later expose him to charges of inappropriateness toward women.[79]

The prosecution assembled an impressive number of eyewitnesses; the culpability of the Columbus whites seemed certain. The defense did little to undermine the prosecution's case. Their strategy was primarily political—to use the trial to rally opposition to northern occupation. On this score, the defense won. On July 21, after the newly elected Georgia legislature ratified the Fourteenth Amendment, which ensured the state's readmission to the Union, Meade recognized the futility of continuing the trial and suspended the military commission. Georgia legal authorities subsequently declined to prosecute the Ashburn murder.[80]

Soon after their release, on July 25, 1868, the Columbus Prisoners composed a public statement. Reviewing the history of their arrest and imprisonment, they claimed that they had been held in violation of their personal liberty, without warrants, and without knowing the charges against them or the evidence until the last minute. Witnesses had been tortured; the testimony of the accused had been suborned "*by torture, bribery, and threats.*" Prisoners had been held at Fort Pulaski in cells that "were as dark as dungeons, without ventilation, and but four feet by seven." Rations had been slim, as well, they claimed. After they were moved to McPherson Barracks, the prisoners continued to suffer ill treatment. "No one who has followed the trial," they commented, "will be surprised at this apparent neglect." Brown, whose "vindictive, ungenerous, and unmanly conduct" characterized the proceedings, had been especially villainous.[81]

FORTY-THREE YEARS AFTER ASHBURN'S MURDER and the release of the Columbus Prisoners, Rebecca Latimer Felton published her memoirs. Through her marriage to William H. Felton, she became one of the most important women in Georgian political life during the post-Reconstruction era. She led reforms endorsing woman suffrage and condemning the convict-lease system, but she also published viciously racist diatribes. In 1922, Felton became the first woman to serve in the U.S. Senate when she was appointed to fill the seat vacated by Sen. Tom Watson's death. Prominent in Felton's memoir was her account of the Ashburn murder. Forty-two years old when Ashburn was assassinated, she remembered the events in Columbus as "a season of fearful excitement." Along with many other southern women, Felton was outraged at Brown's "vindictive treatment" of female witnesses. The prosecution had employed witnesses who had, she claimed, "beat back the truth at all hazards."[82]

The narrative of invasion, violation, and hostile occupation shaped many white Georgians' understanding of Reconstruction itself, and nothing embodied this narrative more fully than the murder of George W. Ashburn and its aftermath. A proposal made by anti-Reconstructionists in 1876—that the boardinghouse where he had been murdered be transported to the Philadelphia Centennial Exposition—exemplifies their celebration of his murder.[83] For a generation, the event continued to be remembered. In the eyes of many whites, Ashburn became a Reconstruction villain, his murderers martyrs. The prevalent understanding was that the Ashburn trial had been part of a larger conspiracy by Radicals, as a Columbus newspaper put it in 1876, to "murder innocent men [in this case, the defendants] for political ends."[84]

In April 1876, the *Columbus Enquirer* launched a campaign seeking a congressional investigation into the case. Someone should answer for the "villainies of Radicalism," the newspaper insisted. Why had the defendants

Joseph Emerson Brown (courtesy of the University of Georgia)

been tortured and persecuted? it asked. Ignoring the fact that the military commission had suspended its trial after the prosecution had made a strong case for conviction, the *Enquirer* portrayed matters differently. The Columbus Prisoners had been acquitted, it inaccurately asserted, "because the utter falsity of the witnesses was exposed." The *Enquirer* also claimed that Joseph Brown had "insulted by innuendo" the honor of female witnesses.[85]

When Brown became a candidate for the presidency of the State Agricultural Society in 1876, the *Columbus Enquirer-Sun* reminded readers that he had "persecuted many of the first young men in Columbus, and insulted ladies on the stand." Was it possible that Georgians could forget these things? "The memory of it still rankles."[86] The Columbus Prisoners' trial remained "one of the blackest chapters in history," commented another white Georgian in 1877. Ashburn's killing had atoned "for the misfortune of his birth."

Innocent young men had been arrested, taken to Atlanta, and tried by military court. Using "every contrivance of cruelty" to extract evidence, the prosecutors had extorted "confession of guilt from the lips of innocence." Brown, with his "blood money," had been only too happy to join forces with the northern despots. Brown's treachery was unforgivable, "akin to the sin against the Holy Ghost."[87]

Memories of the Ashburn murder and the Columbus Prisoners were revived in September 1879, when the Georgia legislature investigated the keeper of the state penitentiary, John W. Nelms, for improprieties. Three years earlier, Georgia had adopted a notorious convict-lease system. In charge of distributing the leased prisoners to private employers, Nelms was accused by Louis Garrard, state representative from Columbus. Brown, who was involved in the mining and transportation industries that used convict labor, defended Nelms, demanding that the legislative proceedings be recorded by a stenographer. When Garrard refused this request, Brown attacked the "star chamber" investigation. Garrard responded in legislative debate by recalling Brown's role in the trial of the Columbus Prisoners. By participating in the prosecution in 1868, he charged, Brown had become "an instrument in the hands of our oppressors to persecute [us] with a degree of malignity and cruelty unparalleled in the annals of history." How, Garrard asked, would the "star chamber" of 1879 compare to the "cruel inquisition" of 1868?[88]

Brown responded with a series of letters published in the *Atlanta Constitution*. He had acted primarily in defense of Georgia's interest, he wrote, hoping to deflect those who held more extreme views. His service on the prosecution of the Ashburn murder defendants, Brown claimed, sought to hasten the departure of northern troops. Outright resistance to them would have been "worse than folly." In the "unprecedented bitterness, madness and vituperation" of the immediate postwar years, white Georgians believed that they "had not only lost all, but that the terms dictated by the conqueror were harsh and rigorous." Brown believed that the best approach was to accept northern terms quickly, elect Georgians to Congress, and have the state recognized as a member of the Union. As long as whites accepted black citizenship and suffrage, they could control the state. Black suffrage was necessary to ensure the "permanent control of the white race."[89]

Brown defended his prosecution of the Columbus Prisoners as an act of political realism. Meade had, to be sure, paid him a large fee—$5,000—for his work but, in his version of the past events, Brown imposed his own terms. In a meeting Brown had with Meade in Atlanta before the trial, Brown urged the general to delay trying the prisoners until the new state government had complied with the Reconstruction Acts. But Meade wanted to make an example of the case. Brown and Meade met several more times, finally agreeing on two conditions: first, that the death penalty would not be imposed, and, second, that Meade would stop the trial after a new civilian government had been formed. Both men realized that if the trial took long enough, the legislature might preempt the ability of the court to administer justice; both agreed to "protract the proceedings until we reached that point." They felt that a "moral effect of prosecution" should be sought "without the infliction of illegal punishment."[90]

THROUGHOUT THE LATE 1860S, the popular reaction to Ashburn's assassination and the trial of his accused murderers had a chilling effect, intimidating scalawags and splitting conservative white Republicans from their African American allies. By the time the military trial of the Columbus Prisoners in Atlanta ended, Reconstruction in Georgia was in shambles. The formation of a new state government during the summer of 1868 resulted in narrow Republican majorities in the legislature, but internal divisions were so severe—and white Republicans so shaken by political violence—that the legislature took the extraordinary action of expelling all of its African American members in September 1868. The rump legislature, purged of its black members, came under the control of anti-Reconstruction forces. But, in March 1869, when the legislature defeated ratification of the Fifteenth Amendment, Congress suspended the state's readmission to the Union. A new legislature was convened that included black members and excluded the whites who were most hostile to Reconstruction, and this new legislature ratified the amendment.

On July 21, 1870—the nineteenth anniversary of the Battle of Bull Run—African Americans gathered to celebrate the achievement of their enfranchisement. Three hundred delegates traveled to Atlanta from Augusta and Chattanooga, along with delegates from other cities and from all the counties of Georgia. In Atlanta, the group organized a parade. Marching with troops from McPherson Barracks, black delegates represented the different states of the Union. Black children from the American Missionary Association's Storrs School marched dressed in white and wearing pink sashes. The marchers kept pace with an African American band. One large banner carried by the marchers read: "A just God has made us free—15th Amendment the law of the land."

The crowd marched down Peachtree Street to a grove opposite the Rolling Mills, northeast of Marietta Street. An *Atlanta Daily Intelligencer* reporter said that the crowd contained some whites, while "all of Atlanta swarmed with an innumerable host of negroes." Henry McNeal Turner, an African American Republican state representative from Bibb County and later an Atlanta resident, addressed the crowd. When the Georgia legislature expelled its black members in September 1868, Turner had vociferously objected. He told the white members that "I shall neither fawn nor cringe before any party, nor stoop to *beg* them for my rights." To seek white sympathy and forbearance, he said, was akin to slaves "begging under the lash." He was there to "demand my rights, and to hurl thunderbolts at the men who would dare to cross the threshold of my manhood." Turner claimed the rights of humankind. "Am I not a man," he said, "because I happen to be of a darker hue than honorable gentlemen around me?" Once skin color was disregarded, there was nothing physiologically to distinguish white from black.[91] Turner was a determined advocate for black equality and a critic of what he later called the "deviltry perpetrated upon my people by a so-called civilized country."[92]

In his Atlanta speech, Turner was fearless. Speaking on the theme of "Progress," he described a pathway for racial advancement. Despite black enfranchisement, he saw little future for blacks in politics. A white reporter praised his "sound advice" as emphasizing African American development through "literature, arts, sciences, and agriculture," as well as in "all the business pursuits of life." Turner was defiantly separatist. He preached a message of independent economic development, urging black people "not to be content with merely imitating the white man but to blaze out new paths." The seeming friendship of whites, northern or southern, Democratic or Republican, was artificial. The future lay in self-reliance: "Root, hog, or die," Turner declared.[93]

Despite the display of black enthusiasm shown in the parade, black political power in Atlanta was circumscribed by white supremacists. Black officeholding in Atlanta lasted only briefly, even though the Georgia constitution of 1868 enfranchised black males, and in 1870 two African Americans had been elected to the city council along with two white Republicans. But in November 1871, the state legislature rewrote the city charter, replacing ward-based council voting with an at-large system. Realizing that they had little chance of being elected under this new system, in November 1871 Republicans ran candidates under an independent slate. All of them were defeated. No other black councilmen were elected to the Atlanta city council until 1953.[94]

In February 1868, the Georgia constitutional convention decided to move the state capital to Atlanta, a change that the *Atlanta Constitution* welcomed.

Local citizens exhibited "an enterprise and energy which augurs well for its future." The relocation of the state capital to Atlanta indicated how far the city had come "from an unbroken forest to a city of the first magnitude."[95] Boosters played a major role in achieving this triumph. By early 1869, entrepreneur Hannibal L. Kimball was leading efforts to construct a new five-story building to house the legislature. The new capitol building—known as "Kimball's Opera House"—was completed in only four months over the shell of a partially finished opera house. It housed the state government for twenty years, after which time a new and more ornate capitol building was erected. Atlanta had quickly become Georgia's social, economic, and political center.[96]

THE REESTABLISHMENT OF WHITE SUPREMACY after the Civil War involved a struggle among the various populations of the South over the significance of the Civil War and the changes that had taken place in the postwar South. Before the end of the war, northerners and African Americans believed that the Confederacy's collapse would lead not only to an end to slavery but to a changed racial system, with the South under temporary northern supervision. But the Confederate defeat obliterated the norms and assumptions of the prewar social system, creating a vacuum. Many southern whites violently resisted a vision of the war's aftermath in which the racial order would be redefined. Black emancipation therefore brought great uncertainty, conflict, and turmoil, as whites regrouped and reimposed racial controls outside the context of the social system of slavery. The preservation of white supremacy, as a bedrock principle, remained fundamental. For many whites, Confederate defeat was also seen as having led to a humiliating occupation that had ended only with the violent overthrow of Republican rule in the South. For blacks, however, the Confederate defeat, the destruction of the old social order, and the federal occupation of the South were interpreted in an entirely different way, especially in the particular context of Atlanta. Yet as white dominance in the South was reasserted, so also there began to emerge a contrasting narrative of the past, which was tied to a contrasting vision of the future. And central to the development of that new vision was the role of the northern missionary enclave and its impact on black lives during the generation after emancipation.

FIVE

We Are Rising

Schooling the City

In the fall of 1868, the commissioner of the Freedmen's Bureau, O. O. How-ard, visited Atlanta. During the Civil War, Howard had risen to the rank of major general, and, as commander of the Army of Tennessee, played a lead-ing role in the Atlanta Campaign. Visiting the American Missionary Asso-ciation's Storrs School, Howard addressed black parents and students. "What shall I tell the children in the North about you?" he asked the black children. A twelve-year-old boy spoke out: "Tell them, General," he said, that "we're rising." George W. Childs, publisher of the *Philadelphia Ledger*, repeated the story to the abolitionist poet John Greenleaf Whittier, who composed a poem entitled "Howard at Atlanta." "And a little boy stood up: Massa / Tell 'em we're rising!" it read. "O black boy of Atlanta!" Whittier continued. "The slave's chain and the master's / Alike are broken / The one curse of the races / Held both in tether: / They are all rising, all are rising / The black and white together!"[1] In March 1869, Richard Robert Wright, the boy portrayed in Whittier's poem, objected to the poet's use of the term "massa." "You made a mistake thinking that I said 'massa,' for I have given up that word," he wrote to Whittier.[2] The "We Are Rising" story has many apocryphal qualities, but it took on a life of its own, and the AMA celebrated the tale among northern audiences. "We Are Rising" was also put to music, becoming the anthem sung by Atlanta University students.[3]

"We Are Rising" served as a rallying cry in the black people's quest for true freedom after emancipation.[4] The song embodied the goals of northern abo-litionist educators who worked in Atlanta during the late 1860s. Establishing an AMA school in the city, they also founded Atlanta University to serve as a beacon of abolitionist values in the age of emancipation. Though these white educators harbored a certain racial paternalism, to an unusual degree for nineteenth-century Americans they exalted equality, economic devel-opment, and an application of the principles of free labor in the employ-ment of former slaves. And so the post–Civil War mission of the northern abolitionists in Atlanta, marked especially by their founding of Atlanta University, had its own, lasting legacy.

Richard R. Wright, the young student who met O. O. Howard, embodied the potential that could be realized by abolitionist-inspired black schooling. He was born a slave in 1855 outside Dalton, in northern Georgia. Family tradition had it that he was descended, on his mother's side, from a Mandingo chief who arrived in the United States from West Africa around 1800; his paternal grandfather, considered rebellious by his master, was sold to owners in Dalton. Wright's family followed Sherman when he occupied Dalton during the Atlanta Campaign, and, after walking three hundred miles, settled in southwest Georgia. Learning about the new missionary schools, Wright and his mother made a three-month trek by foot to Atlanta, where his mother found work as a cook. Later described by his son as "very black," "small of stature," and "bright of mind," Wright enrolled at the new Storrs School, quickly emerging as one of its best students.[5]

Attending Atlanta University, Wright became the valedictorian of its first collegiate graduating class in 1876. Four years later, at age twenty-seven, he became the principal of the first black high school in the state, in Augusta. Wright represented a new kind of emancipated ex-slave: an advocate of racial equality. Solving this "vexing question," he declared, lay in educating African Americans and awarding them full citizenship.[6] Having served as the founding president of Georgia State Industrial College for Colored Youth (later Savannah State), in 1896 Wright was appointed paymaster of the Army—the first time an African American had occupied that position. Although Wright's race meant that his status in Savannah society was exposed and vulnerable, he expressed racial pride and egalitarianism. In 1921, when a Savannah bank teller refused to address his daughter as "Miss Wright," and struck her, Wright abruptly resigned from Georgia State. At the age of sixty-seven, after studying at the Wharton School, University of Pennsylvania, he founded the Citizens and Southern Bank and Trust Company in Philadelphia, remaining in charge of that institution until his death in 1947. His son, Richard Robert Wright Jr., received an undergraduate degree at the University of Chicago and then studied in Germany. In 1911, Richard Robert Wright Jr. became the first African American to receive a Ph.D. at the University of Pennsylvania, and, in 1932, he was elected president of Wilberforce University.[7]

EMANCIPATED SLAVES such as Wright regarded literacy, property ownership, and their attainment of the franchise as the building blocks of freedom.

They enthusiastically embraced schooling; literacy, to them, represented liberation. The spirit that a Freedmen's Bureau official described in August 1867 in DeKalb County, outside Atlanta, illustrates this educational ethic. "The freedpeople in that section," he said, "show a lively interest in their education and have gone to work with a spirit that deserves our sympathy and all encouragement we can give." Local whites, though not all in favor of the school, were "at least not hostile to it."[8] Black people's desire to learn appeared to "undergo no abatement," wrote another bureau official, and they eagerly sought "every available means by which they can be aided in obtaining knowledge."[9]

Missionary teachers committed to freedpeople's education fanned out across the postwar South. A mixture of motivations guided them. Many were abolitionists who had worked with the Union army in ending slavery in the occupied South; others had gained their first experiences in dealing with relief efforts in contraband camps. Subsequent historians have differed in portraying missionary educators as either idealists or paternalist racists, but most agree that their influence shaped the future of black education. The most important group of northern educators that came to Atlanta was the AMA. Founded in 1846 by abolitionists in Syracuse, New York, the AMA was an interdenominational, evangelical, antislavery organization. During the war, its missionaries followed northern armies, establishing schools and churches for freedpeople. Before the war ended, the AMA had sent 320 teachers and missionaries to work among ex-slaves. That number grew rapidly after the war, and, in June 1867, 451 teachers were instructing nearly 39,000 students in both day and night schools. In Georgia, the AMA operated the largest share of missionary schools in the state.[10] The Freedmen's Bureau and AMA collaborated to establish a common-school system that would educate black children.[11] Between 1865 and 1868, the bureau spent $100,000 for Georgia schools, while the AMA contributed $148,000 in cash and $50,000 in clothing and provisions. Usually, the bureau constructed the schools, while the AMA paid the teachers' salaries. Black people, for their part, contributed significant support, paying for 41 of the 199 black schools that were established in Georgia in May 1869.[12]

The AMA ended its financial support for common schools in 1868, after the Georgia constitutional convention created a statewide common-school system. But an AMA enclave remained in Atlanta. While the common schools were being folded into the postwar South's new public school system, the AMA created black colleges that were designed to train a new black leadership class. Among these institutions, none had a greater impact than Atlanta

University. The AMA enclave became essential players in the making of the African American community, in Atlanta and nationally. "This was the gift of New England to the freed Negro," W. E. B. Du Bois later wrote in *Souls of Black Folk*: "not alms, but a friend; not cash, but character." The AMA's educational efforts were the "finest thing in American history, and one of the few things untainted by sordid greed and cheap vainglory." Northern teachers "came not to keep the Negroes in their place, but to raise them out of the defilement of the places where slavery had wallowed them." Du Bois described AMA colleges as places where "the best of the sons of the freedmen came in close and sympathetic touch with the best traditions of New England." At Atlanta University, blacks did not so much learn about the practical world but rather were schooled in "simply old time-glorified methods of delving for Truth, and searching out the hidden beauties of life, and learning the good of living." The AMA's objective was "not to earn meat, but to know the end and aim of that life which meat nourishes."[13]

IN OCTOBER 1865, AMA agent Erasmus M. Cravath visited Atlanta on a scouting mission. An Oberlin College graduate, Cravath served as chaplain of the 101st Ohio Volunteer Regiment and participated in the siege of Atlanta. After the war, Cravath, dedicating himself to black education, became secretary of the Middle West Department of the AMA. Later, he served as president of Fisk University, another leading AMA institution, in Nashville.[14] Unlike most white southerners, many northern missionaries like Cravath believed that Reconstruction depended on changing the status of black people. Atlanta's destruction provided an opportunity to rebuild southern society. North Georgia's hills and valleys, said state Freedmen's Bureau commissioner Rufus Saxton, were "dotted with the entrenchments of contending armies," with the "mark of ruin . . . everywhere." While Atlanta was "building up the ruins," Saxton believed that a truly reconstructed South would only be possible when southern whites "cease to mourn for the lost cause, and are just to the negro and faithful to freedom."[15] Northern missionaries possessed a millennial vision. There was "such a revolution in the hearts & minds of rebels as never was seen before," wrote a Freedmen's Bureau official. In the future, there would be "No more '*nigger*,' '*Cuffee*,' or '*Sambo*.' Our '*colored friends*' '*our colored population*' now!"[16] "What a change has been wrought since 1860!!" wrote another female missionary in Atlanta. "Things have moved in a mysterious way."[17]

The social and economic conditions in Atlanta were challenging for freedpeople, to say the least. In the late 1860s, the city contained what one missionary called a "floating population," their wartime dislocation and extreme poverty having created adverse conditions for the black population.[18] Nonetheless, Cravath found Atlanta an encouraging locale, ripe for missionary work. "I have taken in many new scholars," a female teacher wrote soon after opening school. She wrote that, despite widespread sickness and poverty, her students did "quite as well as we can expect them to do under such unfavorable circumstances," although she found the black community "unsettled" and complained that it was "difficult to keep the children."[19]

There were already a few black schools in Atlanta that were operated by the Western Freedmen's Aid Commission, along with some that Atlanta African Americans operated. But the educational needs of the city's black population were only "*nominally*" being met by these missionaries, and the agent of the Western Freedmen's Aid Commission agreed to cede their ground to the AMA. Cravath promised to supply teachers.[20] On November 15, 1865, Frederick Ayer and his wife, Elizabeth, both veteran missionaries, took charge of the Atlanta outpost. A native of Uxbridge, Massachusetts, Frederick Ayer had worked for twenty years among Indians in Wisconsin and Minnesota as a teacher and church missionary for the American Board of Commissioners for Foreign Missions. In 1862–63, a bloody Indian uprising in the course of the Dakota War drove most of the whites out of western Minnesota, and Ayer became interested in freedmen's education.[21]

Ayer exemplified the mixture of paternalism and egalitarianism that characterized AMA teachers. He emphasized the religious education of black children. Who could "estimate the blessed influence" of hymn-singing, he wrote in June 1866. Only two years before, these children had been "ignorant, Slaves regarded by their owners as but property, and sold and bartered like mules and horses." Under the slave regime, reading was illegal for blacks, and "if one of them was seen with a book it was snatched from him and he was cuffed and kicked and told that 'books were not made for Niggers.'" Ayer saw a "wonderful God-wrought" transformation accompanying emancipation. Black parents sometimes awoke at night, Ayer recounted, and asked themselves: "Am I really free?" "Are my children free?" or "Can I call them my own?"[22]

Ayer's egalitarianism combined with a wariness about blacks. His greatest challenge, he wrote, was to inject a "state of strict & serious discipline & custom" among freedpeople. He believed that they were "restive under restraint, and want to be in perpetual motion." At the same time, Ayer found black people "docile."[23] Elizabeth Ayer shared these attitudes. Black parents, she wrote, expected teachers to whip their children—a lingering effect of slavery's brutalized culture. Whipping was "too common with them" and was "regarded as the panacea for all delinquencies." If a student would not learn, "whip him and make him learn"; black parents wanted their "children whipped to make them good." Black children, she believed, should learn a moral code for its own sake, not from "fear of the lash."[24]

The Ayers' first school was located in the Bethel AME church building on Jenkins Street. In December 1865, the AMA opened a second school known as the "Car-Box." The school met in a railroad car that had previously been used by the United States Christian Commission, which purchased it in Chattanooga for $310 and shipped it to Atlanta. In December 1865, the Ayers were joined in Atlanta by the sisters Lucy and Rose Kinney, both Oberlin College graduates. Frederick and Lucy taught at Jenkins Street, Elizabeth and Rose at the Car-Box. By the end of 1865, six teachers were instructing six hundred black pupils in the two schools. Local whites shunned the northern teachers, and consequently the AMA opened a teachers' home at Houston and Calhoun Streets—now 114 Piedmont Avenue—which they purchased for $5,000 in December 1865. The AMA regarded these schools as temporary, and in the summer of 1866, it purchased a lot next to the teachers' home on Houston Street for $600 and moved the former Confederate commissary building down the street and into this lot in order to make space for more teachers. To finance this move, Cravath and E. P. Smith, another AMA official, raised $1,000 from First Orthodox Congregational Church in Cincinnati, Ohio, and also received $2,400 from the Freedmen's Bureau.

The famous Storrs School—named for the Rev. Henry Martyn Storrs, pastor of the Cincinnati church—consolidated the two AMA schools. The Storrs School became the AMA's headquarters in Atlanta. A two-story building, it boasted four rooms, a hall, and room for 250 pupils. Decorated in the "most tasteful workmanlike style," the rooms contained the latest in school desks, manufactured by Barnes & Rankin. The building also contained a chapel that could accommodate 400 people.[25] O. O. Howard announced that Atlanta had the "first colored school house in the South," made of "Southern pine, handsomely furnished, with some half a dozen school-rooms." The Storrs School was "exceedingly prosperous, and everything in good condition."[26]

By early 1866, Atlanta's contraband camp was closed, leaving a population of dislocated ex-slave children—some of whom had lost their parents in the war or were separated from them. With Freedmen's Bureau money, the AMA established an orphans' asylum, located on five acres on the north side of Cain Street between Fort and Hilliard Streets.[27] In 1866, the asylum contained a population of about twenty-five children, and, within a year, this had increased to eighty-five. Most of these "waifs," according to an account in 1868, were under six years old; some were infants. "No other department of the work appeals so directly to the sympathies of the benevolent, or presents stronger claims for assistance."[28] But the orphan asylum proved to be the AMA's least successful enterprise. Some of the children identified as orphans were immediately reclaimed by their parents, who had been "separated by the cruel, avaricious, and relentless hand of Slavery." Others ran away from the asylum and were absorbed into Atlanta's transient population. Still others were placed in domestic positions, through the AMA asylum, with white families. By late 1867, plans were afoot to build a new two-story building to house the orphanage.[29]

THE DEATH OF FREDERICK AYER, on September 28, 1867, marked a significant moment in the history of the AMA outpost in Atlanta. Held in the Storrs Chapel, his funeral was attended by a contingent of northerners and by "nearly all the colored people in the city, who loved him as a father, and whose grief at his death is very great."[30] Clarence Bacote, historian of Atlanta University, described Ayer's "true missionary spirit," which was essential "for a white person to be a teacher of Negroes." Despite "social ostracism and insults" from Atlanta whites, Ayer had stuck to his principles and continued with his mission of black education. An African American who knew Ayer as a child later said that white hostility to him was acute. "The white people of Atlanta were glad to have Mr. Ayer die," he recalled, "because he was putting ideas into the heads of the colored people." When the city took over the AMA schools in Atlanta in the late 1860s, they renamed the Ayer School—which the AMA had just named in his honor—to Summer Hill School.[31]

In place of Ayer, a new, younger generation of missionaries—most of them associated with Edmund Asa Ware—took over. Having come of age during the Civil War, Ware and his cohort saw the fight for black freedom as lasting beyond emancipation. He arrived in Atlanta in September 1866, not quite a year after Ayer had, to head the new Storrs School, which was dedicated on Christmas Day, 1866. He and Ayer agreed that Ware would manage school operations and that Ayer would handle budget and supplies.[32] After Ayer's death, Ware took charge of AMA activities in Atlanta, while he also served as the Freedmen's Bureau's state superintendent of education from 1867 to 1870.[33] Born in 1837 in North Wrentham, Massachusetts, Ware graduated from Yale first in his class in 1863. He did not serve in the military during the war, but instead applied his energies to freedmen's relief, and then taught school in occupied Nashville. Ware dedicated himself to freedpeople's

Edmund Asa Ware (courtesy of the Atlanta University Center)

education. "His heart was with the colored people," said one contemporary. "His sympathies," said the *American Missionary*, "were strongly enlisted for a race just coming out of the prison house of bondage, and he was ambitious to have a part in laying the foundations of a new and better society in the regions desolated by war."[34]

Ware combined gentleness and determination. A contemporary remembered him as a "slender, long-whiskered man, whose full . . . voice and keen, piercing eyes, though kind and gracious, made their impression on me for life." Ware possessed an "unequivocal positiveness, a loftiness of soul of purpose," along with a "contempt for meanness of any kind."[35] Harboring few illusions, Ware realized that support for black schools would not come from southern whites. AMA workers were dedicated to "enlightening those heathen, and helping them cast off the yoke of bondage," Ware said, that had been imposed on them by their "self-styled 'best friends,'" their former masters. Instead, ex-slaves must look toward "the *North*, for their advising, their helpers and their friends."[36]

A racial egalitarian, Ware dedicated his life to achieving equality for former slaves. His son later wrote that Ware believed that "the blacks were quite equal to the whites in their ability to learn" and that he "had not observed any preference of intellectual ability." Ex-slaves were not "aliens" but people who possessed the "same human qualities as themselves." The South's future depended on "working to make good the cause for which Lincoln and thousands who fell in battle had died."[37]

Like other northern missionaries, however, the AMA educators were also paternalistic. "If the evidence pointing to racial prejudice among the teachers is sporadic and indirect," writes historian Jacqueline Jones, "the problem of cultural conflict between the two groups stands out in stark relief. The teachers' values of evangelical piety, self-control, and hard, steady work formed the trinity of northern-sponsored freedmen's education." The teachers sought to institute "moral character reform and thereby guarantee social stability in the face of increasing fragmentation based on class, political, religious, and racial tensions." But, according to Jones, their sense of "nationalistic individualism clashed with the freed people's 'ethos of mutuality,' which arose during slavery as a protective reaction against white oppression."[38]

Northern female missionaries, despite their racial paternalism, were zealously committed to the cause of black betterment. The missionaries' cultural imperialism was countered by their genuine humanitarian dedication. These post-emancipation AMA missionaries had inherited what James M. McPherson calls the "abolitionist legacy."[39] "My heart was never so nearly full of interest and delight as now," wrote a white female teacher in Atlanta in 1870. Her teaching, rather than being a "novelty wearing away with me," had become a "deep, abiding interest, that increases as I become more and more familiar with the work."[40] Others also found teaching freedmen's children transformative. "I came into the colored schools looking for this and that 'negro characteristic,' but was happily surprised to find the same diversity of intellect, and the same variety of character, that I had seen in my white pupils in the North," wrote another teacher. "If laziness is one of their so-called 'race peculiarities,' there are certainly some noble exceptions."[41] "Which is the most talented, the white man or the black?" asked the AMA journal, the *American Missionary*, in 1870. "Those who think the colored people of the South have had help enough are answering this question. Take a case in point: Before the war, Southern politicians ruled the nation. The mightiest statesmen of the North succumbed to their talents or threats. Now the Freedmen, having the ballot, are called upon to cope with these same Southern politicians, and yet some Northern people tell us that the negroes need no farther education or moral assistance! Is this a concession of superiority, or is it a thoughtless, perhaps culpable, rejection of farther responsibility to the colored man?"[42]

The AMA, the Freedmen's Bureau, and northern whites who were dedicated to black education faced potent hostility from most southern whites. In May 1866, a bureau agent in Henry County reported that white citizens put up "great opposition" to black education by assaulting children en route to school and threatening the teacher. The agent faced the danger of assassination if he continued to support black schools. The bureau subassistant commissioner promised to protect the school.[43] In another community near Atlanta about a year later, local whites ran out a white teacher and then abused a black woman who took over the school. Although those responsible for the abuse were "thoughtless, wild young men," they succeeded in closing down black education in that district.[44] In August 1867, after a black school was burned in Jonesborough, south of Atlanta, bureau official Fred Mosebach became convinced that hostile whites were behind its destruction. Although the "greatest portion and the better class" publicly condemned the burning, many of them "at heart rejoice at it."[45]

The suspicion lingered among most southern whites that the existence of black schools subverted the social order. In Covington, thirty-five miles east of Atlanta, a northern teacher and his wife fled a black school after someone left a note on his door, demanding that they "leave or bear the consequences." Many whites feared that northern teachers were "engaged in sowing ill feeling and hatred among the colored people towards them," said a bureau official, "that they had effectually prejudiced the col. people against them, that they had been holding secret meetings." There was also a pervasive belief that AMA and bureau officials were mobilizing African Americans politically.[46]

The AMA teachers enjoyed the protection of the federal garrison in Atlanta, but they still experienced social ostracism. Local whites called them "N.T.," which stood for "Nigger Teachers." Even in the early 1890s, James Weldon Johnson recalled, the white faculty at Atlanta University remained unwelcome in nearly all white homes; "no observance of caste in India was more cruelly rigid."[47] While serving as state education superintendent, Ware often faced white hostility.

In March 1867, he organized a meeting of African Americans in Macon to form plans to lobby the state constitutional convention, which would meet in early 1868, to adopt common schools for all races. The *Macon Messenger* denounced Ware as one of a number of "Yankee interlopers" and as a "teacher of a negro school in Atlanta." Ware's presence, it continued, indicated his "Yankee impudence and officiousness." The "sole mission" of Yankee interlopers like him was to "stir up strife and sow the tares of hate and evil in the minds of their pupils."[48] Ware remembered later that the white hostility stirred up by the Macon meeting was intense. A few days after the meeting, when he went to Griffin to dedicate a schoolhouse, "the fame of my Macon affair" resulted in his being visited by "leading white men" of the community, whom he described in his diary as "judges, lawyers, colonels, capts., etc., etc., about 40 of them." At least one of them had a pistol, but, Ware recalled, "the Lord guided me," and he was not harmed. But on March 31, 1867, Ware received a threat from the Ku Klux Klan. Take back what he had said in Macon, he was warned, or "the sun will shine on a new made grave." Ware, who described the warning as "somewhat Delphic—and not very alarming," resolved that he would "take nothing back I said."[49]

ACROSS THE SOUTH DURING THE 1860S, missionary schools transitioned into black public schools, which, while suffering from studied white neglect, served as the sole source of African American education. Meanwhile, with the establishment of state-run schools in Georgia, northern missionaries focused their efforts on higher education. Between 1866 and 1869, the AMA founded seven colleges in the South and supported the creation of Howard University, in Washington, D.C., which was federally financed. Like other institutions of southern post–Civil War black higher education, these institutions' primary purpose was to produce teachers. But the AMA colleges also provided the educational foundation of the post-emancipation black leadership.[50]

Chartered on October 16, 1867, Atlanta University enrolled its first students two years later. The university adopted the motto of Yale College's class of 1863—Ware's class—"I Will Find a Way or Make One." The AMA aimed to create "an institution like that of Oberlin," explained the *American Missionary*, which was "founded on the widest possible basis, embracing all sexes, all creeds and all colors, the only requisite for admittance being intellectual ability and moral character." Only a few years earlier, an idea such as this "would have cost a man his head, but now, through the provision of God and the Federal army, it is being accomplished."[51] Ware scraped together funds from various sources. From the Freedmen's Bureau he received $52,000, and $1,300 came from the Peabody Fund. The AMA provided nearly $20,000, and beginning in 1870 the state of Georgia annually appropriated $8,000 from funds that came from the Morrill Act of 1862 (the so-called land-grant funds).[52] A tireless advocate for the institution, Ware constantly lobbied for white support. "I remember him as he came daily from the Capitol," one contemporary recalled, "worn and weary to take his seat as night school teacher, because there was no money to hire another . . . like the faithful soldier, musket in hand and with closed eyes . . . [who marched] on his beat."[53]

On June 1, 1869, the cornerstone of Atlanta University was laid on a sixty-acre site on Mitchell Street, about a mile west of the downtown district. The ceremony was reported in both the *Atlanta Constitution*, soon to become the city's leading white newspaper, and the *American Missionary*, the AMA's official journal. The *Constitution*'s account was dismissive. It described a "considerable crowd of negroes and a few white people" taking part in a ceremony that began with a prayer by a white minister, followed by one read by "a negro." Present also were Republican governor Rufus Bullock and Postmaster James L. Dunning, who listened as "the negro children sang a few songs." The main speaker, John Mercer Langston, was described as "a negro lawyer from Washington." The *Constitution* criticized Langston for his speech, which asserted the "*same rights* to the *whites* that he did to negroes."[54]

The *American Missionary* offered a different account. It noted that the ceremony opened with black children singing the AMA's anthem, "We Are Rising." Ware urged the people of the North to help in removing the "vast cloud of ignorance" that loomed over the South. Countering the dismissive article in the *Constitution*, the *American Missionary* suggested that Langston's achievements should not be summed up simply by calling him a "negro lawyer." Born free in Louisa County, Virginia, to a white planter and a free woman of color, Langston was educated at Oberlin College and participated in abolitionist politics in Ohio. During the Civil War, he organized black enlistment in the Union army, and after the war he became the first dean of the law school at Howard University. In 1888, Langston was elected to Congress from Virginia, the first African American congressman from that state.

Langston's racial egalitarianism was unpalatable to white audiences—this explains the *Constitution*'s adverse reaction. He favored the radical idea of integrated education. Blacks and whites, Langston said, "should be educated together to accustom themselves in childhood to their new relations; to destroy the spirit of servility and fear in the one and arrogance in the other." Citing his experience at integrated Oberlin College, he declared: "Of the practicability of the enterprise there could be no doubt." Langston spoke even more frankly regarding the taboo against social equality and interracial contact. Himself the product of a mixed racial heritage, he believed that no legislation should regulate the "friendship flowing from the palms of another man of different color." The problems of race in America were deep. The nation was on trial, he thought, and its ability to educate its citizens would determine its ability to compete globally. Black people were also on trial in their search for equality, he said, and the true test of success would be their achievements. If black people "produce nothing, they must sink, and justly." Some predicted the extinction of his race, yet Langston hoped that "fifty years might elapse before they lost one curl of the hair, one shade less of their duskiness, that they might prove their title as equals." Atlanta University promised to be a "people's university," and it was "for the people they should erect and endow it." Black people should dedicate themselves to educating their children.[55]

The AMA mission in Atlanta had an important role. Southern whites vastly underestimated its potential—and its subversive impact. Despite its promise, however, Atlanta University progressed slowly. It attracted young black men, mostly from Georgia, but its claims to university status remained tenuous. For the first decade of its existence, the institution remained mostly a high school, with a teacher training (or "normal") department that produced teachers for black schools in Georgia. AMA officials were realistic about the school's immediate prospects. "We hope to gather a class of young men . . . from the various parts of the state, into a Normal Department," one of them wrote in 1868. "There are a few pupils in the state, one here, who have begun the study of Latin & algebra," but this was beyond the preparation of most. "I wish I could report you," he wrote, "a flourishing University."[56]

The university's first building, North Hall, was completed in time to welcome students matriculating in the fall of 1869. The new building was a three-story brick structure that included a dormitory for 40 girls, a large parlor, and a dining room accommodating up to 175 people. The building, constructed at a cost of $24,000, also provided housing for teachers. Much of the support continued to flow from northern whites. The AMA offered to put names over dorm rooms if donors gave at least $25. The donations, it suggested, would be a "constant reminder to us of his love for the work in this part of the Master's vineyard."[57] During the following summer, the university erected a second building, South Hall, which included additional space for teachers, dormitory rooms for 60 male students, and classrooms for 160 pupils. The response was so positive that the boys' dormitory became overcrowded, some rooms housing three boys.[58]

In 1870, the school reported thirty-one boarding students from Savannah, Augusta, Macon, and Milledgeville. Even Ware admitted that the claims that the institution was a university "signified nothing, save as a prophecy."[59] The dormitories lacked much furniture; there was a shortage of desks, books, and musical instruments. The buildings needed doorbells and hall lamps. According to a teacher, the windows needed blinds "to shield us from the hot sun." In addition, bedding, table linen, and towels were reportedly "very scarce with us, and are getting scarcer every day, as our numbers increase." But the students were seen as an asset. There was "about as much white blood as black in our school, variously distributed," according to one of the teachers. The fact remained that "our blackest are just as good scholars as the whitest." White claims of black inferiority, this teacher believed, were "all stuff."[60]

All students were required to work, the boys on the school farm and the girls in domestic work. The AMA leadership wanted a classical curriculum, which included training in ancient languages and emphasized leadership and rhetorical skills. After the school had been open for two years, the state board of visitors attended student examinations at the Normal and Preparatory School on June 26–27, 1871. Former Confederate governor Joseph E. Brown wrote the visitors' glowing report, which told about the success of the new school. Brown, now a Republican, had come a long way in his attitude toward black education, and he was inclined to be positive. Atlanta University, the report declared, was a "novel enterprise concerning the sweep and usefulness of which interest is felt all over the Union." The exams revealed "numerous evidences of the patience, painstaking perseverance and professional skill of the teachers, which the thorough training and admirable demeanor of the pupils demonstrated." The teachers, many of whom were Yale, Harvard, Amherst, and Oberlin graduates, exhibited a missionary spirit and were paid salaries "barely sufficient to supply the necessaries of life." The exams also indicated the "fallacy of the popular idea" that black people were incapable of intellectual achievement. Results indicated that, after their examination in algebra, geometry, Latin, and Greek, many of the students "exhibited a degree of mental culture, which, considering the length of time their minds have been in training, would do credit to members of any race." Notably, the students also displayed "very judicious moral training to which the pupils of the institution are daily subjected," training that had resulted in "polite behavior, general modesty of demeanor, and evident economy and neatness of dress." The students realized that they served a social mission, that they were "being educated for usefulness and not for mere ostentation, or to gratify a selfish ambition."[61]

The Atlanta University students mostly absorbed this ethos. A white visitor from the AMA in 1878 called the students the "flower of the colored race," people who were "eager to fit themselves for future usefulness, and burdened with a longing to help their race." The students worked with "an enthusiasm needing little urging or government." Another white observer would emphasize the "striking degree of refinement among the students," who had developed "rare qualities of earnestness and self-reliance." "A cultivated soul," the first observer concluded, "shines out from these dark faces, and, in our admiration for the soul, we totally forget the color of the skin."[62]

In 1883, a donation from Valeria Stone, of Mahlen, Massachusetts, provided $50,000 for further building expansion.[63] But, for the most part, Atlanta University limped along without a secure financial basis. A black visitor in 1880 maintained that the institution was "crippled for want of funds."[64] The school boasted a school library of 4,000 volumes that existed on the basis of a $5,000 endowment. But except for the library, there was no other endowment, and the school depended on annual contributions from the AMA and northern supporters.[65]

The two buildings constructed in 1869–70, along with the Stone Building in 1882, formed the core of the campus. Within five years, a regular college department opened, in addition to the junior preparatory, or high school, department. There followed what Ware called a "natural and steady growth." In 1878, nine students were graduated with college degrees; twenty-four students had finished the normal program, divided into a "lower" and a "higher" normal. During the same year, twenty-four students were enrolled in the college department and sixty-eight were enrolled in the four-year "higher normal" program. "The home and family feature of the school," Ware explained, was "made prominent," as dormitory life included a matron who assumed a maternal role, "making the house a *home*, instead of a college barrack." The "refining, elevating, and restraining influence of this family life" was "incalculable." The school retained its religious mission. On the Sabbath, church was held in the chapel in the morning, followed by Sunday school in the afternoon, and a prayer meeting during the evening. On Wednesdays and Fridays, students attended more prayer meetings. Every month there was a missionary concert.[66]

Early on, the university sought to transform students' character. The curriculum discouraged frivolity. Schooling would result in "carelessness corrected, punctuality secured, a respect for the rugged virtues as well as the amenities of life stimulated, and, in many cases, a sober and abiding religious earnestness developed." The university tried to remake the students' cultural expectations by separating them from their "old associations and habits" through a "strong and watchful discipline" and by surrounding them with "earnest and aggressive religious influences." Atlanta University attempted to give its students a thorough and rigorous New England-style education, which would "stamp upon them new characteristics" and would help them to become "thoroughly fixed and set in character before leaving school." The most important goal of all, perhaps, was that Atlanta University students challenge white assumptions about African Americans' intellectual capabilities.[67]

Northern whites at Atlanta University in this period were, like Ware, New Englanders of an abolitionist background. Most were educated at Yale or at another Ivy League institution. It was a "hopeful indication of God's purpose to give the Freedmen a high culture in learning and religion," the *American Missionary* declared, that "educated and self-denying young men are moved to consecrate themselves to this field of effort."[68] In September 1867, Cyrus W. Francis, a graduate of Yale Theological Seminary, became pastor of the First Congregational Church and remained closely associated with the school. Pious, austere, and having what one student remembered as "sharp, dark eyes," Francis was never especially popular with students, who regarded him as a "snooper" who patrolled the boys' dormitory at night and spied on students. He was "not far from fanaticism in his religious zeal."[69]

Other New Englanders also helped to run the institution. Thomas N. Chase, a Dartmouth graduate who arrived in 1869, managed the school's financial affairs and buildings and taught Greek and mathematics. Chase was described by a contemporary as "precise, practical, and positive."[70] Possessing keen political instincts, with a "ruddy face" that "held two merry eyes and was fringed by a cropped, reddish beard," he was popular among the students.[71] Like Ware and Francis, Horace Bumstead was in the Yale class of 1863. Bumstead remembered his Yale class as "most interested in the slavery question and the events of the Civil War." With Ware and Yale students, Bumstead used to discuss the war and wonder whether they would have "an opportunity, after we had graduated, to do something for the Freedom—as it seemed certain freedom must come before very long."[72]

Unlike Ware, Bumstead served in the Civil War, as a major of the 43rd regiment, U.S. Colored Troops. He saw action in Petersburg and Richmond during the late stages of the war. Bumstead was gracious but determined. It was later said that he would "fight a circular saw, if he thought it was necessary."[73] In 1870, Bumstead completed seminary training at the Andover Theological Seminary and became a Congregational pastor in Minneapolis.

Horace Bumstead (courtesy of the Atlanta University Center)

In 1875, he joined Atlanta University's faculty, and, on Ware's sudden death by heart attack on September 25, 1885, he became the institution's second president. The quartet of Ware, Francis, Chase, and Bumstead ran Atlanta University in the nineteenth century: all four served as presidents between 1869 and 1907. They were followed by Ware's son, Edward Twitchell Ware, a Yale graduate (class of 1897) who served as president from 1907 to 1922.[74]

Soon after he arrived on campus in the late 1860s, a black student met Ware. He was different from other whites, the student noticed, in the way in which he treated black people and extended common courtesies. "It was a new and strange thing to us to see a white man carrying wood and making fires for us, who had been taught, by precept and example, that it was our business to do the like for his kind."[75] "However you may be mistreated in the city or elsewhere," Ware was said to have informed students, "I want you to know that the moment you set foot on these grounds you are free men in a free country." When a white Atlantan asked him how he could live with black people, Ware responded: "Oh, I can easily explain that; I'm simply color blind."[76]

The early generation of Atlanta University students was especially aware of its role in the emancipated South. Ware's aim, along with that of the abolitionist educators, was to empower the students through education. "How I wish you could have been with us last Tuesday morning, as scholars and teachers marched a few yards, to observe the ceremony of breaking ground for the new building," a white observer wrote in May 1870. The school's students processed to the building site, their faces "beaming with joy and hope." Between the two new buildings were the remains of Confederate earthworks, still surviving six years after the Atlanta Campaign. The moment was not lost on J. W. Alvord, the Freedmen's Bureau general superintendent of education. "I look out upon these entrenchments," he wrote, "in wonder at the change which four short years have made." The Confederate fortifications had "defied the approach of freedom"; in their place stood "walls of brick and stone to shelter the children of the free, and endow them with the power of knowledge." "The roar of batteries," Alvord wrote, was now "exchanged for the music of school songs and recitations."[77]

At the ceremony, Ware read the proclamation of the Fifteenth Amendment, which provided voting rights for black males and was ratified in February 1870. The 100th Psalm was read aloud, and the audience sang Julia Ward Howe's "Battle Hymn of the Republic." "From those hearts," read the account, "there went up a united prayer of gratitude that our country was now not only free in name but in very deed, and that God had answered [our] prayer, in regard to the success of our schools, not according to our faith, but much surpassing it." God would surely hear the "thanks of His poor, despised people."[78]

Ware's racial egalitarianism shaped his organization of the campus. From the beginning, the university was racially integrated—an exceptional situation in the white supremacist South. The belief in racially integrated education lay at the core of the AMA philosophy. As early as 1866, AMA field secretary Edwin P. Smith planned a school open "to all without distinction of color." Smith had found that, throughout the South, young black men were "waiting for such an opening." Smith believed that Atlanta University could help freedpeople to move above the "high wall of prejudice."[79]

There was never more than a handful of whites at Atlanta University as students; most were children of white faculty. Once Atlanta University opened in 1869, a number of thorny issues nonetheless immediately confronted Ware. How would whites and blacks interact? Would they eat together? Would they be in the same classes? How would public spaces be organized? Before the first meal occurred, Ware summoned his faculty. He saw three possibilities: meals could be served at different times and be racially separated; there could be separate tables that were racially separated; or everyone could sit down and eat together. The "last way is the best," Ware declared, "because we have come here to help these people and we cannot do it best at arm's length." An Atlanta University student who attended during the 1880s described this "intimate association three times a day" as exercising "an influence over manners, speech, personal appearance and attitudes that could not be exerted so effectively in any other way and it is that, it seems to me, which has marked Atlanta University graduates outwardly more than anything else." This was "no small decision to make at that time when never before in the lives of those Negro boys and girls had they or any of their kind sat down anywhere with white people on terms of equality. And I know of no other place in Georgia and I am sure there were few places anywhere in the South where a like thing was done." Black students at Atlanta University would often ask each other whether it was possible that any white person would ever believe in racial equality. A "sufficient refutation" was: "Well, what about Mr. Ware?" An early graduate eulogized Ware in this fashion: "Whether you have realized it or not, God gave us for twenty years a character resplendent with virtues and graces, to move in and out among us, that we might see how men are made."[80]

Black activist and intellectual James Weldon Johnson attended the university in the early 1890s. He found Atlanta, as a city, disappointing. With sparse trees and no city parks or squares near his neighborhood, the city was "neither picturesque nor smart; it was merely drab." Johnson found the university, with its stately, ivy-covered buildings, a "pleasant relief," a spot that was "fresh and beautiful, a rest for the eyes from what surrounded it, a green island in a dull, red sea." The university had become a "little world in itself, with ideas of social conduct and of the approach to life distinct from those of the city within which it was situated." When students entered campus, Johnson recalled, "they underwent as great a transition as would have resulted from being instantaneously shot from a Boston drawing room into the wilds of Borneo." At the university, Johnson began to understand the complexities and nuances of race, and to understand how education could prepare him to deal with attitudes of white supremacy. Nearly all of the academic curriculum, remembered Johnson, fit into a "particular system of which 'race' was the center."[81]

When, after nearly two decades at Atlanta University, Ware died suddenly in September 1885, his accomplishments were celebrated with an outpouring of grief expressed even by white Atlantans who had been critical of the northerners' intentions. "In his death the race loses a warm friend," declared the *Constitution*, as well as a "fine instructor and a good adviser."[82] At Ware's funeral and burial in Atlanta, three thousand people paid their respects, including many of the black graduates of Atlanta University. The *Atlanta Constitution*, originally suspicious of the institution, praised Ware for building up the school and "practicing economy, industry, thrift and self-denial, and these principles he earnestly endeavored to impress upon the minds of the hundreds of young people under his charge." While a white pastor presided over the ceremony, "the tears of white and colored mingled together." After two decades' labors, Ware had "laid down his life as a sacrifice on this altar of his own erection."[83]

FROM THE TIME OF THE ARRIVAL of the AMA in Atlanta, whites had expressed unease about its presence. In 1874, a visiting committee appointed by the governor to oversee the $8,000 annual appropriation—which came from federal land-grant funds—recommended terminating the relationship with Atlanta University. The visiting committee reported a "disposition . . . in both precept and example to assert and press the claims of the colored race to social equity with the whites." Over time, whites learned to tolerate the university, considering it an example of how blacks might be "bettered" in their habits. But white suspicions remained. When the board of visitors inspected the campus in July 1876, they noted with surprise that the facilities, despite constant use, were "well preserved." They were also surprised, as southern white visitors often were, at the students' "great craving for knowledge," their longing for a "remarkable and critical accuracy in the use of language, and their acquaintance with the books on which they were examined." The visitors observed that the students exhibited a "quiet and general deference of their deportment." Still, the committee noted with disapproval that, as in previous years, the principle of racial egalitarianism persisted. Although "better counsel" now seemed to prevail, many southern whites continued to see Atlanta University as a subversive institution in their midst.[84]

There were also internal tensions in the black community regarding the university, as some leaders criticized its continued administration by whites. In the early 1870s, Atlanta's black leaders protested the absence of black teachers at the Storrs School. The demand for black teachers to teach black children had become great across the South, and Atlanta was no exception. At the university, despite the racial egalitarianism professed by the whites, there was a flavor of paternalism in their attitudes. No black faculty taught Atlanta University students until 1895, when the institution hired two of its black alumni as instructors. Two years later, W. E. B. Du Bois joined the faculty as a newly minted Harvard Ph.D., and he remained there until 1910. Some years later, he would remark that he had "neither before nor since met so goodly a company."[85] The original northern missionary generation maintained control well into the twentieth century. Not until 1929 did Atlanta University appoint a black president, when John Hope was inaugurated.

The unusual racial policies that the northern white missionaries had instituted at Atlanta University became a matter of public concern in 1887. Annually, the state sent a board to visit the university and report on its activities, as a way to make the institution accountable for the annual $8,000 it was given in federal land-grant funds. When the board of visitors inspected the institution in June 1887, they were shocked to discover the extent of white-black interaction. "There are in attendance white students of various ages, and both sexes," their report read, most of whom were children of white faculty. More troubling still to the visitors was that the "avowed intention" of the faculty was to "receive all white children who apply for admission into the school." This policy indicated, to the visitors, "a desire to break down the existing barriers against the coeducation of the two races." The visitors condemned what they called coeducation as not only "intrinsically wrong," but as an improper use of public funds.[86]

Perhaps most repugnant to them was the attitude of the New Englanders who ran the institution. A day after the visitors' report became public, the *Constitution* sent a reporter to campus to meet with Thomas N. Chase, who was serving as acting university president after Ware's death.[87] Asked if it was true that white pupils attended the university, Chase replied: "Certainly." There were seven such pupils, he told the reporter, and "they have been in attendance for some years." Six of the seven were children of the faculty, one of whom (Ware's daughter) was female; the seventh was the thirteen-year-old son of the white pastor of a black Congregational church. "These pupils sit in the same recitation rooms with the other pupils, and receive the same instruction. There is no special course prepared for them, and no unusual advantages offered for their benefit." When the reporter spoke with Bumstead, he repeated Chase's message: white students shared classrooms with black students and received a common education. Although Bumstead predicted that loss of the $8,000 appropriation would "cripple us," he told the reporter that "we are perfectly fearless in the matter, and have no fear of an investigation."[88]

In his annual message to the legislature, Gov. John Gordon reviewed the history of the appropriation, noting correctly that the annual grant to Atlanta University had existed since 1874. But, he maintained, the "settled policy" of the state was to prohibit "co-education" of whites and blacks in publicly supported schools. No "false principles of sociology or political economy" could change that. The mixing of the races in schools, he said, was "opposed in the interest of the colored as well as of the white race" because it had the "deplorable result of amalgamation so destructive to both races." Ex-Confederate general and former Ku Klux Klan leader Gordon then gave a harangue on racial purity. Although he claimed to favor "the highest elevation of the colored people of this state, of which they are capable," he advised racial separation. All races that had "achieved anything in this world have been homogeneous," he maintained. The state appropriation would continue to support black education, but probably not, in the future, at Atlanta University.[89] Four days after Gordon's message, Rep. W. C. Glenn of Whitfield offered legislation that would prohibit any "school, college or other educational institution conducted for the education and training of colored people" from accepting white students. Teachers who violated the law were subject to fines and a sentence on the state chain gang. Glenn claimed that he was reaffirming the established policy of the state, and that both races stood "on an equal footing before the law."[90]

Rather than buckling, Atlanta University supporters rallied. The assessment of the *New York Times* proved to be correct: "It is certain that the sort of people sent out by the American Missionary Association will not be deterred by ruffianism of this sort from doing what they believe Christian duty requires." The "awful lesson" of the Civil War, after all, had come as a consequence of and remedy for the injustice of "treating men and women as if they were mere animals"; this was a lesson not yet learned "by some who boast that they belong to the new South."[91] Evarts Kent, the white pastor whose son was enrolled at Atlanta University, wrote to the *Atlanta Constitution*. His son attended Atlanta University not in order to be a "playmate of other white children who attend." Rather, his parents believed that the school provided a "technical and intellectual training more thorough and varied than that of any other school in the city; because in practice it accords with the most enlightened public sentiment of the country." Most important, perhaps, his son's enrollment bore "plain witness to a faith in the divine doctrine of a universal human brotherhood."[92]

The Atlanta University leadership reasserted its position. In a letter to the *Constitution*, C. W. Francis reviewed the compromise that had been struck in 1874 over state funding. The Morrill Act funds provided the state with an endowment of $243,000, the entire income—about $17,000—having been turned over to the University of Georgia at Athens. In 1873, there was, according to Francis, "great discontent" among black Georgians because they had been excluded from these federal funds, and some Africans Americans even applied to the all-white state university for admission. In order to forestall further challenges, the legislature appointed a special committee, headed by George Hillyer, Confederate veteran and an Atlanta judge and state senator. The Hillyer committee struck a compromise: the endowment income would continue to flow to the University of Georgia, but a fixed appropriation of $8,000 would go to Atlanta University. It was recognized that these funds were "subsidiary"; Atlanta University received funds from various sources, mostly from northern supporters, and state funds were not its main source of income. That a few white students attended was a "well understood part of the compromise," Francis claimed, and their ability to attend was understood to have been granted in exchange for black students' relinquishing any claim to attend the university in Athens. Moreover, the effective integration of Atlanta University was no secret; it had been "under the direct cognizance of thirteen successive boards of visitors, and no word of criticism, or suggestion even, has ever been given." The university, Francis claimed, had acted in good faith, and it was unwise to "break up a compromise so long accepted and so fortunate in its adjustments without better reasons than have yet been alleged."[93]

The African American community rallied to Atlanta University's support. An "indignation meeting" was organized at the Fort Street Baptist Church on July 19, 1887. The participants denounced the Glenn bill, claiming that it was "oppressive, unjust and unconstitutional."[94] But there was also an undercurrent of resentment about the continued white presence at the university. The Congregational Church, for example, had had a white pastor since its founding; the church's property remained in the hands of the AMA, despite the black majority congregation. The black congregants' discontent was seized on by Atlanta whites.[95] The AME church, long advocating black-run institutions, pressured the city schools to hire more black teachers. Wesley John Gaines, a former slave who became an AME bishop, helped to found Morris Brown College in Atlanta in 1881, and it became the first institution in the state completely under African American control.[96]

The Georgia legislature, meanwhile, focused on the evils of racial mixing. The Glenn bill passed the house, but in the Senate legislation, a substitute bill removed the penalties that had been proposed for faculty who taught at mixed-race institutions, instead penalizing students by prohibiting any graduates of these institutions from employment in Georgia's public schools. The final legislation took yet a third approach: Atlanta University trustees were required to certify that state funds would be used only for educating black students. After the university refused to give such certification, state funding ended. Atlanta University, meanwhile, continued to educate whites and blacks together. When a reporter visited campus in December 1887, Francis confirmed that five whites attended the school, though "we have only the white pupils to whom I have alluded and they will remain where they are."[97]

The loss of the $8,000 could only be made up by an increase in northern financial support.[98] Atlanta University hired a financial agent, C. L. Woodworth of the AMA, and also began publishing its *University Bulletin* to spread the word among supporters.[99] In a meeting at the Park Street Church in Boston on February 26, 1888, Bumstead was joined by Samuel C. Armstrong, president of Hampton Institute, and by Woodworth in an appeal for funds. The loss of the state appropriation, they told their audience, resulted from a "new condition attached by the state, requiring white people to be excluded, a condition which could not be observed without abandoning the principle upon which the institution was founded." The speakers appealed for donations of $1,600 to meet that year's expenses.[100] By the end of 1888, over $18,000 had poured in, all in individual donations from New England supporters. "Who that believes in the Fatherhood of God and the brotherhood of man," concluded the *Atlanta University Bulletin*, "could for a moment doubt that an institution thus persecuted for righteousness' sake would be abundantly provided for by the liberty-loving people of our land?"[101]

DURING THE LAST TWO DECADES OF THE NINETEENTH CENTURY, southern whites wove a story that legitimized their violent imposition of white supremacy. This narrative, intimately a part of what defined the New South, incorporated the themes of southern destruction and rebirth but largely wrote black people out of the story. That narrative found especially powerful resonance in Atlanta, which, as a city, exemplified what the New South meant—and the ways in which it was connected to the past. Despite the withdrawal of state support in 1887, Atlanta University survived, as did the enclave of AMA missionaries in Atlanta. Though most of the original white abolitionists who founded the university had died by the 1920s, the institution continued to serve as an example of racial egalitarianism. At the same time, the university also embodied the contradictory character of the post-Reconstruction New South. Among black people, an understanding of what the Civil War had meant differed from the perspective of most whites. Even while whites' vision of their supremacy had imposed its rules on society, the AMA enclave of educators in Atlanta provided a precedent for the achievement of racial equality—and a competing vision of the South's future.

SIX

Wheel within a Wheel
Competing Visions

In late July 1878, a newspaper reporter observed the anniversary of the Battle of Atlanta, an unsuccessful Confederate assault against Union forces besieging the city fourteen years earlier. A monument marked where Union general James B. McPherson had fallen; not far from that spot, Confederate general William H. T. Walker died on the same day. The anniversary commemorated losses on both sides; surveying the wide battleground, the reporter found little evidence of the carnage of 1864. The old trenches were "almost sunk into common earth," while the forest had "almost repaired the glories which shot and shell tore from it in wrath." The graves in the once bloody ground had "long since been unburdened of their dead," and the grass grew "as if it had never been torn and trodden by two armies." All that remained on that warm July afternoon was "perfect peace," with a radiant sunset and a "tender light" shining through the trees, accompanied by the music of a "faint and sweet" breeze. The day provided a "requiem for the dead."[1]

By the 1880s, the history of Atlanta—a city that had emerged rapidly out of wilderness and then endured near destruction by war—had become linked to its citizens' sense of self-identity. Only a half century earlier, Atlanta had been nothing more than a thick forest, a newspaperman wrote in 1881, with a small stream running through a gentle ravine where later would be located the center of a booming city. In the 1880s some of Atlanta's longtime residents remembered hunting deer near the present-day railroad depot. Lawlessness dominated the frontier town of the 1840s and 1850s, but Atlanta's good citizens triumphed over social chaos.[2] "Where does history chronicle such another rehabilitation after unprecedented disasters?" asked a resident in 1883. Following the "poverty, devastation, the demoralization of civil war, and the depression consequent upon pillage and ruin, bereavement from deaths," he wrote, residents rebuilt their city.[3]

As Atlanta grew into an important urban center in the postwar era, its citizens became more interested in their past. Newspaper pages were filled with early residents' recollections, many of them still living. Local historians gathered those memories; in the 1880s, at least three residents wrote histories of the city. In 1885, the *Atlanta Constitution* called for the establishment of a local historical society. There were people living "who were here when the forests were unbroken and the noble red man had it all his own way," and when the "first white man's cabin was built." They had witnessed "the little village grow into a city," and they had experienced Sherman's siege and the wartime destruction. Still later, they witnessed Atlanta's reemergence and regeneration.[4]

In 1888, a writer for the *Constitution* who used the pseudonym "The Old Colonel" published a series of letters describing life in Atlanta during the Civil War. In late 1864, civilians who had returned to Atlanta experienced the "gloomiest and darkest" Christmas ever. Forty days after Sherman's departure—"the destroyer with his vandal legions"—the city had become a "fire-smitten city." Atlanta lay in ashes; ruined buildings surrounded "the spot where the carnival of war had danced its maddest whirl." The weary returning exiles saw nothing to recall the "festive days which that very hour were girdling the earth." Surrounded by stragglers and looters, wild dogs and birds of carrion, the returning exiles were in despair.[5]

This melodramatic portrait of a prostrate Atlanta served to highlight the city's development as an economic center—and the particular circumstances in which it occurred. In 1889, one of Atlanta's first historians, Wallace Putnam Reed, analyzed the social and economic changes that had taken place in Atlanta's first half century. The city's early development had run contrary to dominant trends in the Old South. A community of free traders, antebellum Atlanta had depended little on slave labor, according to Reed. The "rude lessons" of the Civil War fundamentally altered things. A new Atlanta arose, "built by new men with new ideas, new hopes, and new ambitions." Its citizens welcomed new opinions, encouraged the development of manufacturing and industry, and believed in intersectional harmony—a fusing together "in one solid body, knowing no North, South, East, or West, and all pulling together for the common good."[6]

In 1891, the city "pioneers" organized themselves into a society. The new organization's constitution required that members had lived in the city in 1860 or earlier. In 1902, the pioneer society, which cultivated a vision of the past that reinforced the image they had of themselves as present-day Atlantans, published a history that listed the names of nearly three hundred early residents who still survived. The city, said the society's president, was remarkable because it had two beginnings. The first occurred when "sturdy men of old cleared away the forest, builded the rough cabins, tilled the fields and inaugurated trade, manufacturing, professional and other business pursuits." The second took place after Atlanta's "ruin and destruction following the great war between the states," when "her citizens returned and with unconquerable spirits rebuilt her waste places."[7]

Notably absent in Atlantans' heightened interest in their past was any discussion of slavery and black emancipation. Nor was imposition of white supremacy featured prominently. Instead, white Atlantans fused their memories of ruin with a desire to recreate themselves into a thriving capitalist community. On Memorial Day, 1880, the *Atlanta Daily Constitution* noted that there were "no memories like the memories of the heart." There had been a time of war; that time had passed. The boom of the guns was hushed by thousands of graves. Warring brothers were united in death. Atlantans should "learn from these flower-strewn graves the lesson of love and peace, and not wave above them the signals of anger and hate."[8]

The struggle for meaning in the aftermath of the Civil War helped to shape the emerging, remade New South. The creation of a new southern identity had particular relevance for whites in Atlanta, a city without a long past but with an acute sense of its future. Sherman and the northern invasion, and the events of the war's immediate aftermath, defined the experiences of destruction, renewal, and redefinition. The New South that grew out of the slaveholding South retained many of its essential social characteristics for the white people constructing it.

For white Atlantans in the nineteenth century, the Civil War was still vital and personal. Their own lived history, rather than a distant abstraction, was woven into the fabric of their community, defining their identity. White Atlantans were eager to celebrate their city's postwar economic development. Nonetheless, in a city that eventually became, in the twentieth century, "the city too busy to hate," the preservation of racial hierarchy was the foundation on which the city was rebuilt. It was easy for prosperous whites to ignore the ugliness of white supremacy, but in the aftermath of slavery race was a continuing theme.

ON DECEMBER 22, 1886, Atlanta civic booster and newspaper editor Henry Woodfin Grady took white Atlanta's narrative of the Civil War to a national audience. Speaking before a powerful and rich group of northerners at the New England Society in the City of New York, he described the social transformation that was occurring in Atlanta and the rest of the South. The New England Society annually hosted a dinner and address—the social event of

Henry W. Grady (courtesy of Georgia State University)

the season—delivered at the auditorium of Delmonico's Restaurant. Tickets quickly sold out, with hundreds of people turned away. The first southerner ever to address the Society, Grady saw the event as an opportunity to craft a national message. His delicate task was to engage his listeners while maintaining his credentials as an authentic white southerner. "I have thought of a thousand things to say," he told a reporter, "five hundred of which if I say they will murder me when I get back home, and if I say the other five hundred they will murder me at the banquet."[9]

Understandably, Grady was nervous. William T. Sherman, immediately preceding Grady, offered brief remarks that were greeted with wild applause, while the band broke into a rendition of "Marching through Georgia."

Described as clean-shaven and boyish, Grady was "pale with excitement." Speaking in a slow but clear voice, he quoted Georgia political leader Benjamin Harvey Hill. There had been a "South of slavery and secession," Hill had said, but that world was now dead, replaced by a "South of union and freedom" that was "living, breathing, growing every hour." These words, "true then and truer now," formed the text of Grady's speech.[10]

Grady's view of the past connected to his conception of the future. The end of slavery had liberated southern whites, he announced, just as much as it had slaves. The antebellum landowners had depended on agriculture cultivated by slave labor, unaware that this was an inadequate basis for a healthy economy. The New South, in contrast, was "compact and closely knitted, less splendid on the surface, but stronger at the core." There would be a hundred farms for every former plantation, "fifty homes for every palace," and a diversified industry that met the "complex needs of this complex age."[11]

At the heart of Grady's New South lay his belief in the rejuvenation that could arise out of destruction. "As ruin was never before so overwhelming," he told his audience, "never was restoration swifter." About Sherman, whom he described as a "careless man about fire," Grady said this: "From the ashes he left us in 1864 we have raised a brave and beautiful city"; one could only marvel "that somehow or other we have caught the sunshine in the bricks and mortar of our homes, and have builded therein not one ignoble prejudice or memory." Economy and thrift had taken root and "spread among us as rank as the crabgrass which sprang from Sherman's cavalry camps," while "we have achieved . . . a fuller independence for the South than that which our fathers sought to win in the forum by their eloquence or compel on the field by their swords."[12]

Grady's New South address was an instant success among the largely northern audience. "Before half a dozen sentences had left his lips," commented *Frank Leslie's Weekly*, Grady swept his audience up "by storm."[13] Another reporter on the scene glowingly described his impact as "instant, positive and unequivocal." Representing the South to northern whites, he "carried his audience with him from the first sentence to the last." Southerners present were also impressed with Grady's "manliness and frankness." Any description of the well-decorated hall was "utterly unimportant as compared with Grady's triumph." The audience rewarded Grady with sustained applause and a wild waving of hats and handkerchiefs, until he was forced to his feet in order to acknowledge the adulation.[14]

Born in 1850 in Athens, Georgia, Grady attended the University of Georgia, and, after graduation, spent a year at the University of Virginia. During the early 1870s, he worked in newspapers, writing for the *Rome (Ga.) Courier*. In 1873, he bought part of the newly established *Atlanta Daily Herald*. After that newspaper failed, Grady spent the last half of the 1870s as a correspondent for the *New York Herald*. In 1880, he invested in the *Atlanta Constitution*, becoming its editorial writer and driving force. Grady was a force of nature, a person with intelligence, drive, and entrepreneurialism. "To him was given the power with both his tongue and pen," editorialized the *Atlanta Constitution* after his death, "to move men's hearts as they have rarely been moved." As time passed, it predicted, the memory of his "brilliant, but brief career will become dearer to the people."[15]

Grady was the ultimate New South booster—and an indefatigable promoter of the city of Atlanta. A "greater Atlanta, a greater Georgia," a contemporary later concluded, served as "his monuments."[16] Grady was not simply a "brilliant writer," remembered a contemporary, he successfully promoted Georgia's "great elements of wealth and power."[17] Grady spent his life presenting Atlanta as the center of the New South's economic development and sectional reconciliation. "With a steady rush, like the rolling of some great torrent, Atlanta sweeps on in her grand march," twenty-three-year-old Grady wrote in July 1873. "Nothing can stop her; nothing can swerve her; right as to her noble destiny she hurries." Although the economic depression of the 1870s dampened enthusiasm about the city's rapid growth and "public wonder has become fatigued," Grady wrote, "still we grow just as much."[18] Few southern cities compared with Atlanta, Grady declared in January 1874, the scene of "wondrous change." The city had "waxed from infancy into a fully developed and vigorous maturity, as it were, in a day." Growing from an antebellum railroad city, Atlanta became a wartime center that suffered destruction by "vandal hands" and was reduced to a "heap of ashes and smouldering ruins, her former inhabitants . . . scattered to the four winds." The "spirit of Desolation" cast a pall over "her once busy marts," and the inhabitants were "impoverished and utterly prostate." But the destruction served as a "baptism of fire" that recreated the city. Trade, retailing, transportation, banking, and manufacturing all expanded significantly, and Atlanta became a major cotton center. "With wisdom and well-directed energy," he wrote in 1874, "there is scarcely any degree of prosperity to which she will not attain."[19]

Although Grady popularized the concept, "New South" was already a well-worn term by 1886.[20] "Four years of war wrought mighty changes," wrote journalist Edward Deleon in 1870, "utterly overturning the old system, and out of its *debris* creating what we see to-day—a New South, whose wants and wishes, ends and aims, plans and purposes, are as different from those of

1860, as though a century, instead of a decade only, divided the two."[21] Early in his career, Grady latched on to the term, using it in an editorial appearing in the *Atlanta Daily Herald* on March 14, 1874.[22]

In his New York speech, Grady presented a rosy picture of how the Civil War had transformed white southerners into enterprising capitalists, but it scrubbed clean the discussion of race. Like white Atlantans generally, New South enthusiasts adopted a concept of rejuvenation that ignored racial conflict. Grady and other New South enthusiasts shared a predisposition either to say little about race, or to misrepresent the racial realities of the post-Reconstruction South. Grady emphasized that there were good feelings between the races and that progress had been made. Black people, he said in bland contradiction of the facts, enjoyed equal access to economic resources, schools, and an unbiased legal system. Whites and blacks were working out their future together, he said, in "full and exact justice." The Emancipation Proclamation had assured northern victory because it had shown that the North was committed to the cause of human liberty, "against which the arms of man cannot prevail." Slavery had doomed the Confederacy, "committing us to a cause that reason could not defend or the sword maintain in the sight of advancing civilization." Grady asked northerners to trust southern whites, whose affectionate relationships with black people were "close and cordial."

Grady's New South speech in 1886 succeeded not for its originality but because of its timing. The wildly positive reception by its northern audience helped to persuade northerners to formulate a new understanding of what the post–Civil War South might be. "No postprandial oration of any recent occasion has aroused such enthusiasm in this city," declared the *New York Times*. It noted that Grady's delivery was "exceedingly forcible, and his clear, high, musical voice carried home every word with telling effect." He delivered a welcome message, demonstrating his "thankfulness at the death of slavery, and at the better condition of the South now that the bondmen were free." Grady's promise of a new intersectional fraternalism had evoked "boundless enthusiasm."[23]

SEVEN YEARS EARLIER, IN JANUARY 1879, William T. Sherman had returned to Atlanta for the first time since he left it a burning heap in 1864. Occupying the position of commanding general, Sherman served as the U.S. Army's highest ranking officer, a position that he held until his retirement in 1883. Although his visit brought back to white Atlantans memories of their wartime poverty and distress, it also reminded them of the "learned patience" with which white southerners had set themselves "firmly to the future." The *Atlanta Daily Constitution* continued to insist that the city's residents would never forget Sherman's path through Atlanta; memories of Atlanta's destruction figured crucially for southerners. When Sherman departed in 1864, he had left the city without "visible hope of resurrection or recovery." Now the general would hardly recognize a city that embodied the prosperity of the rejuvenated South.[24] The visit occurred "when Atlanta has made a history she need not blush to own."[25]

The careers of both Grady and Sherman became wrapped up in efforts to define contending postwar visions of the New South. In 1879, the two men were already well acquainted, and in fact it was Grady who facilitated Sherman's return to Atlanta. The general took up residence at the Kimball House, the finest hotel in the South. Constructed in 1870 in only six months, the Kimball House, in the center of the city at Pryor and Decatur Streets, rose six stories and contained 317 elaborately furnished guest rooms. Its vestibule was three stories high, and it was decorated with pillars and a marble floor. The hotel was the creation of Hannibal Ingalls Kimball, a Maine native and carriage maker who had immigrated to Atlanta in 1866 to manage George Pullman's railroad sleeping car operation in the South. The *Atlanta Daily Constitution* aptly called Kimball a "steam engine in breeches."[26] Although a northern carpetbagger, Kimball became one of Atlanta's most important boosters. A tireless promoter, he persuaded the state agricultural society in 1870 to meet in the city, and in six months he prepared a sixty-acre site and successfully managed the event. At one time president of nine different railroad companies, Kimball suffered a financial collapse in November 1871, lost control of the Kimball House, and left the city under a cloud of suspicion for fraud. Three years later, however, he returned to the city, and, in a rapid rehabilitation, was successfully acquitted of the charges.[27]

Soon after his arrival in 1879, Sherman toured the city and was entertained with a ball at the McPherson Barracks. The next day, about 1,500 people attended a seventeen-gun salute to the general, who reviewed the nine companies of the Eighteenth Infantry. That evening Sherman and his party dined with federal judge and future U.S. Supreme Court justice W. B. Woods at his home on Peachtree Street. From Woods's veranda, Sherman viewed the hills near Peachtree Creek, recalling details of the heavy fighting of late July 1864. Sherman had few regrets. The war had been necessary, he said, and "we ought to be thankful that it came so soon" because it resulted in the abolition of slavery, an institution "antagonistic to the very principles of our government."[28]

As for the city itself, Sherman praised Atlanta's postwar progress. "I see the streets are the same," Sherman declared, "but the city is wonderfully changed, and has an appearance of enterprise and thrift that is admirable." His visit attracted the intense interest of the *Atlanta Constitution*, which announced that the general's visit to the city would likely be "one of the most interesting points in his trip through the south" because the destruction of Atlanta had become "one of the most noted features of his long triumphant march to the sea." Sherman's Atlanta Campaign was a "matter of memory" that would be preserved forever.[29]

With Grady as his sponsor, Sherman arrived on January 29, 1879, having traveled the same route south from Chattanooga—140 miles on the Western & Atlantic Railroad—that he followed during his Atlanta Campaign.[30] The symbolism of his choice was not lost on observers. A newspaperman contrasted how Sherman had entered the city in 1864, after a month of heavy bombardment, the city's residents hiding in cellars and "bombproofs." Sherman was remembered for his ruthlessness in expelling the population and leaving the city a "mass of ruins." When he returned in 1879, several hundred residents greeted him. As the train pulled in, one of them shouted: "Ring the fire-bells! The town will be gone in forty minutes." Most of those greeting his arrival were simply curious.[31] A reporter for the *New York Tribune* who accompanied Sherman on his trip saw his return to Atlanta and the "great and generous sentiment" that met him there as evidence of sectional reconciliation.[32]

Although Sherman assured reporters that he was being treated generously, not all Georgians were welcoming.[33] In Macon, the *Georgia Weekly Telegraph* noted that white and black Georgians greeted the returning conqueror differently. African Americans remembered him as a liberator; those who shook his hand seemed to regard him as "something like the moon, which, by association with his majesty the sun, imbibes some of his brilliancy." But white Georgians remembered him as a cruel invader. If Sherman's recollections of events were truthful, the newspaper concluded, they would include "unpleasant reminiscences" of the "misery and suffering" that he caused.[34]

Sherman left Atlanta in early 1879 only partly convinced that the city's prosperity had solidly been reestablished. Soon after he left, E. P. Howell, the *Constitution*'s editor, asked him to write about his views of Atlanta's future. Howell urged Sherman to promote Atlanta and the region by advertising the advantages it could offer to northern capitalists and immigrants. Sherman complied, but his response, published in the *Constitution*, provided no example of Grady boosterism. Sherman had visited north Georgia for the first time in 1843, he recalled, before Atlanta existed; his next visit had occurred in 1864, when he led his massive army through the region.

Now, thirty-six years after his first visit, Sherman offered some perspective. Economic development in New South Atlanta was no more significant— and probably less impressive—than in western states such as California, Iowa, Wisconsin, or Kansas. Despite its abundant natural resources and a transportation infrastructure, Georgia had not kept pace with the rest of the country because of its inability to attract immigrants. "All you need to make it teem with prosperity," he said, was to attract "that class of Northern farmers and manufacturers" that had "converted the great Northwest from a wilderness into comfortable homes for its millions of contented people." In order for immigrants to feel welcome, Georgians should shed their fear of outsiders. Atlantans often scornfully referred to "carpetbaggers," but what major urban center was not built by people who were nonnatives? An immigrant should "feel and realize that his business and social position result from his own industry, his merits and his virtues, and not from the accidental place of his birth."[35]

Nearly two years later, in December 1880, Grady had another encounter with Sherman on a visit to New York City. In a Fifth Avenue theater, Sherman and Grady watched actress Mary Anderson perform in Irish playwright James Sheridan Knowles's *Love*. Anderson was renowned for her beauty; Grady was smitten. In a description he wrote afterwards, he let his words carry him away, combining his response to Anderson's sexual presence with his wonder at being in Sherman's company and watching his reactions. He wrote that Anderson had the "slouching stride of a race-horse." Her neck arching "as prettily as ever," her lips would "flicker and tremble." The "same dewy spring-like freshness hangs as the breath of morning about her garments." Her arms—"I suppose she has the longest arms in the world"—were both "white and virginal" and "wanton in their very length and loveliness." "So sweet a necklace," Grady gushed as he imagined her arms around a man's neck, "had never been designed for the bliss of man and the envy of all the others." Grady had been observing not only Anderson, but also Gen. Sherman, the "sternest and most grizzled of soldiers," as he admired Anderson from a stage box. Sherman, Grady wrote, had watched "every curve of the milk-white neck, every upflying of the glistening arms and every tremor of the red lips."[36]

Grady was amazed that Sherman could be both the person who led the applause "with all the zeal that ever led his veterans" and the "most merciless invader since Alaric, and the man who swept through Georgia like a scourge of God." In the old general's character, Grady observed, admiration for aesthetic beauty was present as well as fury. He had fought with a "mailed hand, and sowed desolation in his path," but had only been in search of a "speedy and all-embracing peace."[37] Grady, who had first met Sherman a few years earlier, in December 1880 interviewed him at Sherman's New York hotel. The old conqueror expressed little sentimentality about the war. To him, "war meant cruelty—it meant death—destruction—and the sooner this was realized the sooner was there chance of peace." Warfare required giving sharp and decisive blows that would destroy the enemy. He was not interested in "glossing its horrors over with a show of pity." Sherman openly discussed with Grady what his purpose at the time of the Atlanta Campaign had been. He maintained that the destruction was targeted rather than indiscriminate. Rather than deliberately burn the city to the ground when he left in November 1864, he had intended only to burn the public buildings in the city center. "As far as burning the city in the sense of wanton destruction," Sherman said, "I never thought of such a thing."[38]

On November 15, 1881, Sherman returned to Atlanta a final time as a guest at the city's international cotton exposition. With Kimball serving as one of its driving forces, the exposition of 1881 advertised Atlanta's arrival on the national economic stage. In October 1880, Boston capitalist Edward Atkinson, visiting Atlanta, proposed a cotton exposition to bring together manufacturers and planters. With the support of Grady's *Atlanta Constitution*, Kimball campaigned to bring the event to the city. The industries that were prominent in Atlanta, Grady wrote, "have their representatives in every portion of Georgia and in almost every portion of the south." The economy of the South, though developing greatly, was "not as marked as that which has manifested itself in Atlanta." According to Grady, Atkinson believed that Atlanta served as the "best example of the energy and the enterprise of the new south" and was "thoroughly representative of the new south."[39] Grady became convinced that the exposition would "bring to Atlanta such a crowd as she has never seen or dreamed of before."[40]

Kimball energetically served as director-general of the exposition, traveling across the country in what the *Constitution* called an "exposition pilgrimage" to drum up support in New York, Boston, Baltimore, Philadelphia, and Cincinnati. He even persuaded Sherman to head up a northern subscription drive and to buy shares in the exposition.[41] With his typical efficiency, Kimball had the exposition ready in seven months. The grounds boasted twenty-seven structures housed on nearly sixty acres of the city's

International Cotton Exposition, 1881 (courtesy of the Atlanta History Center)

Oglethorpe Park, two and a half miles from the city center on the Western & Atlantic Railroad line, and site of the 1870 state agricultural fair.

The 1881 exposition served as a significant chapter in Atlanta's postwar history. The *New York Herald* said that the fair was "as great and important an event in an industrial way as the firing on Sumter and the close of the civil war were in a national and political point of view."[42] Two lakes with promenades were joined by ornamental fountains. The main building, a replica of a one-story cotton textile factory, was constructed in the form of a Greek cross, and in such a way as to admit light throughout the building. A two-story, square central section, one hundred feet long on each side, connected the two wings. The building housed cotton cleaners, gins, and presses, all the latest designs in cotton textile machinery. Nearby was a 23,000-square-foot building containing railroad exhibits. Most of the newly opened southern railroads were represented. An arts and industrial pavilion displayed jewelry, art, furniture, and sculpture as well as designs of industrial and commercial buildings. Another building exhibited the South's agricultural, mineral, and wood products. There were also annexes in which horticulture, machinery, and new inventions were featured.[43]

Hotels were constructed to accommodate 10,000 visitors to the fair, which was open from October 5 to December 31, 1881. Special trains with first-class accommodations offered at reduced rates ran from downtown Atlanta to the exposition grounds every fifteen minutes. By the time it closed in December 1881, 430,000 tickets had been sold, 1,113 exhibits had been displayed, and six countries were represented. The 1881 exposition was followed by expositions in 1887 and 1895. C. Vann Woodward has said that this series of "solemn circuses" with their structures of "plaster and iron were temples erected to the alien gods of Mass and Speed," temples that invoked the "spirit of Progress and . . . the machine" and served as "modern engines of propaganda, advertising, and salesmanship geared primarily to the aims of attracting capital and immigration and selling the goods."[44] The exposition enhanced intersectional economic and cultural exchange, serving as the first event in what Woodward called the "inaugural ceremony" of New South boosterism.[45] The fair, said the *Augusta Chronicle* at the time, revealed the "unparalleled advantages of our state." Atlanta promoted the exposition with its "characteristic enterprise," according to another observer, demonstrating its "public spirit, energy and far-seeing business sagacity."[46] Through its hosting of the exposition, Atlanta displayed itself, in the words of one of its earliest historians, as the "leading representative city of the New South." There was "no place in the South . . . more thoroughly American."[47]

Significantly, during his 1881 visit to Atlanta, Sherman's only public appearance was at a reunion of Mexican War veterans, a group whose members tended to emphasize North-South unity and make little mention of the Civil War. The group's featured speaker, Henry R. Jackson, had served in the Mexican War but had also been a member of Georgia's secession convention and a major general in the state troops during the Civil War.[48] On this occasion, Jackson said that he would avoid recalling the "painful memories of the more recent past"; he preferred to discuss the Mexican War, a "bright spot in our own history." Sherman came unprepared to speak, but he relented in response to calls from the audience, and he was warmly received. He was happy to be in Atlanta, Sherman said, because he and his audience were "all Americans." They now represented "the same nation, the same soldiers, the same government, the same flag, and, so far as I am concerned, I am just as friendly to Georgia as I am to my own native state of Ohio." The exposition was situated "where once we had battle-fields." Now that the war was over, "we are all now in a position to say, every one of us, that we thank God that we are, each and every one of us, great and small, young and old, American citizens."[49]

LONG AFTER THE CIVIL WAR, Sherman's march through Atlanta continued, in the minds of white Atlantans, to serve both as an emblematic event of Atlanta's past and as a foil against which its bright future could be seen. For the rest of his life, Sherman insisted that his own military intentions had had little to do with the city's destruction in 1864, and that he had been unfairly portrayed as a heartless conqueror. But white Atlantans believed otherwise. "Thousands of men now living," declared the *Atlanta Constitution*, were "able to contradict him from their own personal knowledge." The general might be "simply forgetful instead of deliberately inventive" and perhaps was also admittedly "old and in affliction," but Sherman, in his dotage, was both "amusing and irritating."[50]

Though he attended Grady's New South address in 1886, Sherman left no record that indicates what he thought of it. There is ample evidence to suggest, however, that Sherman was uncomfortable with the idealization of the Confederacy that was manifest in the notion of the Lost Cause, and that he was suspicious of Grady's vision of the New South because it seemed to paper over the negative aspects of the Civil War's aftermath. By the late 1880s, the "Old General" had become a lightning rod for controversy, and his tendency to shoot from the hip in his public statements often fanned southern white sentiments.

During the Civil War, Sherman had opposed enlisting black troops and had not favored giving civil and political rights to freedpeople. "A nigger as such is a most excellent fellow," he once said, "but he is not fit to marry, to associate, or to vote with me, or mine."[51] Although this statement would seem to be in harmony with the white supremacist views held by many southerners, southern white attitudes toward Sherman hardened after his views about race and about African American enfranchisement were revised toward the end of his life. Sometime during the 1880s, according to one of his biographers, Sherman experienced a "change of heart" about black people.[52] In October 1888, nearly two years before his death, Sherman, in an article in the *North American Review*, endorsed the idea that federal protection for black voting rights ought to be given. Feeling "partial to the colored people of the United States," he went on to describe in sympathetic, if paternalistic, terms his memory of a freed slave who had served as the steward of Gen. James B. MacPherson. Sherman went beyond his usual platitudes. African Americans, he wrote, were now "not only free, but entitled by the Constitution and law to all the privileges of American citizenship." Saluting the "old bondsman who staid at home" during the Civil War to look after the plantation mistresses while the planter was "away fighting to destroy his own government,"

Sherman noted that black males were being prevented from voting because their enfranchisement disturbed the "judgment of the white majority" and altered "the verdict of their former masters." He called on the white South to "let the negro vote, and count his vote honestly." White northerners, who were "slow to anger, but once aroused not easy to allay," would not continue to tolerate black disfranchisement. Sherman warned that there might be another war "more cruel than the last, when the torch and dagger will take the place of well-ordered battalions."[53]

Sherman's prediction of an impending conflict over black rights aroused the ire of Henry Grady. "What possible good can come of General Sherman's terrible words?" he asked in the *Atlanta Constitution*. He denied that African Americans suffered political oppression, and even if southern whites were frightened by Sherman's predictions, "they could not right a wrong when there is no wrong." Sherman's words would only arouse a "blind and unreasoning rage" in black people. The *Constitution* cited a recent uprising of African Americans in December 1888 in Wahalak, Mississippi, where the "great name" of Sherman had inspired blacks to revolt against white rule, his prediction of northern intervention having emboldened them. There is little evidence that Sherman's words actually had this effect, but the event in Wahalak—in which a group of armed African Americans resisted white police officers—was unnerving to southern whites. Sherman's sword had been "terrible in war," said Grady, and "ruin and the torch went with it." "Let us hope," it continued, "that his pen will not be deadlier in peace, and ruin and the torch be invoked from its point."[54] But Sherman's call for the protection of black voters also attracted northern support. Grady's blaming him for the eruption of racial violence in Mississippi, argued a northern newspaper, was a "very flagrant instance of a most absurd attempt to shift responsibility to wholly innocent shoulders." Like the lamb in Aesop's fable who was blamed by the wolf for befouling his drinking supply, Sherman, who had done so much to save the Union, was now being told that he possessed "no right to express any opinion about the country that is displeasing to the South."[55]

Sherman reminded his audience of the persisting significance of race— and of the fictions that whites had created around it. Rebuilding after the Civil War required rebuilding the productive relationship between northern and southern whites—but in this process southern whites had rewritten and reimagined the past by scrubbing clean the memory of slavery and disregarding the significance of black emancipation and black freedom. In promoting his vision of national reconciliation and southern economic development, Grady had said little about race. Disavowing slavery and slaveholding, Grady held dear the southern view of the racial past. But in remembering this past and envisioning his New South, he also smoothed over the harsh realities of white supremacy, past and present.

In Grady's vision, there were clear limits to the societal role that should be played by black people in his New South. While visiting New York City in 1881, Grady had watched at Booth's Theater a performance of *Uncle Tom's Cabin*, "that classic of hate and slander." Harriet Beecher Stowe's portrayal of the slaveholding South was a "false picture," he believed, of a system that, though "wrong in itself, had been made tolerable by the people on whom it was saddled." White slaveholders had been sympathetic toward the enslaved, Grady contended, while slaves had been content in their enslavement. The "plantation darkey," he said, was the "happiest laborer on all the earth." A "strange tenderness" bound together masters and slaves. White slaveholders had provided slaves "for a century a happiness and contentment to which the servants of New England were utter strangers, and which we fear the negro will never see again."[56]

Grady was committed to the maintenance of white supremacy, and, in the late 1880s, the moment arrived when he admitted this principle explicitly and truthfully. In October 1887, Grady spoke at the Texas State Fair in Dallas, telling his audience that the "hope and assurance of the South" was the "clear and unmistakable domination of the white race." Before this audience of southern whites, he laid out the rationale of white supremacy: the white race, he said, would "never submit to its domination, because the white race is the superior race." Black enfranchisement and officeholding would pollute the political system, separating emancipated slaves from the protection of the slaveholder class. The race issue emerged "wherever the Anglo-Saxon touches an alien race." Grady offered these opinions even as he invoked his familiar modernizing, New South message, making the specious assertion that he had a kindly intent toward black people. His white supremacist views came not out of "passion . . . but in reason; not in narrowness, but in breadth; that we may solve this problem in calmness and in truth."[57]

After Sherman's *North American Review* article appeared in 1888, Grady more explicitly fused his belief in white supremacy with his conception of the New South, for Sherman had forced Grady's hand. His breach with Sherman suggests that the gulf between Grady's vision of the New South and the perceptions of others—such as Sherman—was widening. Though he continued to describe Sherman as a great soldier, Grady told his Texas audience that "as careless as he was with fire twenty five years ago he is now more careless with words."[58] In another speech delivered in late 1888, Grady told a group of Georgians that the white South would remain monolithic "as long as the menace of negro domination" remained, and as long as northerners demanded that the African American vote "be cast and counted in a mass against the white vote." Maintaining white supremacy had to take precedence over all other considerations, he believed, because the New South could only progress with the subordination of African Americans.[59]

Much of Grady's outrage was directed at Sherman's charge that the South had, in effect, reversed the accomplishments of Reconstruction. In an editorial published in December 1888, Grady attacked Sherman in even more personal terms. In a piece entitled "The Old General At It Again," Grady charged that Sherman, in "his declining years," was defensive and inconsistent. Grady maintained that Sherman's "particular craze" was his "desire to vindicate himself," but that he felt no compunction to be "hampered by the facts of history." To some extent, Grady was right. When Grady interviewed him in 1888, Sherman denied with "vigorous emphasis" that he had destroyed Atlanta. Instead, he maintained that he had burned only the railroad depot, though eight years earlier he told Grady that he had burned the city's public buildings. Sherman's understanding of the past contradicted the memories of thousands of living survivors, however, for the city had been totally destroyed. Nothing, Grady claimed, had remained but a ring of five hundred dwellings and perhaps a half dozen stores. If this was Sherman's version of history, he should publish it so that "grown men would laugh over it and the children would cry for it."[60]

GRADY REALIZED THAT THE FUSING of his vision for the New South with the notion of white supremacy depended upon the acquiescence of the North and on an intersectional white racial brotherhood. As he had done for his famous New South speech in 1886, Grady traveled north with a large entourage of white southerners to sell his ideas. Less than two weeks before his sudden death in December 1889, he delivered an address before the Boston Merchants Association in which he laid out the contours of his idea of white supremacy and intersectional white reconciliation.[61]

The Boston banquet hall where Grady delivered his address was filled with flowers and flags and featured a head table with fourteen men, a group equally divided between northerners and southerners. Grady was greeted by applause lasting several minutes. He spoke for nearly an hour and a half in response to the effort by Massachusetts senator Henry Cabot Lodge to sponsor a "force" bill that would provide federal protections for black voting rights. Grady had become discouraged by the outbreaks of racial violence and by the random lynchings that were increasingly occurring across the South. His solution to the race crisis was to reach out to northern whites, seeking their support to help white southerners stabilize the social tensions.

Why, Grady asked, did the South remain underdeveloped and unattractive to migrants from the North? In 1880, the South counted fewer northern-born residents than it had in either 1860 or 1870. Fewer men had crossed the Mason-Dixon line "than when it was crimson with the best blood of the republic, or even when the slave-holder stood guard every inch of its way." The reason, Grady asserted, lay in the problem of race, a problem that could only be solved through an intersectional alliance of southern and northern whites. Southern slaveholders bore responsibility for having maintained slavery, but so did northern whites, whose ancestors had transported slaves from Africa. "You will not defend the traffic," Grady told his audience, "nor I the institution." But the white slaveholder had nonetheless elevated the black slave, he claimed, to "heights of which he had not dreamed in his savage home."

Grady welcomed the fact that slavery had been abolished but felt that black emancipation had led to a racial crisis. Describing the racial violence that was widespread and accelerating across the South, he said that the two antagonistic races were poised against each other in an "experiment sought by neither, but approached by both with doubt." The crisis, he said, demanded white racial unity across sectional lines. Never before had North American whites not rallied around the concept of racial unity. Grady then used his address to elaborate his views on white supremacy, in an openly racist diatribe. No two races, Grady asserted, had "ever lived anywhere at any time, on the same soil with equal rights in peace." Indians had been "cut down as a weed," because they "hindered the way of the American citizen." Asians were excluded from America because they were "alien and inferior." Black people were by nature "pinned to the soil," yet the federal government had taken the stance that they possessed "full and equal heirship of American privilege and prosperity." The very concept of racial equality violated what Grady claimed was a national policy of American prejudice. To change that policy and that practice contradicted the "universal verdict of racial history."

Grady urged northern and southern whites to unite around the banner of white supremacy. Southern whites were "as honest, as sensible, and as just as your people," and if northern whites could admit this, "we may reach an understanding tonight." Northern intervention to protect African American rights would only stiffen southern white resolve, Grady asserted. Whites, North and South, should instead unite in the face of a "tremendous menace," the threat of black rule.[62]

Grady extolled the paternalism of the slaveholder regime because it provided a model for how whites should treat blacks. His version was mostly romanticized nonsense. The "love we feel for that race," he declared, "you cannot measure or comprehend." Drawing a link between the present and the past, Grady praised the trusted slaves who had accompanied the Confederate soldiers to their dying days. He described the death of his own father, William S. Grady, killed at Petersburg, who had been comforted by a slave who bent "his trusty face to catch the words that trembled on the stricken lips," administering help with "uncomplaining patience" and, in his grief, "suffering for the death of him who in life fought against his freedom."

That Grady revealed himself in the end to be an aggressive white supremacist is perhaps unsurprising. More surprising to us from a present perspective, however, is the enthusiastic reaction of his mostly northern audience, which interrupted him twenty-nine times with applause and cheers. Halfway through the speech, according to a New York reporter, two-thirds of the audience had been moved to tears. This was, the reporter declared, an "oratorical triumph of the first magnitude." When Grady finished, according to the *Boston Herald*, the "audience rose en masse and joined in one great cheer." The speech was celebrated by white Bostonians as one of the ablest pieces of rhetoric ever delivered in the city. Grady reached the "sensibilities as the master hand sweeps the harp," claimed another reporter, "evoking now laughter, now wild applause, now tears."[63] "It has opened the eyes of the people here as to the race question," said an Atlantan who was accompanying Grady; the applause greeting the speech was "earnest and prolonged."[64]

Grady's Boston address marked an important chapter in his development of a vision for the New South. His compromise seemed to offer racial peace in exchange for a partnership between southern and northern whites—but only if northern whites acknowledged without question the legitimacy of southern white supremacy. Southern economic development depended upon establishing a new order in the South, but the South was willing to welcome northern investment only if the white North allied itself with southern whites. The northern whites present at Grady's speech seem to have received the message. "The subject has never before been presented so vividly or with such broad intelligence before the public in this section," said the *Boston Post*, suggesting that Grady's speech deserved "careful reading and thought by all." Grady had made an appeal "from a southern man to his northern brethren on the basis of rationality common to them both," declared the *Boston Herald*.[65]

Atlanta provided a stage where the actions taken by whites and blacks after black emancipation were on display. Grady's conceptualization of a New South was linked to selected themes of southern renewal that he had chosen to develop. While his vision involved an element of exaggeration, nowhere was his vision more fictitious than on the particulars of race. Even while he declared that the natural relationship between whites and blacks was a relationship of peace, racial warfare was raging within earshot, as it were, of Atlanta. Lynchings and legal executions of innocent Georgia blacks had become commonplace and were regularly reported in the pages of Grady's own *Atlanta Constitution*. While consistently dismissing as a northern exaggeration the charge that southern whites were grossly unjust to African Americans, he collaborated with political allies in creating and establishing the convict-lease system, which was used to exploit and oppress blacks in horrific ways. Political exclusion and suppression of African Americans had long been a feature of Georgia politics, something that Grady well realized. And racial segregation in the expanding railroad system and in other areas of life had become entrenched, despite the objections of African American leaders.[66]

Many African Americans rightly denounced Grady's New South vision as a sham. In an article reprinted in the *Atlanta University Bulletin*, the *Boston Pilot* declared that Grady's Boston speech was "pleasant to the ear, but unsatisfactory to the judgment and hopeless to the heart." Grady had offered "love and union" to the white North, but "suppression of the legitimate rights of the Southern blacks." He had treated black people as aliens; the *Pilot* would prefer to see equal rights for all. African Americans were not "divided from white men by an inhuman line." Rather, they were "largely bone of the bone and blood of the blood of the Southern whites." The historical reality of "illicit union" between the races made white claims of racial purity instances of "hypocrisy and scoundrelism." Grady had urged black people to abandon hopes of full citizenship. The "skeleton under the rhetoric" of Grady's New South vision, the *Pilot* said, was that he sought to reestablish society's acceptance of white supremacy. "The manacles and chains, and even the scourges" would remain in place, with the "sheriff or constable for the executioner instead of the master." In reality, southern blacks did not "love and trust" southern whites; they were unwilling victims of the racial order that was imposed upon them.[67]

Grady's 1889 Boston speech is largely forgotten or ignored in the historical literature written about him and the New South. For the most part, Grady is remembered for the speech he gave three years earlier in New York City, in which he celebrated and popularized the notion of the New South. His Boston speech unveiled the true meaning and intent of his New South boosterism, making clear the connection between his vision of southern development and his grim determination to maintain white supremacy. Grady's visit north was the last act in his interesting rhetorical career. Struck with a bad cold before the trip, Grady traveled to Boston against his doctor's orders. By the time he returned to Atlanta, he had contracted pneumonia, and he died at the age of forty-nine. Sherman outlived him, but not by much; he died about a year later, in February 1891.

Grady's vision of the New South was rooted in a particular narrative that grew into a larger social truth. This narrative, like white Atlanta's vision of itself, arose out of the southern white experience of the Civil War and the linked experiences of destruction and renewal. But the southern white narrative was hotly contested. The debate between Sherman and Grady about the past and future of the South illustrates one dimension of this struggle. Certainly not all Atlantans nor all southerners purchased what Grady was selling; the city became a battlefield of competing visions. In particular, blacks and whites drew different meanings from the Civil War, and both populations used these meanings to assert their own understanding of the South. Atlanta's history embodied a contestation over the meaning of the Civil War and over what the South might become.

IN LATE DECEMBER 1881, the black people of Atlanta appeared "in force" at the International Cotton States Exposition. The occasion was Freedmen's Day, which planners of the exposition had designated in order to highlight African American achievement. Of particular interest at this occasion were the speeches delivered by AME bishop H. W. Warren and Edmund S. Morris, a white Philadelphia businessman. Both men avidly supported the proposition of black colonization to Liberia. Warren emphasized the strength and power of Africa—with its 200 million inhabitants—both at home and abroad. In Atlanta, Warren stated, the presence of black schools made possible "equal chances for both races during the future." Recalling the Atlanta University anthem, Warren reminded the audience of the story about the origins of "We Are Rising," with its theme of black progress and autonomy. Morris similarly delivered a message of black self-reliance. When he unfurled the Liberian flag, he was greeted with cheers. "In company with the colored people of America," he said, "I can truly say, . . . we, too, are rising."[68]

The final speaker, William A. Pledger, was born the son of a slave and a white slaveholder. Originally from Athens, Pledger graduated from Atlanta

University and practiced law in Atlanta. One of the most important black activists in post–Civil War Atlanta, Pledger had served as chairman of the executive committee of the Georgia Republican party and as the U.S. surveyor of the port of Atlanta. He had also edited several newspapers during the 1870s and 1880s, including the *Athens (Ga.) Blade*, the *Atlanta Journal of Progress,* and the *Atlanta Defiance*.[69] Pledger joined in the self-congratulatory rhetoric of Freedmen's Day. "I can say that we present to the world such a spectacle as is seldom seen," he told the audience. Fifteen years from slavery, black people had been "lifted from servitude and placed side by side in the race of life with the ex-master." "We feel at home in these southern lands and amongst friends," he declared.[70]

Throughout the 1880s, African American leaders lobbied for their own, separate black exposition that would match the flurry of world's fairs that had been held across the United States during the last quarter of the nineteenth century. In 1886 and 1887, organizers in Birmingham and Montgomery, Alabama, argued for congressional funding of $600,000 to finance a black exposition.[71] Pledger led the campaign to host a Colored National Exposition, proposing in June 1887 that the Atlanta Driving Club host the event. Pitching the idea to the club's directors, Pledger promised, with their support, to bring the exposition to Atlanta. He maintained that a renewed effort to obtain a congressional appropriation would succeed, and he promised a national petition drive.

The Driving Club's directors also heard from the Rev. Philip Joseph of Mobile, director general of the black exposition. Like Pledger, Joseph was a veteran of Republican politics, having run twice for Congress. Thirty-five years old, fluent in Spanish and French, Joseph had been in charge of the black exhibition for Alabama at the New Orleans World's Fair in 1884. By the summer of 1887, Joseph had come to favor Atlanta as the best site for an African American world's fair, perhaps because of its Oglethorpe Park facilities.[72] Like Pledger, Joseph assured the Atlanta Driving Club that Congress was on the verge of providing an appropriation. Congressional funding would finance the construction of two hotels, one on the fairgrounds and the other in downtown Atlanta, to house black visitors, excluded from white hotels. Joseph proposed that if the club granted permission to use their facilities he could promise a contribution of $150,000.[73]

The black world's fair would exhibit black progress in trade, industry, and the arts during their two decades of American freedom. Predicting large crowds, Pledger proposed opening the exposition in November and keeping the gates open for the next eighty days.[74] Not only did the Driving Club grant permission for the use of its facilities, the city council, chamber of commerce, and the editors of the *Atlanta Constitution* all endorsed the exposition. Grady was a supporter, as was Gov. John B. Gordon. Joseph sought support from the black community in Atlanta and nationally.[75] The "manhood of the colored race" depended on their "material welfare," he announced at a mass meeting held in June 1888. The federal appropriations that were given for expositions "under the auspices of Anglo-Saxons" should be matched by federal support for a black world's fair.[76] Black leaders, such as New York newspaper editor T. Thomas Fortune and Virginia congressman John M. Langston, lined up behind the idea. The organization incorporated and offered capital stock for the Colored World's Fair Association.

Despite the high hopes of its supporters, the bill for federal support of the black world's fair died in Congress, where, in 1887 and 1888, it never left committee.[77] But the campaign marked a significant moment in Atlanta's coming-of-age as a political and cultural center of the black South. As an aspect of that coming-of-age, African American Atlanta had articulated a vision of the New South that was at odds with Grady's version.

IN 1894, EDWARD RANDOLPH CARTER, pastor of the Friendship Baptist Church, the oldest and most powerful black church in Atlanta, published *The Black Side*. Born enslaved in 1858 in Athens, Georgia, Carter enjoyed the sponsorship of his master, Edward Randolph Harden, for whom he was named. Having learned to read as a young slave, Carter obtained under Harden's patronage three years of schooling after the Civil War. At age eleven, he was apprenticed to a shoemaker; five years later, he taught school. He continued to attend white churches, after the war, as he had done as a slave, and had an experience of religious conversion while listening to a sermon from the University of Georgia's chancellor, Patrick H. Hall. Having been called to the ministry, in 1879 Carter moved to Atlanta, with fifty cents in his pocket, to enter the Atlanta Baptist Seminary (later Morehouse College), where he supported himself and his family as a cobbler. In 1880, Carter became pastor of Stone Mountain Baptist Church, and, two years later, was called to Friendship Baptist Church, where he remained until his death in 1944. An avid prohibitionist who became known as the "dean of Atlanta ministers," Carter led efforts to create a "New Black Man" in post-Reconstruction Atlanta.[78]

In his introduction to *The Black Side*, Henry McNeal Turner elaborated on Carter's vision of African American leadership. Born free in South Carolina in 1834, Turner became an itinerant AME minister, traveling throughout the South in the 1850s. By 1861, he had moved to the North, and during the war he helped to organize the 1st Regiment of U.S. Colored Troops. The experience of the Civil War helped to reinforce Turner's strong sense of self and his lifelong commitment to racial equality. Having served as a military chaplain, after the war he moved to Georgia, where he participated in the 1868 constitutional convention. Elected AME bishop in 1880, Turner advocated black self-reliance and black nationalism, and he promoted late nineteenth-century back-to-Africa movements.[79]

White supremacists, Turner wrote, claimed that black people were incapable of achievement, that they were "degraded, non-intellectual," and inferior. Whites maintained that African Americans "either had no history or had been too incompetent to preserve it." But there existed an authentic African American history, said Turner, that documented black people's "genius, skill, bravery, adventure and enterprise." Under slavery, African Americans had been compelled to experience dehumanizing conditions that led to their degradation. Was this any wonder? White slaveholders were equally degraded, even as they closed "the doors of every avenue that looked toward our elevation." African Americans had "outlived them all, and our duty now is to look to the future," while never entirely forgetting the past. "Greatness has no color; learning is neither white nor black." God was neither white nor black; there was "no such place as a white heaven, where every angel, cherub and seraph is white."[80]

Though Carter was more of a racial accommodationist than Turner, his book reiterated Turner's message of racial equality, self-reliance, and autonomous black economic development. In Atlanta, he enjoyed white sponsorship. According to subsequent accounts, as a young man during the 1870s Carter had met the young Henry Grady, a fellow Athens native who had also just moved to Atlanta. What was later described as a "strong friendship" emerged, and Grady found Carter a "powerful colleague in every fight for righteousness." Years later, in 1941, the white pastor of Atlanta First Baptist Church called Carter "of inestimable value to us" in "leading his own people and in his attitude toward the whites."

Carter also articulated blacks' frustrations. He wrote about the hostility that prevailed between the races in Atlanta, as whites tried to block black economic progress. White dominance resulted in a black "feeling of unrest and everlasting perturbation, which unsettles all permanent thought and action." Even those whites inclined to help African Americans were "clasp[ed] in fetters so binding" that they were prevented from working on an equal basis with black people. Despite having the system geared against them, however, Atlanta blacks had overcome obstacles, "leaped over impediments, gone ahead, purchased the soil, erected houses of business and reared dwellings." Given an equal chance and left to their own devices, Carter said, African Americans could "accomplish what any other race has accomplished or can accomplish."[81]

Atlanta blacks, Carter wrote, had shaped their past and could determine their future. Andrew Montgomery, whom Carter described as the "oldest living Afro-American in this city," had been born in 1808 and was still living in 1894. He arrived in Atlanta when it was Terminus, a small village of several hundred residents containing about fifty African Americans, only two of whom were free. The two free blacks, Mary Combs and Ransom Montgomery (Andrew's brother), had accumulated property. In July 1849, Ransom Montgomery rescued from a burning bridge over the Chattahoochee River more than one hundred passengers aboard a Western & Atlantic train. The Georgia legislature rewarded Ransom by buying him from his master; property of the state of Georgia, he became effectively free, and the state ordered the state-owned Western & Atlantic to employ him. The state also provided Montgomery with a home, while the city council authorized him to sell coffee and cakes in the railroad depot. The Montgomery brothers became early members of an emerging black elite in Atlanta.[82]

Carter's view of the past in *The Black Side* differed significantly from the white version. He remembered living close enough to Atlanta during the war to hear cannon fire. Atlanta's destruction in "torrents of fire, as in the days of Sodom," was a biblical punishment on the slaveholder state. For African Americans, the northern conquest meant freedom, a story "more of gain than loss." Sherman's shells struck the "hammer of liberty, unfastening the fetters of the accursed and inhuman institution of slavery." Black people rejoiced when they saw the Confederate flag "fall like Lucifer and trail in the dust, and in its stead the Union flag floating in the breeze." Atlanta's fall meant that a "diabolical temple of traffic in human blood had been overthrown and buried in everlasting oblivion, and the temple of the Goddess of Liberty had arisen."[83]

Carter's version of the history of Reconstruction—what he called the Black Side—also differed from Grady's New South narrative. The true history of Reconstruction remained untold, he believed. These were years, he wrote, "difficult to narrate, especially when referring to the feeling which existed between the races." White supremacists had portrayed Republicanism as a picture of northern tyranny, southern white perfidy, and black insolence; *The Black Side* saw Republican victory in 1868 as a "year of jubilee." Emancipated slaves were the "backbone and life-giving power of the Republican party." Ex-slaves who had only recently been handling plows, saws, shovels, and picks were now members of the Georgia state legislature. Under the capitol dome, freed slaves enjoyed "protection and security" under the Stars and Stripes.

Carter emphasized that African Americans should understand their past. Every child needed to be told "of the hands which aided in the reconstruction of the government of this grand old Empire State of the South." They should be told, Carter said, "of the honors conferred upon their fathers, and the high positions to which they were chosen, notwithstanding their insufficiency in many instances." This composed a "history of the race, and is therefore worthy of repetition." Remembering their history also enabled black Americans to envision their future, Carter maintained. African Americans, "standing alone, possessing nothing," could only rely on themselves. All black people wanted was a "citizen's privilege, the rights of a tax-payer and free access to the public positions of the city."[84]

THE COTTON STATES INTERNATIONAL EXPOSITION of 1895 is best known for the speech that opened it. Famously, Booker T. Washington delivered an address at the exposition that electrified the white audience because it seemed to promise African American acquiescence in their political exclusion in exchange for some measure of economic independence. Washington's presence at the exposition symbolically represented the image of the New South that white Atlanta wanted to present to the outside world, as well as the image black Atlanta perceived for itself in the post-emancipation world.[85]

Chicago's Columbian Exposition in 1893 had been criticized for lacking black representation, and organizers of Atlanta's Cotton States Exposition were determined not to repeat this mistake.[86] In April 1894, exposition promoters brought Washington, along with AME leaders Wesley J. Gaines and Abraham Grant, with them to lobby Congress. Their efforts yielded a $200,000 appropriation, and organizers promised a Negro Building housing exhibitions organized by black people—the first time that an exposition would host a separate African American facility.[87] The decision to include a Negro Building was "one of the most significant signs that feeling between the two races is becoming more and more fraternal," declared a group of black leaders in March 1894.[88] Black achievement would not be "huddled in an obscure corner, nor scattered over a hundred widely separated sections," said a Chicago newspaper.[89]

Still, many black leaders regarded the Atlanta exposition suspiciously. William S. Scarborough, a former slave from Macon, Georgia, attended

Atlanta University and Oberlin College and later became a professor of Latin and Greek at Wilberforce University in Ohio. Scarborough objected to the exposition's being held in Atlanta because black visitors would have to travel in Jim Crow railroad cars and be housed in segregated hotels, and, along with other black leaders, he urged a boycott. African Americans should keep their "hands off" and "virtually treat the invitation that has been tendered our race . . . with silent contempt."

Turner offered a spirited defense of the proposal for an Atlanta exposition. No one had more contempt for Jim Crow cars than he, Turner said, "or more disrespect for any legislature that would enact laws favoring such an institution." He denounced, as he had in the past, the decision of the United States Supreme Court in the civil rights cases of 1883, which narrowly limited federal intervention on behalf of black civil rights, as "revolting" and "nauseating." Past exhibitions had excluded black visitors entirely. The Philadelphia Centennial Exposition in 1876, he pointed out, had exhibited a painting by a black artist, but a "sensation" resulted when the painter won a prize. At the Columbian Exposition, "the only recognition that was given to the negro was to take care of the toilet rooms," although the fair's managers had been besieged with requests to provide a black exhibition. Turner lobbied the Columbian Exposition on three separate occasions, to no avail. Those black visitors who attended "got jimcrowed or saw their race jimcrowed." But a black boycott of the exposition, Turner maintained, would achieve nothing. African Americans would be "idiots" to refuse participating; the exposition provided too good a chance to "vindicate our honor, and set before the world our intelligence and skill." "Merit wins, worth tells; endeavor, stir and activity achieve better results and not a surly, snarlish, morose inertness."[90]

Representatives from eleven southern states met in Atlanta in January 1895 and chose twenty-six-year-old I. Garland Penn, an attorney who ran the black school system in Lynchburg, Virginia, as exhibit commissioner.[91] As had been the case during the 1880s in the black world's fair movement, in 1895 state committees were organized with representatives in a central executive committee.[92] Booker T. Washington attended the meeting, as did Isaac Montgomery, leader of the Mound Bayou, Mississippi, black settlement, a man whom the *Atlanta Constitution* described as a "brainy negro." Under Penn's watchful eye, the Negro Building was designed by black architect Bradford L. Gilbert and constructed by black artisans. The Negro Building, declared the *Constitution*, was "built by negroes, under the supervision of negroes, and filled with exhibits showing the progress of the colored race." The building, whose construction costs were borne by the exposition, covered 25,000 square feet and featured a central, seventy-foot tower encircled by pavilions at both ends. Located between Buffalo Bill Cody's Wild West Show on one side and the midway on the other, the Negro Building formally opened on October 21, 1895.[93]

The first exhibit in the world to promote African American accomplishments, the building contained the work of black inventors, artists, businessmen, artisans, and farmers. Black sculptor A. C. Hill depicted an enslaved man in chains with the caption, "Chains broken, but not off." Another exhibit, under Turner's control, illustrated black "development" in Africa. A longtime supporter of the idea of American black recolonization to Africa, Turner asserted the "savagery" of black Africa even while he vigorously disputed the assertion that slavery represented an improvement over African origins.[94] Though his portrayals of West Africans were insulting, Turner became outraged when he discovered that whites had assembled a racially derogatory Old Plantation exhibit. Located on the midway, the Old Plantation contained stereotyped representations of passive, happy slaves. It featured a log cabin that had originally been constructed in 1821, torn down for its lumber by Sherman's troops, and then reassembled at the fair. The exhibit, which became one of the fair's most popular attractions, contained "living negroes" who played mammies and "pickaninnies."[95]

Near the close of the exposition, on December 26, a Negro Day celebrated American black accomplishments after slavery. The featured speaker was Robert R. Wright, who, as a boy in 1868, had told O. O. Howard that "we are rising." There could be no solution to racial problems, Wright said, without "exact and untrammeled justice to all its citizens." The "spirit of universal liberty and fair-dealing," he said, will [have] no truer worshipers than her southern votaries, white and black." Having "by his sweat and blood identified himself with every phase and fiber of American life and history, his highest ambition is to unite with the other people of our union in developing a noble manhood and a beautiful and prosperous and contented country."[96]

Booker T. Washington's so-called Atlanta Compromise speech is best understood within the context of a particular moment in the struggle between blacks and whites over what the New South meant. Grady's vision demanded a racial settlement based on the notion of white supremacy, but black Atlanta was expressing a differing vision, of racial accomplishment and independence. Against this context, Garland Penn successfully persuaded the all-white board of directors in August 1895 to invite Washington to speak at the opening exercises on September 18, 1895. A parade of black people, the largest ever held in Atlanta, escorted Washington from the segregated, all-black Howell Hotel to the exposition grounds. Black military groups marched, in addition to Atlanta black ministers, such as Wesley J. Gaines and Henry H. Proctor. The parade lasted for three hours in the sweltering Georgia sun. When Washington finally reached the exposition auditorium, he was cheered on by a vocal black contingent who were sprinkled in among the largely white audience of perhaps 3,500 people.[97]

The exposition grounds, with three hundred buildings spread over two hundred acres, were completed just before the fair's opening, much of the labor having been provided by black convicts.[98] Open for one hundred days, it was constructed at a cost of $3 million and attracted a million visitors. The exposition stood as a visual symbol for Grady's New South. Atlanta was shown to be the "heart of the great South" and to embody the "spirit which has made the New South," declared the *New York Times*. The exposition was "an Atlanta enterprise," created to display the city's coming-of-age.

At the center of the exposition Lake Clara Meer, which had been expanded from a pond built for the 1887 exposition, contained a large electric fountain, Atlantis. Florida railroad and steamboat magnate Henry B. Plant built a pyramid whose exterior was made of phosphate mined in Georgia and Florida. The Alabama state building exhibited the products of the state and included a model of a coal mine. A Confederate Relics Hall displayed items related to Confederate history, though, perhaps ironically, federal soldiers guarded its contents. The Woman's Building, designed by Elise Mercur, a female architect from Pennsylvania, featured the public accomplishments of women. The Manufacturers and Liberal Arts Building, on the eastern side of the central plaza, rose three stories high and covered 103,000 square feet of space in which both Americans and Europeans presented exhibits. The second-largest structure, with 58,000 square feet of exhibit space, was the U.S. Government building, which represented the federal presence in the South.[99]

Washington's speech at the Cotton States Exposition of 1895 eventually overshadowed the exposition itself. According to one newspaper account, he was a "Negro Moses" prepared to lead his people from the wilderness. Washington fully realized the challenge facing him in delivering the speech, which had to navigate between the competing visions of white and black southerners while appealing for sectional reconciliation. Few orators could have pled their case "with more consummate power than did this angular negro standing in a nimbus of sunshine surrounded by the men who once fought to keep his race in bondage." His speech was of "extraordinary significance." There had been nothing like it since Grady's "immortal speech" in 1886, which had embodied "so profoundly the spirit of the New South."[100]

As historian David Blight notes, Washington's Atlanta Compromise speech marked an attempt "to merge sectional and racial peace into a single cause of black progress."[101] The speech, long regarded out of context, should be considered historically as part of a complex thematic mosaic whose subject was Atlanta's place in the New South. At the center of this mosaic was the theme of the Civil War, a theme exemplified by the prominence of veterans at the exposition. As Washington spoke, Union and Confederate veterans gathered on the Chickamauga battlefield 150 miles to the north to dedicate a national military park. On September 21, the exposition honored veterans with a Blue and Gray Day, featuring a speech by Ohio governor, Union veteran, and future U.S. president William McKinley. The Chickamauga reunion at the exposition, described as the "grandest occasion of its kind ever before known in the history of the two sections," was attended by thousands of veterans. Many of these veterans came to Atlanta, according to an observer, to view the "green hills of Atlanta, where Sherman's breastworks still stand." The city stood as an example of how the "ruined" South had remade itself despite "almost hopeless problems." In a gesture of national reunion, on October 9 Philadelphia had sent the Liberty Bell to the exposition, where it was officially received and remained until the end of December.

Washington did not disappoint his audience. Interrupted three times because of applause from cheering, he waited on one of these occasions for five minutes for the crowd to quiet.[102] Washington so electrified the audience that their roar was "as if it had come from the throat of a whirlwind."[103] As historians have often noted, the speech appealed both to northern and to southern whites because it acknowledged black accommodation to a racial order in which white supremacy was solidified. "The wisest among my race understand," he declared, "that the agitation of questions of social equal[it]y is the extremest folly and that progress in the enjoyment of all the privileges that will come to us, must be the result of severe and constant struggle, rather than of artificial feeling." Washington also developed his own vision of the past, present, and future of the South. In the "heart of Georgia," where white men had fought and then fashioned a narrative of the New South, Atlanta had provided an "example of fair play to the Negro." The existence of the Negro Building, and Washington's prominent place in the proceedings, were both acknowledgments of the justice of black emancipation. Though the path along which African Americans made their way was not "trodden without contact with thorns and thistles," Washington claimed "just pride" in "our own independent efforts."[104]

With the opening ceremonies concluded, the exposition began. President Grover Cleveland, from his summer residence in Cape Cod, pushed a button that, by electric signal, switched on the electric power at the Machinery Hall. In the center of the exposition, the Atlantis fountains burst on, spraying fifteen thousand gallons of water a minute; the entire exposition came alight with electric power. The thirteen bells in the Chimes Tower rang out the song, "Nearer My God to Thee," whistles blew, and the beating of drums announced the beginning of the exposition. "The Exposition was open," declared a correspondent, "and the people swarmed into the buildings—black and white, Georgia Colonels and all."[105]

A day after his speech, Washington was giddy. This had been the "most hearty and overwhelming reception in the history of my public speaking," he declared. Sitting on the platform, with "black men who were slaves" next to "ex-Confederate soldiers" who "were the masters of these slaves and on this very ground fought to keep enslaved these black men," he had looked over the audience of whites and blacks and was "carried away in a vision." It was, Washington wrote, "hard for me to realize as I spoke that it was not all a beautiful dream, but an actual scene, right here in the heart of the South."[106]

IN HIS CLASSIC *The Souls of Black Folk* (1903), W. E. B. Du Bois offered his take on Atlanta's position in the New South. "South of the North, yet north of the South," the "City of a Hundred Hills" peered out from the "shadows of the past into the promise of the future." Despite their defeat, Atlantans had turned resolutely toward a future that "held aloft vistas of purple and gold." The city crowned itself with "factories, and stored her shops with cunning handiwork, and stretched long iron ways to greet the busy Mercury in his coming." But the determination to make money—to create a prosperous New South—existed side by side with a determination to maintain the hierarchy of white supremacy. The goals of economic progress and the enforcement of racial hierarchy were sometimes in conflict with one another.

Atlanta's reputation as a center of the New South masked more crass realities, according to Du Bois. On the one hand, it was a place consumed with money-making and materialism. In the rush to create wealth, Atlanta had forgotten the manners of the Old South, the "grace and courtliness of patrician, knight, and noble," replacing them with "men busier and sharper, thriftier and more unscrupulous." The production of wealth had become the "mighty levers to lift this old new land; thrift and toil and saving are the highways to new hopes and new possibilities." This materialism also shaped black people. It made "little difference" to white Atlanta, or to the white South, what black people thought or felt. They would "naturally. . . long remain, unthought of, half forgotten."

Shaping the crass New South, meanwhile, was the "Veil"—the barrier of race that defined and dominated most aspects of life in Atlanta as a southern city. Behind the Veil, African Americans learned "to lisp" by embracing for themselves the values of the white New South. Black striving toward self-realization had become a "wheel within a wheel: beyond the Veil are smaller but like problems of ideals, of leaders and the led, of serfdom, of poverty, of order and subordination, and, through all, the Veil of Race." The old black leaders—teachers and preachers—were eclipsed by a new class of farmers, artisans, gardeners, porters, and businessmen. "And with all this change, so curiously parallel to that of the Other-world," Du Bois said, "goes too the same inevitable change in ideals." The disappearance of the "faithful, courteous slave of other days, with his incorruptible honesty and dignified humility" was but an indication of larger changes coming to the New South. The "sudden transformation of a fair far-off ideal of Freedom into the hard reality of bread-winning and the consequent deification of Bread" had changed both whites and blacks alike.[107]

Du Bois's denunciation of Grady's New South illuminates the two men's starkly different understandings of the meaning of the Civil War. The differences between whites' and blacks' perspectives were obvious. The future model of economic development represented by the New South posited industrialization, agricultural modernization and the abandonment of the plantation, and the development of cities, all fueled by white partnership with northern capitalists. Whites refused to recognize any basis for racial coexistence other than white supremacy, which became an article of faith to which even the goal of prosperity was subordinated. For whites, the war meant there was a need to rebuild the racial order as well as the economic order.

Black Atlantans wanted to buy into this model, but racial inequality remained an obstacle. They saw the relevance of the Civil War in terms of the end of slavery, and they wanted economic independence. Through the 1880s and 1890s, black leaders, remembering the Civil War and emancipation, put less emphasis on black freedom in the abstract and more emphasis on material improvement. Yet black leaders were far from presenting a united front about how to proceed. The death of Frederick Douglass in February 1895 represented the end of a leadership style that had arisen out of the struggle to destroy slavery. Washington's Atlanta Compromise speech, delivered in the same year as Douglass's death, catapulted him to a role as the single most important leader of African Americans. Washington's call for black autonomy, racial peace, and black accommodation with white supremacy was steeped in an African American perspective on the heritage of slavery and freedom, but it was not intended exclusively as an exercise in memorialization. Rather, for African Americans, the aftermath of slavery had ushered in a racial crisis. The black struggle for meaning in the shadow of the Civil War would focus on leadership. Once again, the bustling city of Atlanta provided an uncertain stage for a wider struggle.

SEVEN

The New South in Crisis

On September 22, 1906, Atlanta erupted in an unprecedented racial cataclysm that paralyzed the city for four days and, according to one assessment, "alarmed the entire country and awakened in the South a new sense of the dangers which threatened it." Reacting to lurid accounts in the Atlanta tabloid press about an alleged epidemic of black sexual assaults on white women, white mobs rampaged in the city's downtown, indiscriminately attacking African Americans. On the second and third days of violence, Atlanta's blacks took up arms in resistance, repelling a white invasion of the Dark Town and Brownsville neighborhoods. State militia subdued the armed black community, arresting three hundred black residents, even while the troops did little to apprehend the white rioters. The violence cost an unknown number of black lives, with estimates ranging from twenty-five to more than a hundred. Officially, there were only two white deaths, although black leaders claimed that many more had actually died.[1]

Coming two decades after Grady's speech to the New England Society of New York, the explosion in Atlanta reminded people across the country of the importance of race in the post-emancipation South. Black independence and cultural power in Atlanta, which had grown with the city's development in the late nineteenth century, threatened to undermine the power of white supremacy. Although white fears of black progress became focused on white anxieties about the black rape of white women, they also reflected the ongoing conflict between white and black expectations about the future. The racial massacre of 1906 was profoundly troubling because it upset long-standing white assumptions and cast the New South narrative about Atlanta into doubt.

ATLANTA'S BREAKDOWN OF LAW AND ORDER followed decades of rapid social and economic change, as the city grew into a major transportation, financial, and manufacturing center. By the early twentieth century, twelve

POPULATION OF ATLANTA, BY RACE, 1850–1910

Year	Total Population	White	Black	% Black
1850	2,572	2,060	512	19.9
1860	9,554	7,615	1,939	20.3
1870	21,789	11,860	9,929	45.6
1880	37,409	21,079	16,330	43.7
1890	65,533	37,416	28,098	42.9
1900	89,872	54,090	35,727	39.8
1910	154,839	102,861	51,902	33.5

Source: http://www.census.gov/population/www/documentation/twps0076/twps0076.html.

railroad lines converged there; banks had expanded significantly; the cotton trade was booming; and manufacturing in cotton textiles, furniture, lumber, foundries, and machine shops was rising. Invented in the 1880s in Atlanta, Coca-Cola became a national popular drink by the early 1900s. Between 1880 and 1910, the city's population more than quadrupled, with a stream of new migrants arriving from the surrounding southern countryside. More of these migrants were white than black, and the city's population, which was almost 44 percent black in 1880, declined to slightly more than a third black by 1910. White migrants, arriving mostly from rural Georgia, formed a new urban proletariat composed of young, single men and women working in low-wage occupations. Still, in absolute numbers the African American presence in Atlanta, with nearly 52,000 black inhabitants in 1910, remained significant.[2]

Like other southern cities, as Atlanta physically expanded, it also became more racially segregated. Particularly after the 1890s, the city rigorously separated public spaces. In 1891 and 1899, the Georgia legislature mandated segregated transportation, and, in 1900, Atlanta also enacted a municipal ordinance requiring it.[3] The streetcars were successfully segregated, despite black protest and boycott, over the next several years.[4] Other public accommodations were either segregated or excluded blacks entirely. In 1903, the city council prohibited black college football players from participating in games in Brisbane Park; all city parks erected separate, Jim Crow entrances. Black prisoners were segregated from white, while black witnesses were sworn into court on separate Bibles.[5]

The Jim Crow world reinforced an existing reality: black Atlanta had already fashioned its own institutions, resulting in an unusually well-developed black economic, cultural, and political community. White journalist Ray

Stannard Baker, who conducted a thorough investigation of racial conditions after the 1906 violence, was astounded to discover the existence of a parallel black society in Atlanta, and especially an expanding, self-confident black middle class. By the end of the nineteenth century, the black Atlanta community possessed social, cultural, and political institutions and leadership that set it apart from other urban black populations of the South. Baker reported that a new racial consciousness existed in a vibrant and prosperous black community in Atlanta, whose members were driven together "for offence and defence." This new racial consciousness stressed black self-sufficiency; "feeling that the white man was against him," black people patronized their own dentists, doctors, and storekeepers.[6]

Older black enterprises, such as undertaking and barbering, provided capital for new black-owned businesses. Alonzo F. Herndon, who operated a prosperous barbershop, reinvested his capital in insurance. Atlanta had witnessed the establishment of numerous small mutual aid and makeshift insurance operations in the black community. In 1905, however, the Georgia legislature required that all such organizations pay a $5,000 deposit with the state—which would effectively have driven these same enterprises out of business. Herndon provided this deposit for small operators, amalgamating insurers into the new Atlanta Mutual Life Insurance Company. Within a decade, the company had become one of the big four among African American insurance companies nationally. By the time of his death in 1927, Herndon was one of the richest black men in America.[7]

Other black businesses also prospered. Black dentists and doctors sent their patients to black-owned drug stores. Baker described a prosperous shoe store in Atlanta that was owned by a black-controlled stock company. The manager was a "brisk young mulatto" who was an Atlanta University graduate. Black capitalists had found a niche, the manager reported, because white shoe stores were contemptuous in their treatment of African Americans of the "better class." Black women were handed shoes without being given the chance to try them on and were served only after the last white customer was done. All black people wanted, he said, was protection and justice.

Atlanta's black population was spread across the city, but confined to segregated enclaves. In 1905, Du Bois described African Americans as stretching "like a great dumbbell across the city, with one great center in the east and a smaller one in the west, connected by a narrow belt." The west end of the city around Atlanta University was home both to middle-class blacks and the worst slums in the city. A larger middle-class neighborhood existed around the old Fourth Ward, stretching from an area of black businesses on

Decatur Street and extending along Auburn Avenue.[8] The growing black working class, in contrast, was concentrated in the Dark Town and Pittsburg neighborhoods. In dives, bars, and pawnshops on Decatur Street, white and black workers congregated, and police controlled the restive population by exerting an iron control and using brutal force against the black population. In 1906, Baker found that, of the 21,702 arrests in the city, 62 percent were of blacks, significantly higher than their proportion of the population. Baker visited the court of Judge Nash Broyles on Decatur Street, where he described a "staggering" number of cases. During the morning when Baker visited, the court docket contained more than a hundred cases; the court's work concluded by two in the afternoon. Although many of the cases involved violent crime, Judge Broyles also busied himself enforcing racial etiquette. When a six-year-old boy insulted a white girl, he was whipped in the police station in a fashion, according to a newspaper account, "that will make him remember to be good."[9]

Criminal justice in Atlanta was linked to the state's convict-lease system. The Atlanta police arrested about 17,000 people a year, a figure equaling that in New Orleans, which had twice the population and police. Most Atlanta arrests, not surprisingly, were of black people; many of the convicts were found guilty of minor property offenses but were unable to pay the fines. According to Baker, there were strong incentives for the courts to imprison young African Americans. The courts convicted as many men as possible, Baker wrote, because a high conviction rate provided cheap labor to the contractors and profits to government.[10] Others agreed with Baker's assessment. As northern white reformer Mary White Ovington concluded, there were "two kinds of justice in the city."[11] According to Du Bois, because of the convict-lease system, Atlanta, and other parts of Georgia, shaped the criminal justice system into a moneymaking enterprise. The way to reduce crime was by "just courts, a decent, honest police force," Du Bois wrote, "and a system of punishment the object of which is to stop crime and reform criminals and not to make money."[12]

Du Bois's description of the heinous convict-lease system pointed up the dark side of Atlanta's growth and development. The city had grown rapidly during the four decades after the Civil War, becoming one of the most important cities in the New South. Economic growth depended on racial subordination and the exploitation of black people, a fact that was eclipsed in white perceptions by the material growth of the era. Because Atlanta also had a self-confident black community, with strong underpinnings of political independence, the dynamic of the black response to the enforcement of white supremacy was different from that of the rest of Georgia. For black Americans, Atlanta was a stage on which differing responses to white supremacy could be tested, debated, and articulated. Black Atlantans actively contested the monolithic white vision of the South's past and future.

AFRICAN AMERICAN PUBLIC OPINION remained deeply divided between advocacy of open black resistance and legal and political challenge, and black accommodation, autonomy, and economic empowerment. Famously, these divisions became focused in the debate between W. E. B. Du Bois and Booker T. Washington, but this strategic and ideological tension had roots in the post–Civil War era. Du Bois had initially endorsed the Atlanta Compromise, writing to the *New York Age* that it might provide the basis of a "real settlement."[13] In turn, Washington was an avid supporter of Atlanta University, many of whose graduates taught at his Tuskegee Institute. When Du Bois arrived in Atlanta in 1897, he and Washington remained cordial. Several times, Washington tried to hire Du Bois to come to Tuskegee.[14] Washington attempted to justify his position by claiming that the meaning of his message about racial compromise had been distorted. There was a "wrong impression in many cases of my position," he wrote in December 1895. "I believe in the highest development of the black man and I also believe thoroughly that we must constantly keep before the whole South the fact that there can be no real progress until law and order prevail in every corner of the Southern States."[15]

Du Bois, educated at Fisk, in Berlin, and at Harvard, described Atlanta University, which he joined as a new faculty member in 1897, as a "green oasis" in the white supremacist South. There, he began his "real life work," discovering himself and his mission in life.[16] But Du Bois gradually became alienated from Washington. In truth, the styles, objectives, and tactics of the two men differed fundamentally. Du Bois later described Washington as a difficult person to know. "Wary and silent," Washington "never expressed himself frankly or clearly until he knew exactly to whom he was talking and just what their wishes and desires were." In contrast, Du Bois described himself as "quick, fast-speaking, and voluble."[17] In many ways, these personality differences were reflected by the difference in the educational philosophies of Tuskegee Institute and Atlanta University. While Tuskegee sought to uplift rural blacks through industrial education, Atlanta University offered a more rigorous academic curriculum designed to train an educated black elite. While Tuskegee was rugged, Atlanta was effete. Atlanta University's avowed purpose was to extend the abolitionist legacy of equality in education;

Tuskegee, reflecting Washington's vision for black progress, masked its purposes in the vague concept of "industrial education."

The differences between these institutions found symbolic expression in a football game, the last of the season, played by Tuskegee Institute and Atlanta University on December 17, 1900, in the city's Brisbane Park, three years before blacks were excluded from playing football in the park. An observer described how the physical characteristics of the two teams seemed to reflect their institutions' differing educational philosophies. While Tuskegee athletes were characterized by "muscle and brawn and fine physical development," the Atlantans were "shorter men, with well-knit, compact bodies, agile, and quick as lightning in their movements." The crucial factor in the game, according to this account, was whether discipline and agility could defeat raw physical power. In a close game, Atlanta prevailed, finishing the season with a record of 4-0, Tuskegee representing the only team that had scored against the Atlanta defense all season. "And is this not more than a football victory?" wrote the commentator. "May we not see in the results of this game another vindication of the power of higher education to mould men for conquest over their physically stronger opponents in the game of life?"[18]

During the decade after Washington's 1895 Atlanta Compromise speech—in which Washington had proposed to relinquish political power, civil rights, and an equal form of university education in exchange for greater black economic autonomy—unhappiness grew among other black leaders who feared that his policies amounted to a surrender to white supremacy. Washington represented black public opinion to whites, who in turn provided financial and political support that provided the "Wizard of Tuskegee" with power. Using this power, he tolerated little opposition. Du Bois's critique of Washington in *The Souls of Black Folk*, which appeared in the spring of 1903, included the observation that Washington responded to criticism harshly by squelching his critics. Some opponents were silenced and paralyzed as a result, while others "burst into speech so passionately and intemperately as to lose listeners." Washington deserved praise as the "most distinguished Southerner since Jefferson Davis, and the one with the largest personal following." His vision and his sincere purpose made him one of the leading men of his time. Yet educated and professional black people, like Du Bois, harbored feelings of "deep regret, sorrow, and apprehension" about the Atlanta Compromise. Washington's compromise had been followed by disfranchisement, segregation, and reduced white financial support for black higher education. Washington, Du Bois wrote, favored racial self-respect but proposed counseling "silent submission to civic inferiority." He endorsed industrial

William Monroe Trotter (courtesy of New York Public Library)

training even though industrial schools could not survive without the teachers provided by liberal arts black colleges. In reality, Du Bois asserted, black people could not possess economic power without having political rights. Education should serve the masses, but it should also sustain a black elite, a "Talented Tenth." How could African Americans progress economically if they were disempowered, "made a servile caste, and allowed only the most meagre chance for developing their exceptional men?"[19]

Boston editor William Monroe Trotter sided with Du Bois when he and Washington clashed. In 1895, the same year Washington announced the Atlanta Compromise, Trotter graduated magna cum laude from Harvard, joining a small but vocal group of black militants in Boston who were opposed to Washingtonian policies. With Amherst graduate George W. Forbes, he founded the *Boston Guardian* in November 1901.[20]

Washington later described Trotter and the radicals as a black elite who were unrepresentative of the black masses. For the most part, the Boston radicals were graduates of New England colleges, he said, "coddled" and subsidized by their white sponsors. They had not "had to work their way up from the bottom," Washington wrote. They believed that they could assert leadership for the "whole colored race" by placing it "in the same artificial position that they themselves are in."[21] But the Boston radicals had grown frustrated with Washington's heavy-handed domination of the black press and monopoly over leadership. At the meeting of the Afro-American Council in Louisville, Kentucky, in July 1903, the Boston radicals protested against Washington's philosophy. Firmly in control of the meeting, the Washingtonians silenced the insurgents.[22]

Washington had previously avoided speaking in Boston because it was hostile territory—a citadel of black radicalism. Trotter charged cowardice, however, goading Washington into addressing the local branch of the National Negro Business League on July 30, 1903. Trotter's militants were well prepared for Washington. When he attempted to speak, they heckled him and shouted him down, and a general melee ensued.[23] In the aftermath, with Washington insisting that the Boston radicals be punished,[24] Trotter was prosecuted as the protesters' ringleader and given a thirty-day prison sentence. The Washingtonians also pursued a libel case against Trotter and Forbes. Thus concluded what became known as the Boston Riot.[25]

Washington suspected that Du Bois supported Trotter's protest tactics. In reality, Du Bois had no role in organizing the uprising, though he admired the radicals' bravado. The Boston Guardian, Du Bois recalled in his autobiography, was "bitter, satirical, and personal," but also "well edited" and "earnest." Although he disagreed with the radicals' intemperate tactics, he regularly read the newspaper.[26] The Boston Riot was a turning point for Du Bois in his assessment of other contemporary black leaders.[27] He suspected that Washington's supporters had provoked the conflict.[28] He also condemned the vindictiveness with which Trotter was prosecuted, defending him as a "clean-hearted utterly unselfish man whom I admired despite the dogged and unreasoning prejudices" that some harbored against him.[29]

In December 1903, Du Bois defended himself in a long letter to white philanthropist and Atlanta University trustee George Foster Peabody. Declaring his disapproval of the "unfortunate occurrence" in Boston, Du Bois could no longer defend Washington. His faith in the "Wizard" diminished, Du Bois agreed with Trotter's main contentions. He admired his courage, "his unselfishness, pureness of heart and indomitable energy, even when misguided." Du Bois conceded that there was a "vast difference between criticizing Mr. Washington's policy and attacking him personally." Trotter was simply "nearer the right" in his view, however, and in Trotter's

George A. Towns (courtesy of the Atlanta University Center)

controversy with Washington, Du Bois admired his "sincerity and unpurchaseable soul."[30]

Other African Americans in Atlanta agreed with Trotter's protest tactics. George A. Towns graduated from Atlanta in 1894 and attended Harvard, from which he received a B.A. and an M.A. He later returned to Atlanta University as a faculty member. Like others of Du Bois's circle, Towns was excited by Trotter's protest. Impatient with Washington's philosophy and tactics, Towns wrote a strong letter of support that was published in the *Boston Guardian* on October 17, 1903. Towns applauded Trotter for his struggle against a "subsidized Negro press and against the Mammon of unrighteousness." Washington alienated elite, educated blacks by forcing Trotter's imprisonment, Towns believed. The Boston Riot exposed Washington's tactics and his reliance on "his friends for revenue only." Although many black leaders were too timid to oppose Washington, most of them were prepared to "use the knife which is up their sleeves upon him." Towns disagreed with Trotter's methods of protest, but he believed that he was correct in principle.[31]

The disaffection with Washington placed Atlanta University in a difficult position. President Horace Bumstead, who took office after the end of state support in 1887, had skillfully cultivated northern white philanthropists. In a delicate balancing act, Bumstead exercised racial diplomacy but privately disparaged the notion of white supremacy. There were obvious internal contradictions in the logic of white supremacy, he wrote in 1903. His sarcasm was obvious: "The Negro is inherently and hopelessly inferior to the white race, and yet it will not do to educate him much lest white supremacy be endangered! The Negro could not be less of a factor in the political life of the South if disfranchised than he now is, and yet to insure white control it is necessary to still further disfranchise him by repealing the constitutional amendments! The extermination of the Negro is the only solution of the problem, and yet the South will never find it necessary to resort to this solution!"[32]

Du Bois's and Towns's criticisms of Washington attracted the ire of the "Tuskegee Machine." Towns's criticism in the *Boston Guardian* had been a "weak dirty letter," wrote one Washingtonian supporter, while the "Wizard" himself privately wrote that he possessed evidence that Du Bois was behind the attacks.[33] Northern white benefactors became disturbed. Peabody warned Du Bois that his "unfrank and vague words of depreciation of others" were injuring his work and reputation. Though privately supportive of Du Bois, Bumstead thought Du Bois's and Towns's publicly declared support for Trotter brought "serious trouble" to the university. It was one thing to support Trotter's principles, but another to endorse his methods.[34] Bumstead gently informed Du Bois about the dangers of alienating white supporters, such as Peabody, who were "willing to work with us and with whom we can work amicably without necessarily holding the same views, if we only can avoid giving him needless irritation." Bumstead spent effort over the next months defending Du Bois before the white trustees.[35]

Bumstead was less willing to protect the younger upstart. Towns maintained that his "very strong feelings" prompted him to speak out, and, he said, "the unwisdom of my act" lay in publishing his letter, not in his formulation of its thought. While admitting that his letter had been "impolitic," Towns refused to back down.[36] Bumstead then took discussion of the matter to the board of trustees, which condemned Towns's "ill-advised expression of sympathy for a man serving a sentence for a violation of the law" and for his "discourteous utterances" about Washington.[37]

IN 1903, WHEN ATLANTA'S NEW CARNEGIE LIBRARY OPENED, Du Bois and eight other people issued a protest. Having heard that black people would be excluded from the library, Du Bois explained, "we thought it well to ask why." Du Bois spoke for the group, which demanded "justice to the black people of Atlanta by giving them the same free library privileges that you propose giving the whites." To spend public money in a discriminatory way, Du Bois believed, was illegal; the spirit of the endowment founded by Andrew Carnegie for the establishment of libraries admitted "no artificial differences of rank or birth or race." Any argument that could be made of the need for libraries for whites applied to black people to an even greater degree. They needed "instruction, inspiration and proper diversion; they need to be lured from the temptations of the streets and saved from evil influences, and they need a growing acquaintance with what the best of the world's souls have thought and done and said." While Atlanta lacked enough schoolroom seats to house half its black children, the city possessed "ample provision for them in her jails." Du Bois's protest, perhaps predictably, had little effect. The trustees of the Carnegie library rejected Du Bois's claim but promised to seek the establishment of a separate, all-black library. However, it took white officials nineteen years to open a library for African Americans in Atlanta.[38]

Du Bois's protest in 1903 was yet more evidence of black disfranchisement, segregation, and the general deterioration of African American civil and political rights in the South. Du Bois and his allies, many of them from Atlanta, increasingly saw activism and protest as more effective tools than Washingtonian compromise and accommodation. In July 1905, Du Bois and other prominent black Atlantans founded an organization they named the Niagara Movement. Disgusted with Washington and his heavy-handed repression of black dissent, Du Bois was convinced that his accommodationist policies had failed.[39] The Niagara Movement, with Du Bois and Atlanta black editor J. Max Barber as its driving forces, called for full civil and political equality for blacks. The organization was deliberately small—about two hundred members in seventeen states—and was composed of elite, educated black males like Du Bois. He described the group proudly: "In all modesty," he wrote, "no organization in the United States, white or black, represents . . . a higher grade of character and efficiency." In a slap at the Washingtonians, the Niagara Movement would advocate the establishment of a "free unsubsidized Negro press."[40]

Du Bois, who became the Niagara Movement's general secretary, also promoted an emancipationist view of the past. In November 1905, he urged members to celebrate the 100th birthday of William Lloyd Garrison and to honor other heroes of the struggle for freedom, including Frederick Douglass and Albion W. Tourgée. The Niagara Movement's second meeting convened at Storer College, a state-supported black normal school in Harpers Ferry, West Virginia. The group celebrated John Brown's 100th birthday and commemorated the fiftieth anniversary of the attack by pro-slavery whites on the town of Osawatomie, Kansas.[41] The choice of Harpers Ferry as a venue for the meeting, said Barber, represented a gesture made by men for the sake of whose freedom Brown had died to "show reverence to the man and the place where he dared to die." The attendees left with strong feelings of respect for "those who died for freedom."[42]

In Georgia, Du Bois helped to organize the Georgia Equal Rights Convention meeting in Macon in February 1906, which attracted five hundred participants from around the state. Du Bois wrote the meeting's address, which pointed to the inferiority of black schools; to the "network of debt and petty crime" that was oppressing rural blacks; to white restrictions on black voting and to the need for federal enforcement of the Fourteenth and Fifteenth Amendments; and to the existence of lynching and other racial violence. With black political rights should come the right for blacks to serve on juries and to be in the state militia. The address condemned the segregation of railroads and streetcars, which reduced black people to uncomfortable and humiliating accommodations. The convention also condemned what it called the "open traffic in Negro crime" through which thousands of blacks were unjustly imprisoned in the convict-lease system, where they were sold "body and soul to private capitalists for the sake of gain." Du Bois criticized white assertions about the prevalence of black rapists, pointing out that it was white men who were "openly taught disrespect for black womanhood." The address conceded that shortcomings could be found in the behavior of some black people, but asserted that "we are not . . . as bad as the willfully distorted and criminally unfair press reports picture us."[43]

The Niagara Movement never sought a mass following; its main goal was to rally the "Talented Tenth." Despite these efforts, in 1906 the Georgia legislature joined the rest of the South in voting to disfranchise most black voters. No federal intervention to protect voting would occur for another half century. The Niagara Movement widened Du Bois's breach with Washington; Du Bois temporarily effected an alliance with the mercurial Trotter and charted a different path of black leadership. The Niagara men remained bitterly opposed to Washingtonian compromise and to the northern white allies of the "Wizard" who wanted black people to "shut their eyes to our humiliations." Members of the Niagara Movement charged that the "paid" black press attacked any kind of open black opposition to white supremacy and attempted, as Barber expressed it, to "put a quietus on our ambitions for equality."[44]

THE OUTBREAK OF RACIAL WARFARE IN ATLANTA IN SEPTEMBER 1906, resulting in the indiscriminate massacre of innocent black people by whites, shook the confidence of Atlanta's black leadership. The white business community, in the aftermath of the riot, was mostly interested in restoring business as usual. The *Atlanta Constitution* realized that northern white investment depended on confidence in Atlanta's racial stability. There was no greater racial chaos in Atlanta than elsewhere in the country, the *Constitution* claimed. The northern press was paying undue attention to the South's race problem, it said. There was only one solution: the white South had to raise its "standards of respect for the law and obedience to its precepts above those of other states." The New South was in the midst of a "commercial and industrial progress that has startled the world." The *Constitution* assured northerners that "nothing will be done or tolerated that will destroy the peace, the happiness and the plenty that prosperity has brought."[45]

At first, Atlanta's white leaders blamed the violence on the black community's supposed toleration of black sexual assaults on whites. The violence resulted from a series of rapes, said the *Atlanta Constitution*, which had taxed "Anglo-Saxon patience and endurance to a preternatural tension." While condemning the fury of the white mob, the newspaper declared that the city's "mettle," "courage," and "reverence for law and order" were "on trial—before themselves, first, and, at the last analysis, before the nation."[46] White reformer and Presbyterian minister Alexander J. McKelway wrote in the national periodical *Outlook* that the violence had cleared the air. Atlanta whites, he wrote, could breathe more easily than they had for weeks. The "thunder-storm" of racial violence was therapeutic and would bring a new era of racial peace and stability. Atlanta blacks had been "taught a needed lesson" about the need for white supremacy and the necessity of cooperating to prevent black rape of whites.[47]

But Atlanta's uncontrolled racial violence also undermined its New South image of social stability and economic development. The vision of unqualified progress was in competition with other narratives of the past and was undermined by racial conflict. The unrestrained violence had exposed the contradiction between the New South narrative of thriving economic development and the violence of white supremacy. Although Atlanta should be regarded as a progressive city, said a contemporary commentator, "it had forgotten its public duties."[48] A few observers noted ironically that the epicenter of the riot, in the middle of downtown Atlanta, had been at the feet of the statue of Henry W. Grady that had been erected in 1891 in his honor.

The breakdown in law and order reflected a looming racial crisis and a new degree of racial radicalism that undermined the intersectional comity promoted by Henry Grady. In this tense atmosphere, white Baptist minister, playwright, and novelist Thomas Dixon offered a view of the South's past and future that broke with the prevailing white racial norms by advocating a radically aggressive posture of violence toward southern blacks. In the months before and after the eruption of violence in Atlanta, Dixon promoted a highly successful touring stage production of his novel, *The Clansman*. The play attracted throngs of people across the country.[49] According to a black leader, *The Clansman* was an "exquisite piece of deviltry" that provided a "psychological impulse" for white mob violence.[50] Despite black protests, which shut down the play in some northern cities, Dixon presented the play as a justification of white supremacy to a national audience. *The Clansman* constructed a new narrative of the past, suggesting that the abolition of slavery had caused inevitable racial conflict, which no measure of white moderation and paternalism could solve. *The Clansman* presaged a new, uglier mood.

Soon after the Atlanta Riot, the *New York Times* interviewed Dixon. The violence resulted from black "insolence," he claimed, and white attempts to enforce the law proved unable to solve the problem. Whites' desire to dominate was inherent, Dixon maintained, as a racial subconsciousness compelled their insistence on inequality. The only solution to conflict, Dixon believed, was the removal of the black population, which, as a race, was "4,000 years behind the Aryan race in development." Removal would mean mass relocation of blacks to colonies in the West Indies, South America, and Africa. Ships filled with black deportees from the United States, Dixon suggested, could return with "Aryan immigrants."[51]

Dixon's radical racism seemed to observers to be consistent with the events in Atlanta. *Outlook* described the violence in Atlanta as equivalent to a Russian-style pogrom that amounted to "government by murder." The violence differed from Russian massacres only in that the government did not directly organize it, but the events ought to make the entire nation ashamed.[52] The *Chicago Tribune* called the violence "mob murder" that had "no other result than the slaughter of innocent negroes." The racial massacre reflected badly on Atlanta's ability to govern itself. The events should make the South ashamed that it harbored a race prejudice "so bitter and undiscriminating that guiltless persons may be killed and maimed just because they belong to the negro race."[53] Atlanta was not a typical southern city, said the *New York Times*, because "elements of trouble exist there that do not exist in most other cities." The newspapers believed that the city's large proletariat was responsi-ble for the violence because of their lawlessness and lack of social restraint.[54]

The most pronounced critique of events came from African Americans, who were outspoken and embittered. Having visited Atlanta the previous summer and predicted trouble, *New York Age* editor T. Thomas Fortune blamed the prominence of black disfranchisement as an issue in Georgia's gubernatorial election of 1906. Fortune also saw deeper, more structural reasons for the violence. Atlanta's booming economy had drawn in a white working class, a demographic change that had fanned competition between white and black workers. The police only minimally protected black people and had let racial tensions career out of control. Although Atlanta had be-come the "centre of the intelligent negroes of the South," the white press focused on the alleged problem of black bestiality. Fortune emphasized that Atlanta blacks had acted in self-defense. White mobs had ruthlessly killed innocent people; he only hoped that blacks had "slain as many whites in re-turn." Racial violence would continue until black people resisted white mob violence.[55]

Black leadership in Atlanta remained divided, however, as black moder-ates sought to reestablish racial harmony by assuaging white opinion. The *Atlanta Independent*, a Republican newspaper, urged the black community to self-police criminals while instituting their own measures against black rapists. Although this conceded the white supremacist claims of black sexual criminality, the *Independent* also asserted that whites should insist on law and order by restraining white mob violence. "We hope those who are eager to misjudge our racial motives and charge the infamy of the rapist to the entire race," it editorialized, "will not mistake our position" by assuming that this meant an acceptance of white mob violence. While condemning the "beast who brutally assault[ed] innocent women," the *Independent* also as-serted that nothing justified lynch law. Any society tolerating it rested "their superstructure upon an eruptive volcano."[56]

J. Max Barber, editor of Atlanta's *Voice of the Negro*, was even more forth-right. On September 26, he wrote to the *New York World*, saying that the violent mob had been "as lawless and as godless as any savages that ever shocked civilization." Gubernatorial candidate Hoke Smith, who had won the Democratic nomination, subjected black people to steady abuse and dis-tortion. The real cause of violence, rather than the commission of rape by blacks, was a "frightful carnival of newspaper lies" that were designed to benefit Smith's campaign. Barber claimed that some of Smith's agents had blackened their faces and knocked down white women in order to inflame the situation. When bloodhounds were put on the scent, he added, the scent led to a white man's house, though the posse targeted an innocent black man instead. One white woman who claimed assault, Barber wrote, later admitted fabricating the story. The days leading up to the racial massacre were fraught with tension; any black male encounter with a white woman became suspect. The remedy, said Barber, was impartial enforcement of the law.[57]

Barber suffered badly for his candor. Although he had written to the *New York World* anonymously, an Atlanta telegraph operator identified him as the author. The day after the letter was published, he was visited by Gov. Joseph M. Terrell's chief of staff, who informed him that he was being accused of having made a "vile slander on Atlanta." Facing a choice of either leaving the city or incurring a sentence on the chain gang, Barber fled, moving the editorial offices of the *Voice of the Negro* to Chicago. Like Du Bois, Barber was accused by the Washingtonians of cowardice for having fled the city so quickly. But Barber's authorship of the letter was known generally among the white leadership. He had crossed the line of behavior that was acceptable to whites, and, wrote Barber, "there could be no question of my fate had I remained in town."[58]

Another black resident, writing to the northern periodical *Independent* about a week after the violence, described the situation in Atlanta. The city, he wrote, had once again revealed that it was "not a civilized community." Its tabloid press competed among themselves to manufacture charges of rape committed by blacks—charges that remained unproven—in order to sell newspapers. The alleged assault on the day of the riot had been nothing more than a verbal altercation between a black man and a white woman. "It se[e]med only necessary for a white to see a negro meeting her in the same street or looking at her on her front porch," he wrote, "to make her cry out, 'Assault.'" On this slender evidence Atlanta's white press had advocated mob retaliation against "peaceable negroes."

This observer claimed that the violence was planned, premeditated attacks having been made against black shopkeepers. Black barbershops were demolished, the barbers dragged out and beaten while they were shaving white customers. According to some accounts, the attacks were perpetrated by competing white barbers. The mob violence had served as a "cover to destroy their competitors." The growth of Atlanta's black middle class, according to this account, had become an "eyesore" to some whites who could "in no peaceable way prevent progress." Lawless whites, running amuck without any restraint as police watched, were uninclined "to hate the negro less when he beats them in competition, as in the case of the barbers."

The violence, the writer continued, exposed the hypocrisy of white Atlanta's New South ethos. The massacre represented a breakdown in the ability of the police to maintain order; it also demonstrated the failings of the "conservative, good white people." On the Sunday of the riot, white pulpits had been vacant and white ministers had stayed silent. The ostentatious display of Christian piety in white homes was meaningless. "If the white people of the South are going to expect negroes to co-operate in catching negroes accused of crime . . . when experience proves that such persons have no hope in the world of a fair trial," he concluded, "then the white people are doomed to disappointment."[59]

With the Atlanta violence assuming national significance, white journalists of the city attracted an audience. John Temple Graves, editor of the *Atlanta Georgian*, was one of the tabloid journalists most responsible for inflaming opinion about black rapists. A newspaperman since the 1880s, Graves was known for his public speaking, a reputation gained from his memorial address on Henry Grady in December 1889, an address in which he had described Grady's "diamond pen" that "flashed like an inspiration on every phase of life in Georgia." Grady, Graves had said, "caught the heart of the country in the fervid glow of his own," and the "forces of statesmanship have not prevailed for union like the ringing speeches of the bright, magnetic man."[60]

Graves's 1889 memorialization of Grady was so successful that he went into public speaking full time, spending much of his time on the road on the after-dinner circuit. His message reiterated Grady's New South vision. Atlanta, he told the Southern Commercial Congress in 1911, had witnessed a resurrection from its wartime destruction that stood as the "miracle of all civic recuperation." The city's success embodied an ethos of "Progress" and "Enterprise" that made the city a "model and example for every ambitious town in all the South." What Graves called the "Atlanta Spirit" embodied the city's development and resurrection, and it reflected, he claimed, Grady's compelling vision.[61]

But Graves's message was not always so full of positive boosterism: like Grady, he came to see white supremacy as linked to southern progress. In 1902, he returned to Atlanta and became editor of the *Atlanta News* and then founded the *Atlanta Georgian* in 1906. His style was inflammatory, especially on issues of race. Barber later called him "one of the worst enemies the Negro has."[62] In 1903, addressing an audience at Chautauqua, New York, Graves defended lynching as the "sternest, the strongest, and the most effective restraint that the age holds for the control of rape."[63] In the summer of 1906, he wrote in the editorial pages of the *Atlanta Georgian* that he favored a program of segregation, black colonization, and disfranchisement. Adopting Dixon's radical racism, he asserted that white domination was "a racial instinct of the Anglo-Saxon." God had never intended "two opposite and antagonistic" races to coexist equally, he said, for Anglo-Saxons had always been a "dominant and conquering race" that was intolerant of "an equal in its own territory of existence." Black people, claimed Graves, had little hope of political equality. The only solution was white supremacy and, he believed, black removal and colonization. Without this radical settlement, the alternatives were racial separation, black annihilation, or amalgamation of the races.[64]

During the months before the outbreak of violence, Graves urged white Atlantans to defend white womanhood. A month before the riot, he lashed out at black males' "torrid wave of lust and fiendishness." In particular, Graves stirred fears of black rape of white women, something which would "always stir to frenzy the Caucasian blood." Portraying New South economic development as in conflict with African American assertiveness, he claimed that there was a threat to white womanhood in Atlanta, the "heart of progress and development." Black leadership had failed to deter sexual violence, the "black shadow of the fiendish passion of these ebony devils"; Atlantan African Americans were "shamefully and criminally silent" in condemning the black rape of white women. Having lost patience, whites should now refuse to endure a "siege in which our women are the prisoners" and in which the white man was the "anxious sentinel at the outpost of his fireside and the shrine of his home."[65] In another editorial, while not endorsing mob violence, Graves ominously pronounced that "desperate diseases require desperate remedies."[66]

In the aftermath of the riot, Graves refused to back down from his aggressively white supremacist views. Arguing that mob violence and the black raping of white women were morally equivalent, he urged northern white critics "to help us by giving two words in condemnation of rape where they gave one to the condemnation of lynching." Northern newspaper editorialists should temper their "limitless and boundless sympathy with the negro" by acknowledging blacks' criminal behavior.[67] Graves pursued his case before a national audience. Provided space in the *Washington Post* two days after the riot began, Graves composed a piece that was subsequently distributed across the country through Associated Press syndication. He blamed the violence on a "tidal wave of crime" that was occurring with "unspeakable audacity" in Atlanta, the New South's capital. The white mob violence had resulted from genuine provocation, he claimed. Complete separation of blacks and whites was inevitable; the two races could "never live together in the same government under equal laws."[68]

In the months after the Atlanta violence, Graves continued to develop his argument. In November 1906, he participated in an exchange with Du Bois that was published in the national journal, the *World To-Day*. Graves disingenuously claimed that he had been mischaracterized as a "radical extremist" on the race issue. He ought rather to be portrayed as a social scientist, "absolutely devoid of passion, temper or prejudice." Like many southern whites, he wrote, he claimed many black people as friends, and he even declared that he had sheltered African Americans from the mob during the September violence. Then Graves delivered a familiar message: the racial massacre, he claimed, was the fault of black people. Blacks and whites, as he had frequently asserted, were inherently and naturally at odds. Mob violence, he announced, was indefensible, but the white mob had been provoked, acting on the same instincts that compelled animals to protect their young. Like McKelway, Graves claimed that the riot had put an end to black sexual violence in a new era of peace. The "shadow of terror" had been lifted from the "hearts and minds of our women."[69]

Du Bois was shaken by the racial violence. Seven years earlier, in 1899, he had reacted with horror when he learned of the torture, dismemberment, and lynching of Sam Hose in nearby Coweta County. Atlanta's indiscriminate racial violence was, he later said, the "greatest disillusionment which ever faced the Atlanta Negroes."[70] Rushing back to Atlanta during the first day of the riot, he wrote a mournful "Litany," which he published on October 11 in the *Atlanta Independent*. White Atlantans complained about black crime, but the "word was mockery, for thus they train a hundred crimes while we do cure one." Black men were told to "work and rise" but were randomly maimed and murdered. Like the Old Testament's Job, Du Bois cried out for divine justice. Did white justice "stink in Thy nostrils, O God?" "Sit no longer blind, Lord God, deaf to our prayers and dumb to our dumb suffering. Surely Thou too art not white, O Lord, a pale, bloodless, heartless thing?"[71]

Du Bois avoided responding directly to Graves's invective in the *World To-Day*, instead considering the underlying causes of the racial crisis in Atlanta. As background context, he pointed to black disfranchisement, which left African Americans powerless to defend their lives and property peacefully. Without a true republican government, only radical actions could prevent future violence. The alleged cause of the violence was the rape of white women by black males, but Graves's own newspaper acknowledged that none of the four alleged assaults on September 22 had involved a true case of rape. The four cases instead amounted to "two cases of fright and two cases of intentional or accidental violence." A similar wildness of exaggeration, Du Bois suggested, might have been responsible for the so-called epidemic of alleged rapes that had been reported in the newspapers in the six weeks prior to the riot.[72]

Du Bois offered another explanation for the supposed epidemic of African American criminality. Arguing that black rape of white women was fictitious, he maintained that whites projected their own fears and anxieties onto black males. In general, he wrote, the assumption of black bestiality was a distortion of the true fears harbored by whites. A "general fear" of blacks prevailed among whites in the rural and urban South. This was the "fear the oppressor has of the oppressed; the fear of the man who is always looking for insurrection from beneath because he knows that the lower class has been wronged." This was the same fear that dominated white thinking under the slave regime.[73]

The real source of Atlanta's explosion of violence, Du Bois asserted, was the two-year campaign of "vituperation and traduction" against black people that was conducted by candidates for the Georgia governorship, combined with the ineffectiveness of Atlanta's police and the oppressiveness of its criminal justice system. Hoke Smith, eventually elected governor, had deliberately aroused the "deepest hatred of the Negro, fear of his aspirations, and determination to keep him down." Du Bois pointed also to a deeper, structural problem. Most African Americans regarded the police as their oppressors; white police spent much of their time arresting and harassing blacks. The Atlanta police also had done nothing to stem the chaotic violence of September 1906. Only two policemen were injured in the melee; the police had stood by, permitting the white mob to have its way.

Du Bois was obviously shocked by the extent of the violence in Atlanta; the event dimmed his hopes for racial progress. But he also noted that during the racial massacre Atlanta blacks fought back, and that their armed resistance seemed to have protected them. Although the unwritten law was that African Americans should not resist white violence, in Atlanta they had resisted. During the second day of the riot, a white mob had entered Dark Town, but were met by gunfire as black residents shot out the electric lights. The gunfire turned back the mob. The white police, suddenly moved to action, had entered the black neighborhoods but were also met by gunfire, with the resulting death of a white police officer and the wounding of three others. The state militia restored order only after three days of violence, but it had expended most of its energy in rounding up the black resisters.

From Du Bois's perspective, white leaders bore a primary responsibility for the riot because they were engaged in a "criminal procedure" by inflaming racial hatred. Although black crime existed, the way to stop it was by having a "decent, honest police force." There could be no racial peace if the black population remained oppressed and ignorant. Moreover, Du Bois again saw the black franchise as essential. Only with the vote could an African American "peacefully defend his life and property, help the best class of whites defend theirs and put down the criminals of both races." Atlanta, and the South, needed a massive program of federal intervention that would penalize states that disfranchised blacks and provide aid to black southern public education.[74]

Eventually, Du Bois left Atlanta. The reasons for his self-exile were rooted in the racial cataclysm of September 1906. Barber, his fellow traveler in the Niagara Movement, was an even more embittered refugee. There would be no peace in Atlanta in the aftermath of the violence, Barber predicted from his Chicago exile. Black people might in the future be outwardly "humbler and more polite," but their true feelings were hidden. Profound dissatisfaction would remain as long as current conditions prevailed. Barber went further, ridiculing Atlanta's New South ethos. Atlanta represented the modern South, he wrote, but "coming events always cast their shadows before them." The shadows, in this case, were foreboding. Let Atlanta remember the "fate of the Harlot, Babylon, and desist from this species of political drunkenness and stupidity."[75]

ATLANTA'S RACIAL VIOLENCE IN 1906 closed a chapter in its evolution. The breakdown in law and order tarnished the city's image, undermining its carefully crafted narrative of orderly growth and economic development. Grady's vision of a New South based on intersectional harmony and the advance of civilization was tattered and frayed, and was generally rarely used thereafter. The violence had highlighted an ugly racial hatred and the degree to which the principle of white supremacy dictated affairs in the city, even with the existence of a strong, prosperous, and reasonably autonomous black community. Despite their significance, the troubling events of September 1906 do not represent the final chapter in the contestation over the South's future. Throughout the twentieth century, Atlanta's importance as a southern cultural center continued to grow. Yet what the lasting significance of black emancipation would be was unclear in the early years of the twentieth century.

The Propaganda of History

Writing in 1922, Atlanta historian John R. Hornady offered evidence of the power that memory of the Civil War still held. Like many others, he believed that the city exemplified the modernizing South, but felt also that the war had left a lasting imprint. A lifelong resident of Atlanta, Hornady grew up among material reminders of the war. As a child, he used to play in a swimming hole in Peachtree Creek, surrounded by Civil War–era earthworks. By the 1920s, trolley cars and automobiles had extended beyond the suburbs, intruding on this historically hallowed ground. A long boulevard now crossed the creek and Hornady's swimming hole. He saw this as a mark of progress, part of a "beautiful and truly marvelous transformation," but the physical alteration of the landscape was so profound that he felt completely lost. Nearby, throngs of people poured out of a passenger station; streetcars clanged; mowers cut velvet lawns. The setting where men had fought and died—and "made glorious history"—no longer existed. The stark nature of the change illustrated how Atlanta had seemingly mastered its past.[1]

Elsewhere, material reminders of the war blended with indications of the city's progress. In downtown Atlanta, at the busy intersection of Whitehall and Alabama Streets, Hornady noted an old lamppost that survived as a reminder of Atlanta's bombardment. At the base of the lamppost was a shell hole, marked with an inscription on a bronze tablet. Around the lamppost were buildings and an "endless stream of pedestrians, or automobiles and street cars," joined by the "roar and din of a great City that throbs with the noise of boundless energy." All evidence of Atlanta's destruction had been erased, "save the slender iron pole, with its gaping hole and its tiny tablet of bronze." The scars of war had "disappeared, vanished, gone like an evil dream," and the process by which this had occurred was "one of the wonders of Atlanta."[2]

Atlanta represented the larger South, a place where, on the one hand, Sherman's "war machine attained the maximum in destructive force," while, on the other, the city was to become the "most dynamic power in the reha-bilitation of the South." Atlanta represented for the South a "shining light, leading an exhausted and impoverished people into peaceful conquests out of which came wealth and happiness." There was something in Atlanta that was "impervious to shot and shell and flaming torch—a spiritual something that lived and loved and hoped and wrought when ashes filled the nostrils and scorched the feet and no green thing seemed to hold out hope of a bright and happier day."

In the postwar era, a prosperous vision of the New South was born in Atlanta.[3] Hornady described Atlanta's urban ethos, a quality that could be felt everywhere. "Let him attend a meeting of some civic organization in any Southern city," he wrote, "and the chances are about ten to one that before the meeting is over, some one will arise to suggest that 'If we had the Atlanta Spirit we could put this over in a jiffy.'" This mentality had spread through-out the South, and few could "inhale this atmosphere without feeling some of its contagion."[4] To Hornady, Henry Grady was the embodiment of the At-lanta Spirit and the ethos of the New South. He was close enough to the Old South "to feel all the sweetness and tenderness of its softer moments, and to know all the sternness and gallantry that characterized its conflicts." At the same time, he also understood the New South and "every impulse by which it was stirred." Grady's most significant success was his ability to reveal At-lanta and the South "as he revealed himself—devoid of bitterness because of the things that had gone before, and filled with a great and just pride because of the things that were and which were yet to be."[5]

By 1922, this narrative of war and reconstruction had become dominant. The city's image as the cradle of a New South had become firmly implanted in collective national memory. It was a narrative, as Hornady suggested, that exerted its appeal beyond the confines of Atlanta. In a larger sense, the nar-rative of Atlanta's journey from the Civil War had become a way to explore the meaning of the New South.

TWELVE YEARS AFTER HORNADY'S HISTORY APPEARED, Margaret Mitch-ell published her epic *Gone with the Wind*. Within six months of publication, it had sold a million copies, and, since then, more than thirty million copies, making it one of the most popular novels of all time. In 1939, the book was made into a film that had the largest gross box-office income of any film in history, a record that stood until 1966. Winning the Pulitzer Prize for fiction, the book provided an accessible popular history of the Civil War in Atlanta in the form of a romance novel. Mitchell spent a decade writing the novel.

She avidly researched the topic, piecing together a narrative that included long portions of the story set in the presecession era, as well as an account of the Civil War and Reconstruction. Mitchell's narrative conveyed white Atlanta's understanding of the Civil War's significance. Slavery was portrayed in a favorable light; the domestic slaves were depicted as simpletons who remained loyal to their masters. Mitchell's portrayal of Reconstruction followed the interpretation of Columbia historian William Dunning and his followers. In particular, the enfranchisement of black Georgians, according to Mitchell, led to their manipulation by the greedy northerners who had invaded and occupied the state.

Born in Atlanta in 1900 and raised there, Mitchell internalized the white construction of the significance of the Civil War and its aftermath, a narrative that persisted long into the twentieth century. As a child, she had played in the surviving military fortifications, and she watched numerous Confederate memorials go up in the city. Her brother recalled watching parades of old rebel veterans. "Nobody said a word," he wrote, "but tears just flowed down everybody's cheeks." It was "your nation that you were crying over, and you knew it." Atlanta, he observed, was a "Confederate town," and "that was its history."[6] Margaret Mitchell used to joke that it was not until she was ten years old that she realized that the South had lost the war. She remembered that she "heard so much when I was little about the fighting and the hard times after the war that I firmly believed that Mother and Father had been through it all instead of being born long afterward." Surrounded by these memories, Mitchell learned from an oral tradition in the preservation of which her family "didn't talk of these happenings as history nor as remarkable events but just as a part of their lives . . . And they gradually became part of my life."[7]

One of Mitchell's earliest memories was the racial massacre of 1906. Living on the northern end of the Fourth Ward, she and her family were up the hill from Dark Town, the black neighborhood whose residents, during the violence, had had to defend themselves against the white mob. Rather than recalling the fury of white violence toward innocent people, Mitchell remembered her family's fears that an army of African Americans was about to invade. Though no black attackers ever appeared, her father, Eugene Mitchell, prepared to protect his house and family, armed only with an iron waterkey and an ax. Margaret heard the sounds of guns in the conflict between the African Americans and the white mob. "No sight has ever been so sweet to these eyes," she wrote, "as when I crawled from under the bed where I had prudently taken refuge to see the militia tramp up Jackson Street and camp on our lawn and the street."[8]

Readers of *Gone with the Wind* learned and relearned the lesson of how the city fell victim to the ravages of Sherman's invasion and how, in his departure in November 1864, his army destroyed the city. The book's heroine, Scarlett O'Hara, fled the city before the advancing Yankee troops, escaping to the family plantation, Tara. On her departure from Atlanta, Scarlett witnessed the burning of warehouses, supply depots, and ammunition. Declaring that she thought "our boys" burned Atlanta, Scarlett was informed by another rebel, "We'd never burn one of our own towns with our own folks in it!" The real damage was done by the Yankees. Much stood intact when Sherman first occupied the city, and he cruelly expelled the remaining residents. There were old and sick who "ought not to have been moved," but who were forced out. After Sherman had rested his men for two months in the depopulated city, "he set fire to the whole town when he left and burned everything." It was unthinkable that this "bustling town they knew, so full of people, so crowded with soldiers, was gone," with its "lovely homes beneath shade trees, all the big stores, and the fine hotels—surely they couldn't be gone!" But the defeated city had entirely been destroyed, as Mitchell told the story. There were "acres and acres of chimneys standing blackly above ashes, piles of half-burned rubbish and tumbled heaps of brick clogging the streets, old trees dying from fire, their charred limbs tumbling to the ground in the cold wind." The city's cemeteries were robbed and looted, with skeletons and corpses "flung helter-skelter among their splintered caskets . . . exposed and so pitiful." Cats and dogs left homeless were "frightened, cold, ravenous, wild as forest creatures, the strong attacking the weak, the weak waiting for the weaker to die so they could eat them."[9]

The story of *Gone with the Wind* then described Atlanta's rebirth. It would "take more than Yankees and a burning" to keep city residents down, said Scarlett's beau, Frank Kennedy. The city's residents were "stubborn as mules about Atlanta." When Scarlett returned to Atlanta after the war, she was cheered by the sight of a flurry of new building construction. "They burned you," she told the city, but "they couldn't lick you. You'll grow back just as big and sassy as you used to be!" Though shocked by the sight of the ruined city blocks, she also noticed an atmosphere of "rush and bustle about the resurrecting town." The sidewalks were jammed, the streets filled with horses, people, and wagons. The story of *Gone with the Wind* perfectly embodies the New South narrative of Atlanta's destruction and rebirth.[10]

WHILE *GONE WITH THE WIND* was capturing the national popular imagination, W. E. B. Du Bois returned to Atlanta. In 1910, he had left Atlanta

Staging the burning of Atlanta in *Gone with the Wind*
(courtesy of the Atlanta History Center)

University for New York City, where he then edited *The Crisis*, the monthly publication of the National Association for the Advancement of Colored People (NAACP), an organization that Du Bois and others had founded in 1909. He remained in New York for twenty-three years, but resigned from his editorship and moved back to Atlanta in 1933. He was persuaded to return by his good friend, John Hope, whom Du Bois had known since he was a young faculty member at Atlanta University. Having been a member of the Niagara Movement and later joining the NAACP, John Hope became president of Atlanta Baptist (later Morehouse) College. In 1929, he led the merger of five all-black colleges in Atlanta into a single Atlanta University Center. Hope tried to persuade Du Bois to return to Atlanta, and Du Bois was receptive to the proposal because of his conflicts with NAACP president Walter White. In its reorganized form, Atlanta University became a center of black graduate education, and Du Bois was recruited to lead the sociology department. He remained in Atlanta for the next eleven years, and continued as the most articulate interpreter of a view of the South's past that differed from the white narrative of the New South.[11]

Du Bois, in a way, relived his earlier experience at Atlanta University by striving to make Atlanta University Center into an institution where the sociology, economics, and history of race could be examined. As he wrote in his autobiography, he had three further goals in his life: to write an expanded study of the history of the African American experience; to establish a scholarly journal on "world race problems"; and to restore Atlanta as a center of "the systematic study of the Negro problem."[12] He tried to inaugurate an ambitious *Encyclopedia Africana*, but could not find financial support; only one preliminary volume appeared in 1945. After John Hope's death in 1936, Du Bois persuaded university authorities to support a new journal, *Phylon*, whose name was taken from the ancient Greek word for "tribe," in the sense of a cultural, racial, or ethnic group. In its first issue, in 1940, Du Bois published a Greek-inspired apologia—a statement in defense of his beliefs and behavior. *Phylon* was to be a journal of "race and culture, and of racial and cultural relations" in which race was viewed as "cultural and historical . . . rather than primarily biological and psychological." This represented a revival of ideas put forth in Du Bois's Atlanta University conferences, in which he had developed a social scientific understanding of race. In the early twentieth century, Atlanta University had stood alone in its interest in this dimension of social science. By the 1930s, the field had grown significantly, as universities around the country began to include the study of race as an academic subject. There was now, Du Bois maintained, a "new orientation and duty which will call not simply for the internal study of race groups as such, but for a general view of that progress of human beings which takes place through the instrumentality and activity of group culture." Du Bois predicted a "new view of social sciences" resulting from considerations of race, a view that would reinterpret history, education, and sociology.[13]

Of perhaps even more lasting impact was Du Bois's insistence on a narrative of the past that differed from the dominant southern white narrative. His later years at the NAACP had been consumed with office politics and infighting; now the time was available for him to write. He produce a series of important works that included *Black Reconstruction* (1935), *Black Folk, Then and Now* (1939), and the autobiographical *Dusk of Dawn* (1940). His magnum opus, *Black Reconstruction*, was deeply ideological and dominated by an often materialistic view of historical change. The position Du Bois articulated concerning the significance of the Civil War and Reconstruction had not changed. He had formulated this approach as early as 1910, when he published an article in the *American Historical Review* stating that a "grave injustice" had been committed to "the negro American in the history of Reconstruction." For twenty-five years after the publication of this article, as Du Bois's biographer David Levering Lewis has suggested, its impact on fellow historians "was as if it had never been written."[14] Though not completely ignored by Du Bois's contemporaries, its challenge to the prevailing view of the significance of the Civil War and its aftermath was only fully rediscovered by later historians. Du Bois originally intended to write another book about African Americans during World War I, but this work was never accomplished. *Black Reconstruction* became one of his most significant works of history. His purpose, as he wrote his publisher, was to tell a story that differed from the prevailing one: he wanted to show "the slave who is being emancipated" as "the real hero and center of human interest" during Reconstruction. Black people, Du Bois wrote—far from lacking capacity or serving merely as passive objects of corrupt northern exploitation—were key actors in the changes that were wrought by the Civil War and Reconstruction. He thus took aim at the scholarly and popular white understanding of the meaning of the national past.[15]

In *Black Reconstruction*'s final chapter, entitled "The Propaganda of History," Du Bois scrutinized commonly held assumptions about African American history. The dominant white understanding of the Civil War was that black people were ignorant, lazy, and dishonest; that their brief political empowerment during Reconstruction had brought corruption and misgovernment. The war had left "terrible wounds," which the attempt to heal had led to an effort to suppress the memory of slavery and to dismiss Reconstruction with "a phrase of regret or disgust." This "sweeping mechanistic interpretation" fundamentally misrepresented history. The past should not be remembered for the sake of "pleasure or amusement, for inflating our ego, and giving us a false but pleasurable sense of accomplishment." Historians

W. E. B. Du Bois at Atlanta University, late 1930s
(courtesy of the Atlanta University Center)

were obliged to "set some standards of ethics in research and interpretation." How could the truth be "omitted or half suppressed in a treatise that calls itself scientific?" No true understanding of slavery could see it as anything but a "cruel, dirty, costly, and inexcusable anachronism, which nearly ruined the world's greatest experiment in democracy." The "fairy tale" about the slaveholding regime—of the sort that would shortly appear in *Gone with the Wind*—continued to exert its power. But could anyone doubt that slavery had been the true cause of the Civil War? "What do we gain by evading this clear fact, talking in vague ways about 'Union' and 'State Rights' and differences in civilization as the cause of that catastrophe?" For four "long and fearful years," the white South fought to preserve slavery, and yet, he noted, a monument in North Carolina announced, "They died fighting for liberty!" Most northern whites had little concern for the slaves, yet the decisive moment of the war occurred when Abraham Lincoln emancipated the slaves and armed them. Rather than having been "inert recipients of freedom," blacks had engaged in self-liberation.

So, too, during Reconstruction, African Americans led a path toward freedom. Although the emancipated slave had been the "chief witness in Reconstruction," he had been "almost barred from court." The African American written record had either been destroyed or was consistently ignored by historians. Only some of the states had even preserved the debates of the constitutional conventions where black political leadership had first been defined. Biographies of black people were non-existent. Black people were assumed always to have been poor and ignorant; their actual accomplishments were ignored. The "unfair caricatures" which persisted portrayed African Americans as "shrewd," "notorious," and "cunning." Every effort had been made by historians of Reconstruction to treat black participation in it "with silence and contempt." The fact that so many white Americans accepted the prevalent southern understanding of the significance of the Civil War meant that "we have got to the place where we cannot use our experiences during and after the Civil War for the uplift and enlightenment of mankind." In the "magnificent drama" of human history, no story was more compelling than the transportation of ten million Africans into the New World—the story of how they "descended into Hell; and in the third century they arose from the dead, in the finest effort to achieve democracy for the working millions this world had ever seen." That truth had been obscured, Du Bois wrote, because of those who "would compromise with the truth in the past in order to make peace in the present and guide policy in the future."[16]

THE STRUGGLE OVER the meaning of the past and future in Atlanta became nationalized, as the South became a subject in popular media and culture. As the success of both *Gone with the Wind* and *Black Reconstruction* suggests, there was an avid audience for stories about the drama of Civil War, destruction, Reconstruction, and reconciliation.[17] The central symbol in this obsession with constructing the past was Atlanta. Even while the city was being invoked as a symbol of a sparkling New South by white civic boosters such as Henry Grady, the city's African American population was articulating a different narrative of the meaning of the Civil War. Establishing themselves in an urban enclave that provided some protection from the limitations imposed by white supremacy, African Americans found Atlanta a relatively hospitable environment. Black Atlanta was at the heart of African American culture. Culturally, economically, and politically, black Atlanta arose out of the distinctive conditions of the post–Civil War era. Atlanta University, together with many other black institutions and movements that came out of Atlanta, extended the educational and cultural legacy of northern abolitionism into the twentieth century to create a new kind of black cultural freedom. These institutions and movements played a major role in establishing a positive black cultural narrative that took root to counter the powerful images about the white South that had once dominated American culture.

Notes

ABBREVIATIONS

AARL   Archives Division, Auburn Avenue Research Library on African American Culture and History, Atlanta, Ga.

AHC   Kenan Research Center, Atlanta History Center, Atlanta, Ga.

AMA   American Missionary Association Archives, Amistad Research Center, Tulane University, New Orleans, La.

AUL   Archives Research Center, Robert W. Woodruff Library, Atlanta University Center, Atlanta, Ga.

DUL   David M. Rubenstein Rare Book and Manuscript Library, William R. Perkins Library, Duke University, Durham, N.C.

EUL   Manuscript, Archives, and Rare Book Library, Emory University Library, Atlanta, Ga.

FB/AC   Records of the Assistant Commissioner for the State of Georgia, Bureau of Refugees, Freedmen, and Abandoned Lands, 1865–1869, Record Group 105, National Archives, Washington, D.C. (Microfilm M798).

FB/FO   Records of the Field Offices for the State of Georgia, Bureau of Refugees, Freedmen, and Abandoned Lands, 1865–1872, Record Group 105, National Archives, Washington, D.C. (Microfilm M1903).

FB/SE   Records of the Superintendent of Education, State of Georgia, Bureau of Refugees, Freedmen, and Abandoned Lands, 1865–1869, Record Group 105, National Archives, Washington, D.C. (Microfilm M799).

LC   Manuscripts Division, Library of Congress, Washington, D.C.

OR   U.S. War Department. *The War of the Rebellion: A Compilation of the Official Records of the Union and Confederate Armies*. 128 vols. Washington, D.C.: Government Printing Office, 1880–1901.

RGD   Georgia (Fulton County), vol. 13, R. G. Dun & Co. Collection, Historical Collections, Baker Library, Harvard Business School, Boston, Mass.

SCC/A   Southern Claims Commission, Allowed Claims, Record Group 217, National Archives, Washington, D.C. (Microfilm M1658, Fulton County, Georgia).

SCC/D   Southern Claims Commission, Barred and Disallowed Claims, Record Group 233, National Archives, Washington, D.C. (Microfilm M1407).

SHC   Southern Historical Collection, University of North Carolina at Chapel Hill Library, Chapel Hill

UGA   Hargrett Rare Book and Manuscript Library, University of Georgia, Athens, Ga.

UMA   Special Collections and University Archives, University of Massachusetts, Amherst

INTRODUCTION

1. Reed, *History of Atlanta*, 18–20.
2. Woodward, *Origins of the New South*, ix.

3. Gaston, *The New South Creed*, 7, 9.

4. Foster, *Ghosts of the Confederacy*, 20–21; Charles Reagan Wilson, *Baptized in Blood*.

5. Blair, *Cities of the Dead*; Bruce E. Baker, *What Reconstruction Meant*; Clark, *Defining Moments*; Janney, *Burying the Dead but Not the Past*.

6. Blight, *Race and Reunion*, 2. For an incisive study that extends consideration of memory forward in time, see Brundage, *The Southern Past*.

7. Warren, *The Legacy of the Civil War*, 3–4, 53–54.

8. Correspondent for the *Cincinnati Gazette*, October 20, 1865, in *Columbus (Ga.) Daily Enquirer*, November 2, 1865.

9. Mixon, *The Atlanta Riot*; Ferguson, *Black Politics in New Deal Atlanta*; Kruse, *White Flight*.

10. Berlin et al., *Slaves No More*; Morgan, *Emancipation in Virginia's Tobacco Belt*; O'Donovan, *Becoming Free in the Cotton South*.

11. Claim of Austin Wright, May 31, 1872, SCC/A.

12. Kantrowitz, *Ben Tillman and the Reconstruction of White Supremacy*.

13. Garrett, *Atlanta and Environs*, 1:676–81.

CHAPTER 1

1. Garrett, *Atlanta and Environs*, 1:493.

2. "The Comet," *Atlanta Daily Intelligencer*, July 4, 1861.

3. *Atlanta Journal*, December 15, 1883, in Reed, *History of Atlanta*, 39–43. According to the *Atlanta Journal*, these locals included Jonathan Norcross, James Collins, Dr. George G. Smith, A. P. Forsyth, Joseph Thomason, Thomas Kile, William Kile, the Joys, David Dougherty, Washington Collier, Cousin John Thrasher, the McDaniels, Col. L. P. Grant, and Judge Hayden.

4. Newman, *Southern Hospitality*, 11–20; *DeBow's Review* 1–10 (1846–51): 381–82; Wooton, "New City of the South," chap. 1.

5. *Atlanta Journal*, December 15, 1883, in Martin, *Atlanta and Its Builders*, 1:39–43.

6. Carlton Rogers was the visitor. Wooton, "New City of the South," 14.

7. Bowlby, "The Role of Atlanta during the War between the States," 179–81.

8. Garrett, *Atlanta and Environs*, 1:304.

9. Jennison, *Cultivating Race*, 270.

10. Martin, *Atlanta and Its Builders*, 1:77; Garrett, *Atlanta and Environs*, 1:329–31. See Norcross entries, June 15, 1854, June 7, 1857, RGD.

11. Reed, *History of Atlanta*, 32–33.

12. "A Terror to Evil-Doers," *Atlanta Weekly Intelligencer*, February 8, 1855.

13. "The place," wrote early historian Thomas H. Martin, "was nothing if not bustling." "At a very early period in her history," he declared, "Atlanta laid the foundation of her great commercial supremacy and rapid upbuilding." Russell, *Atlanta, 1847–1890*, 72; Reed, *History of Atlanta*, 45–46; Martin, *Atlanta and Its Builders*, 1:100; Wooton, "New City of the South," 48. See also "Atlanta Police," *Atlanta Constitution*, August 12, 1888.

14. Wooton, "New City of the South," table V, p. 59.

15. Du Bois and Dill, eds., *The Negro American Artisan*, 34. Jennison makes the important point that antebellum Atlanta sought to exclude black people as part of a larger construction of hierarchy along racial lines. In general, the Georgia upcountry "proved hostile to free people of color," he writes. Jennison, *Cultivating Race*, 311.

16. Reed, *History of Atlanta*, 111–13; Garrett, *Atlanta and Environs*, 1:532–34.

17. "A Delusion," *Atlanta Daily Intelligencer*, July 4, 1861.

18. *Atlanta Daily Intelligencer*, November 14, 1861.

19. Robert Cott Davis Jr., ed., *Requiem for a Lost City*, 44–45.

20. Singer, "Confederate Atlanta," 58–65; Garrett, *Atlanta and Environs*, 1:508–9.

21. Henry S. Campbell to his father, April 19, 1861, Henry S. Campbell Papers, EUL.

22. "Not Burnt Up," *Atlanta Daily Intelligencer*, November 19, 1861.

23. Singer, "Confederate Atlanta," 108–11.

24. Quoted in *Natchez Daily Courier*, November 24, 1863.

25. Singer, "Confederate Atlanta," 240–41; Doyle, *New Men, New Cities, New South*, 35.

26. Taylor, "From the Ashes," 3; Singer, "Confederate Atlanta," 101–5, 112, 137–42; Garrett, *Atlanta and Environs*, 1:532–34 (quotation).

27. Reed, *History of Atlanta*, 106; Garrett, *Atlanta and Environs*, 1:509–10; Singer, "Confederate Atlanta," 108, 148–49 (quotation); Bowlby, "The Role of Atlanta during the War between the States," 179–81. There were also complaints about Confederate seizures of supplies in northern Georgia. "More Outrages—A Remedy Applied," *Southern Confederacy*, February 27, 1863.

28. Elizabeth Wiggins to her mother, September 7, 1861, Elizabeth Wiggins Papers, DUL.

29. Garrett, *Atlanta and Environs*, 1:513. See also *Southern Confederacy*, October 12, 1861, April 3, 5, 1862; "A Card to the Public," *Atlanta Daily Intelligencer*, October 24, 1861.

30. Lucy Hull Baldwin, autobiography, in Lucy Hull Baldwin Papers, SHC.

31. "Speculation," *Atlanta Daily Intelligencer*, November 5, 1861. See also ibid., November 27, 1861.

32. "Speculation," *Atlanta Daily Intelligencer*, November 5, 1861.

33. "Military Regulations in Atlanta," *Atlanta Daily Intelligencer*, May 15, 1862; "Atlanta as a Military Post," *Atlanta Daily Intelligencer*, January 15, 1863.

34. "Martial Law," *Atlanta Daily Intelligencer*, August 14, 1862.

35. Reed, *History of Atlanta*, 119–22; Garrett, *Atlanta and Environs*, 1:525–27; Singer, "Confederate Atlanta," 122–26; "The City Election," *Southern Confederacy*, January 17, 1862.

36. Garrett, *Atlanta and Environs*, 1:558.

37. "An Influx to Atlanta," *Atlanta Daily Intelligencer*, February 27, 1862.

38. S. P. Yancey to Benjamin Yancey, November 11, 1861, Benjamin C. Yancey Papers, DUL.

39. Annie Maney Schor to her sister, March 10, 1862, John Kimberly Papers, SHC.

40. Annie Maney Schor to Bettie Maney Kimberly, May 22, 1864, John Kimberly Papers, SHC.

41. Annie Maney Schor to her parents, May 1, 1862, John Kimberly Papers, SHC; Garrett, *Atlanta and Environs*, 1:572; Massey, *Refugee Life in the Confederacy*.

42. Singer, "Confederate Atlanta," 192–98.

43. Robert Cott Davis Jr., ed., *Requiem for a Lost City*, 86–87.

44. Doyle, *New Men, New Cities, New South*, 34.

45. Dyer, *Secret Yankees*, 5.

46. "Incendiaries Abroad," *Atlanta Daily Intelligencer*, December 14, 1862.

47. Dyer, *Secret Yankees*, chap. 7.

48. Taylor, "From the Ashes," 20; Claim of Christian Kantz, June 3, 1872, SCC/A.

49. Singer, "Confederate Atlanta," 216–17, 229–31; *Atlanta Daily Intelligencer*, February 5, 1863.

50. S. B. Yancey to Benjamin C. Yancey, November 8, 1861, Benjamin C. Yancey Papers, DUL.

51. "Thieving," *Southern Confederacy*, February 26, 1983.

52. Garrett, *Atlanta and Environs*, 1:569–70; *Atlanta Daily Intelligencer*, February 21, 1863.

53. *Atlanta Daily Intelligencer*, November 20, 21, 1863.

54. Singer, "Confederate Atlanta," 164–65; Garrett, *Atlanta and Environs*, 1:573; "The Wages of Labor," *Atlanta Daily Intelligencer*, June 26, 1862.

55. "Crinoline Imitations of the Habits of Certain Officials," *Southern Confederacy*, March 19, 1863; Singer, "Confederate Atlanta," 189–90; McCurry, *Confederate Reckoning*, 180–82. McCurry describes the riot as "highly organized, premeditated, and disciplined." McCurry, *Confederate Reckoning*, 181.

56. Singer, "Confederate Atlanta," 143–44. A "successful end to this war," Samuel Richards predicted, would mean even higher demand and prices for his slaves. In a note in his diary in May 1863 he wrote: "I must make out descriptive lists of my darkies and record in my journal for future reference." Garrett, *Atlanta and Environs*, 1:557.

57. Hunter, *To 'Joy My Freedom*, 21.

58. Russell, *Atlanta, 1847–1890*, 70; Wooton, "New City of the South," 60; Dorsey, *To Build Our Lives Together*, 23–26; Jennison, *Cultivating Race*, 311.

59. Claim of Henry and Polly Beedles, July 12, 1873, SCC/A.

60. Claim of Jefferson Simons, January 30, 1872, SCC/A.

61. Claim of Joseph Holland, January 6, 1872, SCC/A. Holland's brothers, Thomas and William Holland, also self-hired themselves from the same master. Claim of Thomas Holland, February 11, 1873; claim of William Holland, February 11, 1873, SCC/A.

62. Claim of Prince Ponder, January 15, 1873, SCC/A; U.S. manuscript census of population, 1870. Ponder was awarded $3,666.25 out of an original claim of $4,341.25—a substantial allowance by the Southern Claims Commission's stingy standards. It is possible that Ponder was owned by Ephraim Ponder, one of the largest slaveholders in Atlanta, most of whose slaves self-hired. Garrett, *Atlanta and Environs*, 1:511–12.

63. Russell, *Atlanta, 1847–1890*, 71–72.

64. Garrett, *Atlanta and Environs*, 1:511–12, 571; "Strange," *Atlanta Daily Intelligencer*, September 25, 1862.

65. "An Admirable Requisition," *Atlanta Daily Intelligencer*, October 30, 1861.

66. Garrett, *Atlanta and Environs*, 1:557.

67. S. P. Yancey to Benjamin Yancey, November 11, 1861, Benjamin C. Yancey Papers, DUL.

68. Cyrene Bailey Stone Diary, May 27, 1864, UGA.

69. Garrett, *Atlanta and Environs*, 1:553.

70. Mayor's Court Record, May 21, 23, 1861, February 14, 1862, AHC.

71. Mayor's Court Record, February 12, 1862, AHC.

72. Mayor's Court Record, August 25, 1863, AHC.

73. Strikingly, on the same day in March 1864 the mayor's court dismissed several cases of self-hiring while, at the same time, it fined a white man, P. L. Howard, for his slave's keeping an eating house "on his own accord." Mayor's Court Record, March 23, 1864, AHC.

74. "Negro Balls," *Atlanta Daily Intelligencer*, December 13, 1861.

75. Claim of Austin Wright, May 31, 1872, SCC/A; Russell, *Atlanta, 1847–1890*, 110; "A Concert by Negroes," *Southern Confederacy*, August 21, 1861; *Atlanta Daily Intelligencer*, July 3, 1867.

76. Russell, *Atlanta, 1847–1890*, 110.

77. Singer, "Confederate Atlanta," 190–91.

78. Mayor's Court Record, July 5, 1861, AHC.

79. Mayor's Court Record, February 8, 1864, AHC.

80. Mayor's Court Record, March 29–30, 1861, AHC.

81. Mayor's Court Record, May 15, 1861, AHC.

82. Mayor's Court Record, October 18, 1861, AHC; *Southern Confederacy*, October 20, 1861.

83. Mayor's Court Record, February 21, 1863, AHC. Henry, a slave owned by H. L. Lockhart, was charged with "riding a horse in a gallope [sic] and in a faster gait than a walk across the Bridge in Market Street near city market." *Southern Confederacy*, March 25, 1864.

84. Mayor's Court Record, February 23, 1864, AHC.

85. Conyngham, *Sherman's March through the South*, 216–23; T. M. Eddy, *The Patriotism of Illinois*, 1:193.

86. Wooton, "New City of the South," 91.

87. Liddell Hart, *Sherman: Soldier, Realist, American*, 233.

88. Grant to Sherman, April 4, 1864, in Sherman, *Memoirs*, 2:26.

89. "Is Atlanta Safe?," *Atlanta Daily Intelligencer*, April 22, 1862.

90. P. C. Key to E. H. Key, June 21, 1864, Key Family Civil War Papers, UGA.

91. Annie Maney Schor to her parents, April 27, 1862, John Kimberly Papers, SHC.

92. Venet, *Sam Richards' Civil War Diary*, 224, entry for June 10, 1864.

93. "The Fall of Atlanta," *New York Evangelist*, September 8, 1864.

94. On the military history of the Atlanta Campaign, see Castel, *Decision in the West*; McMurry, *Atlanta 1864*; Royster, *The Destructive War*, 296–327.

95. Reports of Brig. Gen. Thomas J. Wood, September 10, 1864, *OR*, ser. 1, vol. 38, pt. 1, pp. 372–89.

96. Sherman to Grant, telegram, May 4, 1864, *OR*, ser. 1, vol. 38, pt. 4, p. 25.

97. Jacob Cox, *Atlanta*, 59–69.

98. Jacob Cox, *Atlanta*; Report of Capt. Orlando M. Poe, July 1–October 31, 1864, *OR*, ser. 1, vol. 38, pt. 1, pp. 127–37.

99. "Cost of the War," *Southern Confederacy*, June 29, 1864.

100. Sherman to Grant, August 4, 1864, *OR*, ser. 1, vol. 38, pt. 5, p. 350.

101. James K. Polk Martin to his family, April 30, 1864, Charles A. James Martin Papers, UGA.

102. Hedley, *Marching through Georgia*, 113.

103. P. C. Key to T. E. Key, August 3, 1864, Key Family Civil War Papers, UGA.

104. "The Heavy Battle of the 28th of July," *New York Times*, August 10, 1864. Confederates resisted Sherman's advance, said an Ohioan, "contesting every inch of ground." John Herr to his mother, May 27, 1864, John Herr Papers, DUL.

105. "Gen. Sherman's Army," *New York Times*, August 11, 1864; "From Sherman's Army," *Chicago Tribune*, August 2, 1864.

106. Peter B. Kellenberger to Friend Pollard, August 29, 1864, Peter B. Kellenberger Papers, LC.

107. Willard Neal, "Hindenburg Line Modeled after Kennesaw," *Atlanta Journal*, September 19, 1926, Jennie Meta Barker Papers, box 2, folder 4, AHC.

108. Alonzo Miller to his family, July 9, 1864, Alonzo Miller Civil War Papers, AHC.

109. William Anthony Stokes to Margaret Rhind Stokes, August 25, 1864, Margaret Rhind Stokes Papers, UGA.

110. A. T. Holliday to Elizabeth Holliday, July 28, 1864, Holliday Family Civil War Correspondence, AHC.

111. A. T. Holliday to Elizabeth Holliday, August 3, 1864, Holliday Family Civil War Correspondence, AHC.

112. James H. Goodnow to his wife, August 21, 1864, James H. Goodnow Papers, LC.

113. William Wallace to Sarah Wallace, August 7, 1864, in Holzhueter, ed., "William Wallace's Civil War Letters," 105.

114. Cyrene Bailey Stone Diary, June 7, 1864, UGA.

115. Edward W. Allen to his parents, August 11, 1864, Edward W. Allen Papers, SHC.

116. A. T. Holliday to Elizabeth Holliday, May 26, 1864, Holliday Family Civil War Correspondence, AHC.

117. George Anderson Mercer Diary, August 24, 1864, SHC.

118. A. T. Holliday to Elizabeth Holliday, July 14, 1864, Holliday Family Civil War Correspondence, AHC.

119. P. C. Key to E. H. Key, August 5, 1864, Key Family Civil War Papers, UGA.

120. Report of Maj. Gen. David S. Stanley, September 1, 1864, *OR*, ser. 1, vol. 38, pt. 1, p. 226.

121. Fleharty, *Our Regiment*, 72. See also the frequent references to the soldiers' routine and to the risks of trench warfare in the James A. Congelton Diary, July–August 1864, LC.

122. Alonzo Miller to his parents, June 14, 1864, Alonzo Miller Civil War Papers, AHC. Another soldier wrote on same day of the "exceedingly wet weather we have been having here for the past two weeks." "Rain! Rain! Nearly every day & night." Robert Goodwin Mitchell to "cousin," June 14, 1864, Robert Goodwin Mitchell Papers, UGA.

123. Fleharty, *Our Regiment*, 69–70.

124. Robert T. Wood to his wife, July 15, 1864, Robert T. Wood Papers, UGA.

125. A. T. Holliday to Elizabeth Holliday, June 22, July 12, 1864, Holliday Family Civil War Correspondence, AHC.

126. Horace Park to J. S. McBeth, August 2, 1864, Horace Park Letter, UGA.

127. Benedict J. Semmes to his wife, August 7, 1864, Benedict Joseph Semmes Papers, SHC. On Hood in Atlanta, see Miller, *John Bell Hood*, chap. 5.

128. Stephens Mitchell, "Defenses of Atlanta," 32–35. See also "Atlanta: Its Occupation by Gen. Sherman," *Chicago Tribune*, September 14, 1864.

129. A. T. Holliday to Elizabeth Holliday, July 12, 1864, Holliday Family Civil War Correspondence, AHC.

130. Fleharty, *Our Regiment*, 96, 99–101.

131. Cyrene Bailey Stone Diary, June 1, July 5, 1864, UGA.

132. Sherman ordered the forces besieging Atlanta to construct earthworks "with special reference to the protection of the artillery." H. W. Perkins to W. T. Ward, August 3, 1864, *OR*, ser. 1, vol. 38, pt. 5, p. 346. See also Stephen Davis, "'A Very Barbarous Mode of Carrying On War,'" 57–90.

133. A. S. Bloomfield to his sister, July 24, 1864, A. S. Bloomfield Papers, LC.

134. Sherman to Thomas, July 20, 1864, *OR*, ser. 1, vol. 38, pt. 5, p. 197.

135. Bonds, *War Like a Thunderbolt*, 115.

136. Old Colonel [pseud.], "A Baptism of Fire," *Atlanta Constitution*, May 6, 1888.

137. Mollie Smith, reminiscences, in unidentified clipping, Jennie Meta Barker Papers, box 2, folder 4, AHC.

138. George H. Thomas, report, August 17, 1864, *OR*, ser. 1, vol. 38, pt. 1, p. 157.

139. William Wallace to Sarah Wallace, July 24, 1864, in Holzhueter, ed., "William Wallace's Civil War Letters," 104; *Louisville Journal*, August 10, 1864, in *Chicago Tribune*, August 17, 1864.

140. John Wesley Marshall Journal, August 14, 16, 1864, LC.

141. Sherman to Thomas, August 7, 1864; Sherman to O. O. Howard, August 10, 1864, *OR*, ser. 1, vol. 38, pt. 5, pp. 412, 452.

142. Sherman to Thomas, August 10, 1864; Thomas to Sherman, August 10, 1864, *OR*, ser. 1, vol. 38, pt. 5, p. 448; McMurry, *Atlanta 1864*, 164.

143. George Washington Baker to his mother, September 3, 1864, George Washington Baker Papers, SHC, http://docsouth.unc.edu/imls/bakergw/bakergw.html.

144. *Richmond Daily Dispatch*, August 16, 1864.

145. Conyngham, *Sherman's March*, 192.

146. Semmes to his wife, August 21, 1864, Benedict Joseph Semmes Papers, SHC. Another young Atlantan described the arrival of the shells, each flying "like a big ball of fire, making

its way towards us," careening overhead "with a shrieking and hissing that must be heard to appreciate its diabolical sound." Wortman, *The Bonfire*, 287–88.

147. Mollie Smith, reminiscences, in unidentified clipping, Jennie Meta Barker Papers, box 2, folder 4, AHC.

148. Thomas L. Clayton to his wife, August 3, 1864, Clayton Family Papers, SHC.

149. Benedict J. Semmes to his wife, August 7, 1864, Benedict Joseph Semmes Papers, SHC.

150. Sherman to Howard, August 8, 1864, *OR*, ser. 1, vol. 38, pt. 5, p. 428; Sherman to Thomas, August 8, 1864, in Martin, *Atlanta and Its Builders*, 494–95.

151. W. W. Hopkins to A. K. Taylor, August 9, 1864, *OR*, ser. 1, vol. 38, pt. 5, p. 437. Another soldier reported that the bombardment was "carried out with mathematical accuracy." One thirty-pound shell was sent into the city every five minutes during daylight and every fifteen minutes between sunset and sunrise. Thomas Osburn to A. C. Osburn, September 19, 1864, in Harwell and Racine, eds., *The Fiery Trail*, 17.

152. Semmes to his wife, August 12, 1864, Benedict Joseph Semmes Papers, SHC.

153. Semmes to his wife, August 21, 1864, ibid.

154. Reed, *History of Atlanta*, 191–93. See also Colin Dunlop to his mother, August 17, 1864, Colin Dunlop Papers, AHC.

155. Semmes to his wife, August 25, 1864, Benedict Joseph Semmes Papers, SHC; *Richmond Daily Dispatch*, August 17, 20, 1864.

156. Reed, *History of Atlanta*, 191–93.

157. *Richmond Daily Dispatch*, August 16, 1864.

158. Singer, "Confederate Atlanta," 253–61.

159. Ibid.; Davidson, *History of Battery A*, 124–25.

160. Old Colonel [pseud.], "A Baptism of Fire," *Atlanta Constitution*, May 6, 1888.

161. Reed, *History of Atlanta*, 182–97.

162. Venet, ed., *Sam Richards' Civil War Diary*, 228, entry for July 23, 1864.

163. Sherman to Thomas, August 10, 1864, *OR*, ser. 1, vol. 38, pt. 5, p. 448; Castel, *Decision in the West*, 464.

164. *New York Times*, August 7, 1864.

165. Stephen Davis, "How Many Civilians Died in Sherman's Bombardment?" This estimate matches that of Sam Richards.

166. Dean, *Shook over Hell*.

167. Bonds, *War Like a Thunderbolt*, 243–51.

168. William Anthony Stokes to Margaret Rhind Stokes, August 28, 1864, Margaret Rhind Stokes Papers, UGA.

169. "Atlanta: Its Occupation by Gen. Sherman," *Chicago Tribune*, September 14, 1864; William H. Sinclair to Nathan Kimball, September 3, 1864, *OR*, ser. 1, vol. 38, pt. 5, p. 779; Castel, *Decision in the West*, 522–24.

170. Ellison, ed., *On to Atlanta*, 83, entry for September 2, 1864.

171. "Atlanta: Its Occupation by Gen. Sherman," *Chicago Tribune*, September 14, 1864.

172. Ibid.; William Wallace to Sarah Wallace, September 5, 1864, in Holzhueter, ed., "William Wallace's Civil War Letters," 109; Castel, *Decision in the West*, 527–29. Also see Andrew J. Taft to his parents, September 16, 1864, Taft Family Papers, UGA, describing the Union entrance into the city.

173. Venet, ed., *Sam Richards' Civil War Diary*, 236, entry for September 9, 1864.

174. Castel, *Decision in the West*, 548.

175. Sherman to Halleck, September 3, 1864, *OR*, ser. 1, vol. 38, pt. 5, p. 777; Sherman to Grant, September 6, 1864, ibid., p. 808.

176. "Atlanta: Its Occupation by General Sherman," *Chicago Tribune*, September 14, 1864. A northern soldier noted in August 1864 that the campaign had lasted 112 days. "So far I am getting tired of this long campaign," he wrote. John Herr to his sister, August 31, 1864, John Herr Papers, DUL.

177. Conyngham, *Sherman's March*, 154–55.

178. James H. Goodnow to his wife, August 21, 1864, James H. Goodnow Papers, LC.

179. "The Fall of Atlanta," *New York Evangelist*, September 8, 1864; "Occupation of the City," *New York Times*, September 19, 1864; William T. Sherman to Henry Halleck, September 4, 1864, in Simpson and Berlin, eds., *Sherman's Civil War*, 699.

180. "Sherman at Atlanta," *North American and United States Gazette*, July 16, 1864.

181. Castel, *Decision in the West*, 565.

182. Gildersleeve, *The Creed of the Old South*, 60–61.

183. Doyle, *New Men, New Cities, New South*, 31.

CHAPTER 2

1. Neely, *The Limits of Destruction*; Megan Kate Nelson, *Ruin Nation*.

2. Doyle, *New Men, New Cities, New South*, 34, notes that Atlanta in the antebellum era had come to be known as a "northern enclave on foreign soil." See also DeCredico, *Patriotism for Profit*.

3. Special field orders, no. 67, September 8, 1864, *OR*, ser. 1, vol. 38, pt. 5, pp. 837–38; special field orders, no. 70, *OR*, ser. 1, vol. 39, pt. 2, pp. 356–57.

4. Sherman to Hugh Slocum, September 3, 1864, *OR*, ser. 1, vol. 38, pt. 5, p. 778; DeCredico, *Patriotism for Profit*, 112; Dyer, *Secret Yankees*, 204. Garrett reports that, by the end of September, 1,565 whites had left the city, accompanied by 79 slaves. Most of the city's slave population stayed in the city, according to Garrett, *Atlanta and Environs*, 1:642.

5. Sherman to Halleck, September 4, 1864, *OR*, ser. 1, vol. 38, pt. 5, p. 794.

6. Gildersleeve, *The Creed of the Old South*, 28.

7. Neely, *The Limits of Destruction*.

8. See Halleck to Sherman, September 23, 1864, in Sherman, *Memoirs*, 2:128.

9. Sherman to Hood, September 7, 1864, *OR*, ser. 1, vol. 38, pt. 5, p. 822.

10. Special field orders, no. 67, September 8, 1864, *OR*, ser. 1, vol. 38, pt. 5, p. 837.

11. Hood to Sherman, September 9, 1864, in Sherman, *Memoirs*, 2:119.

12. Sherman to Hood, September 10, 1864, in Sherman, *Memoirs*, 2:119–21. For a discussion of the Sherman-Hood exchange, see Miller, *John Bell Hood*, 140–43.

13. Hood to Sherman, in Sherman, *Memoirs*, 2:121–24.

14. Sherman to Halleck, September 20, 1864, in Sherman, *Memoirs*, 2:117–18.

15. James Calhoun et al. to Sherman, September 12, 1864; Sherman to Calhoun et al., September 12, 1864, in Sherman, *Memoirs*, 2:124–25.

16. Castel, "Order No. 11."

17. Given these numbers, Castel probably overstates Sherman's expulsion of civilians when he describes it as the "harshest measure taken against civilian authorities during the entire Civil War." Castel, *Decision in the West*, 548–49.

18. Reardon, "Sherman in Postwar Georgia's Collective Memory," 228.

19. "Direct Questions," *Atlanta Daily Constitution*, January 1, 1881.

20. Reardon, "Sherman in Postwar Georgia's Collective Memory," 228.

21. *Atlanta Daily Intelligencer*, quoted in "The Desolation of Atlanta," *Fayetteville Observer*, January 5, 1865.

22. Hood, *Advance and Retreat*, 236–42.

23. Jefferson Davis, *The Rise and Fall of the Confederate Government*, 564, 570. Davis told a reporter than Sherman was a "vain man" but a "man of very mediocre talents." Reardon, "Sherman in Postwar Georgia's Collective Memory," 231. Sherman responded that "not a man, woman, or child was harmed in that removal," and that Davis's assessment was "simply absurd." *New York Times*, June 9, 1881.

24. "Letter from Atlanta," *Cincinnati Commercial Appeal*, September 30, 1864, reprinted in *Milwaukee Daily Sentinel*, October 17, 1864.

25. Doyle, *New Men, New Cities, New South*, 32; DeCredico, *Patriotism for Profit*, 112–13. Dyer, *Secret Yankees*, 208–11, provides the best explanation of how the destruction of Atlanta occurred as a matter of military policy.

26. "Burning of Atlanta," *Vermont Chronicle*, January 7, 1865; Nichols, *The Story of the Great March*, 41; Hedley, *Marching through Georgia*, 257.

27. Howe, ed., *Marching with Sherman*, 57; Trudeau, *Southern Storm*, 85–89. See Henry Hitchcock's original diary in LC.

28. Paskoff, "Measures of War," 35–62.

29. "The Devastation at Atlanta, November 15, 1864," *Daily National Intelligencer*, November 22, 1864.

30. For a detailed description of the Western & Atlantic line, see G. W. Lee to Joseph E. Brown, March 25, 1864, Brown Family Papers, box 1, folder 3, UGA. On destruction and railroads, see Thomas, *The Iron Way*, 87–88.

31. Sherman to Logan, July 23, 24, 1864, *OR*, ser. 1, vol. 38, pt. 1, pp. 237–38, 242–43.

32. Sherman to Howard, August 28, 1864, *OR*, ser. 1, vol. 38, pt. 1, p. 695.

33. Hedley, *Marching through Georgia*, 256. See also DeCredico, *Patriotism for Profit*, 117, for similar descriptions. For an examination of environmental destruction during the Civil War, consult Brady, *War upon the Land*.

34. Conyngham, *Sherman's March*, 216–23.

35. "The South as It Is," *New York Times*, August 22, 1865.

36. Ibid.

37. *Richmond Daily Dispatch*, August 30, 1864.

38. William Wallace to Sarah Wallace, June 6, July 1, 1864, in Holzhueter, ed., "William Wallace's Civil War Letters," 99–100.

39. John Herr to his mother, June 12, 1864, John Herr Papers, DUL.

40. Megan Kate Nelson, *Ruin Nation*, 104.

41. "The Desolation of Atlanta," *Fayetteville Observer*, January 5, 1865.

42. Bonds, *War Like a Thunderbolt*, 211–22.

43. "How Atlanta Looks," *New York Tribune*, September 6, 1864, in *San Francisco Evening Bulletin*, October 26, 1864.

44. Arcada Baker was a widow whose husband, Russell Baker, died in October 1870. During the summer of 1864, Yankee soldiers visited her farm north of Atlanta and took corn, beef cattle, and sheep and also damaged her house in Decatur, about five miles north of the city; she claimed $515.20. The commission rejected her petition, noting that several of her sons had served in the rebel army. Arcada Baker, September 1871, SCC/D. On the demolition of homes, see Megan Kate Nelson, *Ruin Nation*, 102.

45. Claim of Elizabeth Grubb, January 1872, SCC/D.

46. Claim of Henry Holcomb, April 1875, SCC/D.

47. Claim of James Lamar, June 7, 1871, SCC/D.

48. Lee to Brown, March 25, 1865, Brown Family Papers, box 1, folder 3, UGA.

49. Colin Dunlop to his sister, August 13, 1864, Colin Dunlop Papers, AHC.

50. "Atlanta: Its Occupation by General Sherman," *Chicago Tribune*, September 14, 1864.

51. "A Letter from Atlanta," *Lowell Daily Citizen and News*, September 19, 1864.

52. Conyngham, *Sherman's March*, 216–23; "Inside View of Atlanta," *New York Times*, September 16, 1864.

53. "The Desolation of Atlanta," *Fayetteville Observer*, January 5, 1865.

54. William Wallace to Sarah Wallace, September 5, 1864, in Holzhueter, ed., "William Wallace's Civil War Letters," 109–11.

55. W. F. Spencer to Mary and Laura, September 20, 1864, William G. McCreary Papers, DUL.

56. Taft to his parents, September 16, 1864, Taft Family Papers, UGA.

57. Reid, *After the War*, chap. 35.

58. R. J. H., "The South," June 29, 1867, *Boston Daily Advertiser*, August 3, 1867.

59. "Letter from Judge [O. A.] Lochrane," *New York Times*, August 27, 1865.

60. Quoted in Bonds, *War Like a Thunderbolt*, 375–76.

61. "The Condition of Atlanta," correspondent for the *Columbus (Ga.) Times*, in *Daily Richmond Enquirer*, February 2, 1865. See also Andrews, *The South Since the War*, 338–44.

62. W. P. Howard, report on conditions in Atlanta, November 25, 1864, *Houston Tri-Weekly Telegraph*, January 26, 1865, published in Hewett et al., *Supplement to the Official Records*, pt. 1, vol. 7, ser. 7, pp. 154–57; "Burning of Atlanta," *Vermont Chronicle*, January 7, 1865; Wooton, "New City of the South," 222–24.

63. "The South as It Is," *New York Times*, August 22, 1865; Howard, report on conditions in Atlanta, *Houston Tri-Weekly Telegraph*, January 26, 1865. Another report from an Augusta newspaper claimed that three-fourths of Atlanta's buildings had been destroyed. Taylor, "From the Ashes," 31–32.

64. Andrews, *The South Since the War*, 338–44. On Christmas Day, 1865, a correspondent for the *Nation* founded Atlanta streets ankle-deep in mud, with the city "completely cheerless." Quoted in Conway, *The Reconstruction of Atlanta*, 25–26. For another travel account, see Trowbridge, *The South: A Tour*, 452–59.

65. Claim of Henry and Polly Beedles, December 20, 1875, SCC/A.

66. O. S. Hammond to Mrs. Adair, February 10, 1865, quoted in Russell, *Atlanta, 1847–1890*, 119.

67. Wortman, *The Bonfire*, 345.

68. Wooton, "New City of the South," 116, 126.

69. Reed, *History of Atlanta*, 206–9; *Atlanta Daily Intelligencer*, June 14, October 11, 1865; *Macon Daily Telegraph*, June 10, 1865.

70. Taylor, "From the Ashes," 315–16.

71. Chapman Brothers, *Portrait and Biographical Album of Sedgwick County*, 469–71; "From Atlanta," *Chicago Tribune*, May 25, 1865; Dyer, *Secret Yankees*, 224.

72. "Adversity—How to Bear It," *Atlanta Daily Intelligencer*, May 10, 1865.

73. Entries for George Johnston, April 2, 1859, October 28, 1865, RGD.

74. Entry for O. H. Jones, March 8, 1861, October 28, 1865, RGD.

75. Entries for Cox, Hill, and Co., August 15, 1859, October 28, 1859, RGD. The same was true for other merchants closely associated with the war trade. W. B. Lowe and Co. "made considerable money" during the war, and their capital provided a jump-start over competitors. Entry for W. B. Lowe and Co., March 3, 1866, RGD.

76. Entries for Ormond McNaught, December 12, 1859, January 16, 1860, October 28, 1865, February 26, 1866, RGD.

77. Entries for Wylie, Carroll, and Co., April 10, 1866, May 1871.

78. Entry for Adair and Chisholm, January 8, 1857, RGD; Martin, *Atlanta and Its Builders*, 627–28.

79. Entries for Abram Rosenfield, January 15, September 15, 1866, RGD.

80. Entries for G. McGinley, September 30, 1871, June 1, 1875, January 11, 1876, RGD.

81. Entry for Garrett & Bro., November 15, 1865, RGD.

82. Entry for W. H. Brotherton, December 8, 1865, RGD.

83. Entry for J. F. Jenkins and Co., December 8, 1865, RGD.

84. Entry for S. R. McCamry and Co., February 3, 1866, RGD.

85. Andrews, *The South Since the War*, 338–44. When he left Atlanta in late June, Eggleston was praised for "gentlemanly bearing and proper appreciation of what is due our people." He had "won the respect of our citizens, and leaves bearing their good wishes for his future happiness and success." "Col. B. B. Eggleston," *Atlanta Daily Intelligencer*, June 22, 1865.

86. Russell, *Atlanta, 1847–1890*, 126, 127.

87. Reid, *After the War*, chap. 35.

88. Rebecca M. Craighead to Samuel Hunt, January 16, 1866, AMA.

89. *Atlanta Daily New Era*, November 3, 1866.

90. *Cincinnati Gazette*, October 20, 1865, in *Columbus (Ga.) Daily Enquirer*, November 2, 1865.

91. "Our 'Gate City,'" *Atlanta Daily Intelligencer*, April 19, 1865.

92. *Atlanta Daily Intelligencer*, July 4, 1866.

93. Kennaway, *On Sherman's Track*, 115–16.

94. John Stainback Wilson, *Atlanta as It Is*, 9.

95. "From Atlanta," *Chicago Tribune*, May 25, 1865.

96. *Louisville Journal*, in *Daily National Intelligencer*, August 8, 1865.

97. *New York Herald*, September 3, 1865.

98. Martin, *Atlanta and Its Builders*, 21.

99. James Pile Wickersham to Emma, July 17, 1881, James P. Wickersham Papers, AHC.

100. Garrett, *Atlanta and Environs*, 2:131.

101. "Atlanta, Past, Present and Future," August 31, 1865, *Atlanta Daily Intelligencer*, September 2, 1865.

102. S. J. F. to the editor, July 5, 1870, in "A Sound, Sensible Letter—Atlanta Merchants, Read and Ponder—Another Railroad," *Atlanta Constitution*, July 9, 1870.

103. Thomas, *The Iron Way*, 182–86.

104. Garrett, *Atlanta and Environs*, 1:729–30.

105. "New City of the South," 222–24.

106. Reid, *After the War*, chap. 35.

107. Andrews, *The South Since the War*, 33–34.

108. "Atlanta a Fast City," *Savannah Daily News and Herald*, February 14, 1867.

109. "Atlanta," letter to the editor, *New Orleans Tribune*, September 12, 1869, published in *Atlanta Constitution*, September 21, 1869.

110. Report from *Field and Fireside*, in *Natchez Daily Courier*, October 27, 1866.

111. Wooton, "New City of the South," 273–74.

112. King, *The Great South*, 350–55.

113. Russell, *Atlanta, 1847–1890*, 127.

114. "Affairs in the South," *New York Times*, October 11, 1866.

115. Quoted in the *Atlanta Daily New Era*, September 17, 1869.

116. "Atlanta," *Atlanta Weekly New Era*, May 11, 1870.

117. "The Phoenix City of the South," *Atlanta Constitution*, September 2, 1875.

118. Reed, *History of Atlanta*, 18–20.

119. Report from *Peoria (Ill.) Democrat*, "The Condition of Things in Atlanta," *Cincinnati Daily Enquirer*, May 20, 1867. See also *Atlanta Constitution*, April 15, 1869.

CHAPTER 3

1. Mustered out in November 1865, Salm-Salm served—along with other Americans, most of them former Confederates—under Maximilian I of Mexico, an Austrian prince whom Napoleon III of France had installed as Emperor of Mexico. When the Mexicans captured and executed Maximilian, Salm-Salm escaped and returned to Germany. Agnes Salm-Salm, *Ten Years of My Life*, 112. On Agnes Salm-Salm, see Coffey, *Soldier Princess*; *Atlanta Daily Intelligencer*, July 28, 1865.

2. "The South as It Is," *New York Times*, August 22, 1865.

3. *Atlanta Daily Intelligencer*, August 30, 1865.

4. Taylor, "From the Ashes," 318.

5. *Atlanta Daily Intelligencer*, December 2, 1865.

6. Ibid., December 31, 1865, January 4, 1866.

7. Ibid., July 6, 1866.

8. Garrett, *Atlanta and Environs*, 1:676–81; Diary of Thomas Maguire, June 18, 1865, AHC.

9. Diary of Thomas Maguire, May 18, 1865, AHC.

10. Ibid., May 28, 1865.

11. Ibid., June 6, 1865.

12. Martin, *Atlanta and Its Builders*, 1–6.

13. "A Storm Brewing—Action Necessary," *Atlanta Daily Intelligencer*, July 20, 1865.

14. Garrett, *Atlanta and Environs*, 1:676–81.

15. Ibid., 1:689.

16. " 'What Can Be Done for the South?,' " *Atlanta Daily Intelligencer*, June 6, 1865.

17. "Legislation Necessary," *Atlanta Daily Intelligencer*, June 7, 1865.

18. "Vagrancy in Atlanta," *Atlanta Daily Intelligencer*, April 14, 1866. See also "A Most Grievous State of Things," ibid., August 10, 1866.

19. *Report of the Joint Select Committee to Inquire into the Condition of Affairs in the Late Insurrectionary States*, 1:54.

20. Glymph, *Out of the House of Bondage*, 107.

21. Hahn et al., eds., *Land and Labor, 1865*, 22–25.

22. Rev. E. Weaver, "Letter from Atlanta, Ga.," August 2, 1865, *Christian Recorder*, August 19, 1865.

23. "Our Atlanta Correspondence," *New York Herald*, March 14, 1867.

24. Martin, *Atlanta and Its Builders*, 1–6; Hahn et al., eds., *Land and Labor, 1865*, 20–22.

25. "What Shall Be Done with Him?," *Atlanta Daily Intelligencer*, July 21, 1865.

26. "Painful and Strange," *Atlanta Daily Intelligencer*, July 7, 1865.

27. Du Bois, "The Freedmen's Bureau," 357.

28. Bentley, *A History of the Freedmen's Bureau*, 214. For a similar view, see Thompson, *Reconstruction in Georgia*.

29. Hunter, *To 'Joy My Freedom*, 21. For a similar approach, see Scott Nelson, *Steel Drivin' Man*, 46–47; Wooton, "New City of the South," 281–83.

30. Cimbala and Miller, eds., *The Freedmen's Bureau*, xxx. See also Cimbala, *Under the Guardianship of the Nation*; Cimbala, "The Freedmen's Bureau, the Freedmen, and Sherman's Grant," 597–632. On the bureau and black health, see Savitt, "Politics in Medicine," 45–64; Downs, *Sick from Freedom*.

31. These counties included Butts, Campbell, Carroll, Cherokee, Clayton, Cobb, Coweta, Dekalb, Fayette, Forsyth, Fulton, Gwinnett, Haralson, Heard, Henry, Newton, Milton, Paulding, and Polk.

32. Hahn et al., eds., *Land and Labor, 1865*, 27.

33. U.S. War Department, *Report of the Commissioner of the Bureau of Refugees, Freedmen, and Abandoned Lands, November 1, 1866*, 705–7.

34. Poole to Mr. Mason, February 10, 1866, FB/FO, reel 43.

35. Cimbala, *Under the Guardianship of the Nation*, 54.

36. "Papers Wanted," *Atlanta Daily Intelligencer*, June 7, 1865.

37. John Richard Dennett, "The South as It Is," *Nation*, January 25, 1866.

38. "Disturbance in Atlanta," *Savannah Daily News and Herald*, July 6, 1866.

39. Fred Mosebach to C. C. Sibley, September 10, 1867, FB/FO, reel 43.

40. *Atlanta Constitution*, October 16, 1868, quoted in Garrett, *Atlanta and Environs*, 1:793.

41. "Generals Steadman and Fullerton," *Atlanta Daily Intelligencer*, June 7, 1866.

42. In one of many cases in northern Georgia, a bureau official in October 1866 ordered a white man to return an ex-slave's children. The bureau official reprimanded Osborn Lynch, the former master, for having "in your custody two of his children whom you detain contrary to his wishes as a parent and violation of the Laws of this State relating to freedpeople." The official informed Lynch that "parents and children however Black Canot be forcibly seperated [sic] from each other." Orders sent to local citizens and register of complaints, October 29, 1866, FB/FO, reel 45. In early 1866, Thomas Pitts, a planter outside Atlanta, kept the daughter of an Atlanta black woman and refused to return the child. The bureau agent ordered her return. D. C. Poole to Adam Robinson, February 6, 1866, FB/FO, reel 43. For an exploration of the reunification of black families, see Williams, *Help Me to Find My People*.

43. Thomas F. Forbes to Davis Tillson, April 3, 1866, FB/FO, reel 43.

44. Fred Mosebach to C. C. Sibley, November 14, 1867, FB/FO, reel 43.

45. Fred Mosebach to Capt. J. M. Hoag, November 25, 1867, FB/FO, reel 43.

46. Case file, Angeline Ellis, February 5, 1868, FB/FO, reel 43.

47. E. F. Winslow to Captain Griffin, May 31, 1865, *OR*, ser. 1, vol. 38, pt. 1, pp. 939–40.

48. *New York Tribune*, quoted in "The Life of Edmund Asa Ware," in the Edmund Asa Ware Papers, AUL.

49. "Letter from Atlanta," July 17, 1865, from *Daily Georgia Telegraph*, in *Atlanta Daily Intelligencer*, July 19, 1865.

50. Report of the destitute, October 21, 1865, FB/FO, reel 45.

51. Report by Brig. Gen. C. H. Howard of South Carolina, Georgia, and Florida, December 30, 1865, *Report of the Commissioner of the Freedmen's Bureau, March 1, 1866*, 39th Cong., 1st sess., House Executive Document 27. The bureau agent described "great destitution and suffering for want of the necessaries of life in each of the counties comprising the district of Atlanta" as late as 1867. John Leonard to Davis Tillson, April 9, 1867, FB/FO, reel 43.

52. John Leonard to Davis Tillson, August 31, December 21, 1866, FB/FO, reel 43.

53. John Leonard to Davis Tillson, April 9, 1867, FB/FO, reel 43.

54. George R. Waldridge to C. T. Watson, May 9, 1866, FB/FO, reel 43.

55. George R. Waldridge to Davis Tillson, May 7, 1866, FB/FO, reel 43.

56. John Leonard to Davis Tillson, April 9, 1867, FB/FO, reel 43.

57. George R. Waldridge to Davis Tillson, February 28, 1866, FB/FO, reel 43.

58. "Passing Away," *Atlanta Daily Intelligencer*, May 19, 1866.

59. Garrett, *Atlanta and Environs*, 1:792.

60. "Domestic Dramas," *Atlanta Daily New Era*, February 27, 1868.

61. Garrett, *Atlanta and Environs*, 1:689–90.

62. Special field orders, no. 1, August 26, 1865, in *Atlanta Daily Intelligencer*, August 29, 1865.

63. In August 1865, twenty-five prisoners were black, fifty-three white; in September 1865, forty prisoners were black, fifty-seven white; and in October 1865, forty-one prisoners were black, thirty-seven white. Provost Marshal Records for Atlanta, Register of Prisoners at Atlanta, 1865–1866, Record Group 393, National Archives Building, Washington, D.C.

64. Wooton, "New City of the South," 137.

65. Lt. Col. George Curkendall to Maj. Gray, December 7, 1865, in Hahn et al., eds., *Land and Labor, 1865,* 675; Taylor, "From the Ashes," 319.

66. George R. Waldridge to Davis Tillson, March 10, 1866, FB/FO, reel 43.

67. George R. Waldridge to Louis Beckwith, March 15, 1866, FB/FO, reel 43.

68. George R. Waldridge to Davis Tillson, April 29, 1866, FB/FO, reel 43.

69. *Atlanta Daily Intelligencer*, January 5, 1866.

70. Garrett, *Atlanta and Environs*, 1:792.

71. George R. Waldridge to Davis Tillson, March 10, 1866, FB/FO, reel 43.

72. Heather Cox Richardson, *The Death of Reconstruction*; O'Donovan, *Becoming Free in the Cotton South*, 166.

73. John Richard Dennett, "The South as It Is," *Nation*, January 25, 1866.

74. Orders sent to local citizens and register of complaints, January 7, 1868, FB/FO, reel 45.

75. Circular no. 11, Gen. O. O. Howard, in *Atlanta Daily Intelligencer*, July 20, 1865.

76. "Bureau of Freedmen—General Orders No. 1," *Atlanta Daily Intelligencer*, August 8, 1865.

77. Orders sent to local citizens and register of complaints, October, Special Order No. 1, October 13, 1865, FB/FO, reel 45; John Richard Dennett, "The South as It Is," *Nation*, January 25, 1866.

78. Orders sent to local citizens and register of complaints, February 28, 1866, FB/FO, reel 45.

79. Court papers and reports, affidavit of Columbus Allen, December 10, 1865, FB/FO, reel 45.

80. George R. Waldridge to E. L. Jackson, March 9, 1866, FB/FO, reel 43.

81. Orders sent to local citizens and register of complaints, May 22, 1867, FB/FO, reel 45.

82. Orders sent to local citizens and register of complaints, October 29, 1866, FB/FO, reel 45.

83. "Regulations for Freedmen," *Atlanta Daily Intelligencer*, July 9, 1865.

84. George R. Waldridge to Park Arnold, March 15, 1866, FB/FO, reel 43.

85. Orders sent to local citizens and register of complaints, June 10, 1867, FB/FO, reel 45.

86. Fred Mosebach to Daniel Nerd, January 14, 1868, FB/FO, reel 43.

87. Orders sent to local citizens and register of complaints, January 7, 1868, FB/FO, reel 45.

88. Orders sent to local citizens and register of complaints, February 25, 1868, FB/FO, reel 45.

89. John Richard Dennett, "The South as It Is," *Nation*, January 25, 1866.

90. Garrett, *Atlanta and Environs*, 1:689–90.

91. Hunter, *To 'Joy My Freedom*, 21.

92. Garrett, *Atlanta and Environs*, 1:676–81.

93. Cimbala, *Under the Guardianship of the Nation*, 10.

94. Until 1881, the McPherson Barracks—named in honor of fallen Union general James B. McPherson—remained a military garrison. Although the buildings and grounds were sold in that year, in 1886 Congress established an enlarged Fort McPherson in Atlanta that remained in the city for many years.

95. Fred Mosebach to James W. Williams, May 31, 1867, FB/FO, reel 43.

96. Foner, *Reconstruction*, 272; *Ex parte Milligan*, 71 U.S. 2 (1866).

97. Fred Mosebach to C. C. Sibley, August 1, 1867, FB/FO, reel 43.

98. Fred Mosebach to C. C. Sibley, January 24, 1868, FB/FO, reel 43.

99. Fred Mosebach to C. C. Sibley, August 28, 1868, FB/FO, reel 43.

100. Fred Mosebach to Adam Poole, November 23, 1867, FB/FO, reel 43.

101. Fred Mosebach to Thomas H. Ruger, March 4, 1868, FB/AC, reel 43. In H. A. G. Williams to Fred Mosebach, March 5, 1868, FB/FO, reel 43, Ruger informed Mosebach that he would consider the case if Mosebach sent the proceedings.

102. Case file, James Bloodgood, February 5, 1868, FB/FO, reel 44. On the difficulty blacks had attaining justice, see Hahn, *A Nation under Our Feet*, 236.

103. Fred Mosebach to J. R. Lewis, December 4, 1867, FB/FO, reel 43; case file, January 9, 1868, FB/FO, reel 43.

104. "Regulations for Freedmen," *Atlanta Daily Intelligencer*, July 9, 1865.

105. Fred Mosebach to George W. Nolan, February 20, 1868, FB/FO, reel 43.

106. U.S. Congress, *The Condition of the South.*

107. T. B. Thorpe, "Affairs in the South," *New York Times*, June 18, 1866.

108. Fred Mosebach to C. C. Sibley, April 9, 1868, FB/FO, reel 43.

109. Testimony of Amos T. Ackerman, December 19, 1868, in *The Condition of Affairs in Georgia*, 22. Ackerman subsequently served as attorney general and prosecuted Klan depredations in the South.

110. John Leonard to Davis Tillson, September 4, 1866, FB/FO, reel 43.

111. Fred Mosebach to C. C. Sibley, November 6, 1868, FB/FO, reel 43.

112. Fred Mosebach to C. C. Sibley, April 9, 1868, FB/FO, reel 43.

113. Fred Mosebach to C. C. Sibley, November 6, 1868, FB/FO, reel 43.

114. Fred Mosebach to C. C. Sibley, February 15, 1868, FB/FO, reel 43.

115. Fred Mosebach to Davis Tillson, March 8, 1866, in Berlin, Reidy, and Rowland, eds., *The Black Military Experience*, 759–61.

116. Fred Mosebach to C. C. Sibley, January 24, 1868, in Wooton, "New City of the South," 313.

117. Fred Mosebach to C. C. Sibley, January 28, 1868, FB/AC, reel 43.

CHAPTER 4

1. Sarris, *A Separate Civil War*, 166–67.

2. "Minor Topics," *New York Times*, July 30, 1867; *Atlanta Daily Intelligencer*, June 22, 1867.

3. Dyer, *Secret Yankees*, 34–35; Martin, *Atlanta and Its Builders*, 5; "Minor Topics," *New York Times*, July 30, 1867.

4. Martin, *Atlanta and Its Builders*, 68; *Atlanta Daily Intelligencer*, October 1, 1867.

5. Quoted in *Iowa Daily State Register*, August 23, 1867.

6. *Atlanta Daily Intelligencer*, October 1, 1867.

7. Ibid., October 2, 1867.

8. Ibid., October 4, 1867.

9. "That Monumental Vote," *Atlanta Daily Intelligencer*, October 4, 1867.

10. "Disgust" to the editor, *Atlanta Daily Intelligencer*, October 5, 1867.

11. "Stonewall" to the editor, *Atlanta Daily Intelligencer*, October 8, 1867.

12. *LaCrosse Democrat*, quoted in "The Lincoln Monument," *Atlanta Daily Intelligencer*, November 6, 1867.

13. "Indignant" to the editor, October 9, 1867, *Atlanta Daily Intelligencer*, October 12, 1867.

14. "The Lincoln Monument," *Atlanta Daily Intelligencer*, November 6, 1867.

15. Old Colonel [pseud.], "It's Not Here," *Atlanta Constitution*, November 11, 1888.

16. Trelease, *White Terror*, 73–74; *Atlanta Daily Intelligencer*, March 24, 1868. On the Klan and postwar vigilante violence, see Rosen, *Terror in the Heart of Freedom*.

17. Trelease, *White Terror*, 318.

18. *Report of the Joint Select Committee*, 1:64.

19. Testimony of John E. Bryant, December 21, 1868, in *The Condition of Affairs in Georgia*, 27.

20. Petition of the Republican members of the Georgia legislature to Congress, January 1, 1869, in *The Condition of Affairs in Georgia*, 87.

21. "Forney on Atlanta," *Atlanta Constitution*, May 18, 1869. "We cannot stop anywhere else so safely," commented a Greene County freedman who had migrated to Atlanta. Quoted in Wooton, "New City of the South," 277.

22. Columbus Jeter, October 25, 1871, *Report of the Joint Select Committee*, 6:559–63.

23. Testimony of Alfred Richardson, July 7, 1871, *Report of the Joint Select Committee*, 6:1–19.

24. Testimony of Andrew D. Rockefellow, July 25, 1871, *Report of the Joint Select Committee*, 6:249–64; Drago, *Black Politicians and Reconstruction*.

25. Testimony of Andrew D. Rockefellow, July 25, 1871, *Report of the Joint Select Committee*, 6:249–64.

26. Bryant, *How Curious a Land*, 107–8.

27. Testimony of Abram Colby, *Report of the Joint Select Committee*, 7:699–712. The city's black population thus enjoyed a degree of protection as refugees from Klan violence. In the spring of 1871, Warren Davis, a forty-eight-year-old ex-slave from Coweta County, fled to Atlanta after Klansmen nailed a coffin on his fence with the following message (original spelling retained): "LOOK OUT FOR KKK. If you are found in this country in fifteen day this shol be your doom and so you had beter be on look out or the ku kucks will get you and this will be your resting place." Davis had disputed the price of his cotton with local whites, and the result was a nighttime visitation from the Klan, with shots fired into his house. Davis concluded that it "looked like I had better get away, or I would be killed." Coming to Atlanta, he declared that there was "nothing to go back there now for, and I do not intend to go back." Testimony of Warren Davis, *Report of the Joint Select Committee*, 7:727–30.

28. Testimony of Greene Westmoreland, *Report of the Joint Select Committee*, 7:730–31.

29. Whitehead and Bogart, *City of Progress*, 30–37, 98–102, 111; DeCredico, *Patriotism for Profit*, 3–5.

30. *Radical Rule*, 1–14.

31. The census of 1850 listed Ashburn as a Georgia native, though the census of 1860 listed him as born in Tennessee. In November 1865, Ashburn described Georgia as the "place of my birth."

32. *Columbus (Ga.) Daily Enquirer*, January 18, 1848.

33. *Ashburn v. Dempsey*, 15:248–52.

34. U.S. manuscript census of population, 1860, Columbus, Georgia.

35. *Report of the Adjutant General and Acting Quartermaster General of Iowa*, 2:629.

36. Once the war ended, one source described Ashburn as a "Government spy in search of property belonging to the late Confederate States." Daniell, "The Ashburn Murder Case," 297; *Reports of the Committees of the House of Representatives*, 43rd Cong., 1st sess., Report No. 302 (Case of Martha A. Ashburn); *Radical Rule*, 1–14.

37. George Ashburn to Andrew Johnson, April 15, 1865, in Graf and Haskins, eds., *The Papers of Andrew Johnson*, 7:555. See the biographical information on Ashburn in ibid., 5:334, n. 2; "Semper," *Columbus (Ga.) Daily Enquirer*, November 20, 1865.

38. George Ashburn, letters to the editor, *Columbus (Ga.) Daily Enquirer,* November 29, 30, 1865. In September 1866, Ashburn attended a meeting in Philadelphia of southern loyalists who endorsed the Fourteenth Amendment and recommended a harsh policy toward the South. Writing to the *Macon Telegraph,* Ashburn announced that, if he were Georgia governor, his first act would be to "close every Rebel printing office in that Rebellious State that refuses to place at the head of its paper the (36) thirty-six Stars with the Stripes and defend the principles of the American government." Reprinted from *Macon Telegraph,* in "Highly Interesting (!) Correspondence," *Weekly Columbus (Ga.) Enquirer,* September 25, 1866.

39. J. H. Caldwell, October 23, 1871, *Report of the Joint Select Committee,* 6:432.

40. *Weekly Columbus (Ga.) Enquirer,* February 18, 1868; Reed, *History of Atlanta,* 241–43; Trelease, *White Terror,* 76 and 77, n. 39.

41. Trelease, *White Terror,* 76. On March 28, 1868, J. H. Caldwell, a white Republican from Troup County who had served in the constitutional convention with Ashburn, visited Columbus for a political rally. In town for a few days, Caldwell learned that the Klan had issued death threats to local Republicans. A drawing in one of these death threats represented Ashburn lying in a coffin. J. H. Caldwell, October 23, 1871, *Report of the Joint Select Committee,* 6:432.

42. "Murder of Ashburn by Rebels," *Milwaukee Daily Sentinel,* April 14, 1868.

43. Trelease, *White Terror,* 76–78.

44. "The Killing of G. W. Ashburn," from *Columbus (Ga.) Sun,* in *Savannah Daily News and Herald,* April 4, 1868; "Beginning of the End—The Killing of the Notorious Ashburn," *Savannah Daily News and Herald,* April 4, 1868.

45. *Western Christian Advocate,* April 8, 1868.

46. "The Killing of G. W. Ashburn," from *Columbus (Ga.) Sun,* in *Savannah Daily News and Herald,* April 4, 1868; "The Ku-Klux Klan," *New York Tribune,* April 7, 1868.

47. Trelease, *White Terror,* 76.

48. "The Ku-Klux Klan," *New York Tribune,* April 7, 1868.

49. General Order No. 51, in "The KuKlux Klan: Gen. Meade's Order for Its Suppression," *New York Times,* April 9, 1868.

50. *Washington Chronicle* account, reprinted in "Murder of Ashburn by Rebels," *Milwaukee Daily Sentinel,* April 14, 1868.

51. "Political Murders in the South," *New York Times,* April 7, 1868.

52. "A Deed of the Kuklux-Klan," *Chicago Tribune,* April 10, 1868.

53. William Mills to John E. Hosmer, March 31, 1868; William Mills to George Meade, April 10, 1868, in U.S. Army, Department of the South, *Report of Major General Meade's Military Operations,* 6.

54. These men included Columbus Bedell, a bank clerk; policemen W. D. Cash and Kirk Roper; clerks Robert Ennis and James W. Barber; E. J. Kirksey, a physician of Muscogee County; merchant William Bedell; and Thomas Grimes Jr., an attorney.

55. George Meade to Ulysses S. Grant, April 4, 1868; William Mills to George Meade, April 6, 1868, in U.S. Army, Department of the South, *Report of Major General Meade's Military Operations.*

56. U.S. Army, Department of the South, *Report of Major General Meade's Military Operations,* 3.

57. "Killing of G. W. Ashburn," from *Columbus (Ga.) Sun,* in *Daily National Intelligencer,* April 10, 1868.

58. Quoted in Daniell, "The Ashburn Murder Case," 301.

59. "The Killing of G. W. Ashburn," from *Columbus (Ga.) Sun,* in *Savannah Daily News and Herald,* April 4, 1868; Thompson, *Reconstruction in Georgia,* 361–62; Trelease, *White Terror,*

76–79; Conway, *The Reconstruction of Georgia*, 158–59; Almand, "The Ashburn Murder Case and Military Trial," 43–48.

60. "The Reason Why," *Atlanta Constitution*, June 20, 1868.

61. "Affairs in Atlanta," *Georgia Weekly Telegraph*, July 10, 1868.

62. Quoted in "Beginning of the End—The Killing of the Notorious Ashburn," *Savannah Daily News and Herald*, April 4, 1868.

63. According to the account given in the broadside, white Republican A. G. Bennett, who was present at the murder, had bragged that he "would have killed him if the mob had not." As further evidence against Ashburn's character, the authors of *Radical Rule* explained that only Ashburn's son and a "local Jew" had appeared to claim his remains and to ship them to Macon. *Radical Rule*, 1–14.

64. *Radical Rule*.

65. "What Does It Cost?," *Atlanta Constitution*, July 12, 1868.

66. "The Atlanta Military Commission," from *Cincinnati Enquirer*, July 13, 1868, in *Georgia Weekly Telegraph*, July 24, 1868.

67. *Columbus (Ga.) Sun*, quoted in "The Reign of Terror," *Atlanta Constitution*, June 22, 1868.

68. *Radical Rule*.

69. H. C. Whitely to George Meade, June 27, 1868, in U.S. Army, Department of the South, *Report of Major General Meade's Military Operations*, 33–34.

70. "The Murderers of Hon. G. W. Ashburn," *Chicago Tribune*, June 22, 1868.

71. Roberts, *Joseph E. Brown and the Politics of Reconstruction*.

72. Joseph E. Brown to William D. Kelly, March 18, 1868, Joseph E. Brown Papers, box 3, folder 9, AHC; Parks, *Joseph E. Brown of Georgia*. See also Joseph E. Brown to W. A. Bedell, June 17, 1868, Joseph E. Brown Papers, box 3, folder 9, AHC.

73. The following discussion is based on the trial transcript available in *Radical Rule*, 15–199.

74. *Savannah Daily News and Herald*, June 20, 1868. After the murder, Marshall recalled, he was provided with a gold watch and chain and a $100 loan, unsecured and unpaid, supplied by the Columbus mayor.

75. "Killing of G. W. Ashburn," *Savannah Daily News and Herald*, April 2, 1868; report from *Macon Telegraph*, in "Killing of G. W. Ashburn," *Savannah Daily News and Herald*, April 2, 1868.

76. "The South," *Chicago Tribune*, July 3, 1868.

77. Ibid.

78. Daniell, "The Ashburn Murder Case," 307.

79. "The South," *Chicago Tribune*, July 11, 1868.

80. "The Ashburn Murder Trial Suspended—The Prisoners Retained in Custody," *New York Times*, July 23, 1868.

81. *Radical Rule*. See also "The Military Trial at Atlanta," *Atlanta Constitution*, July 19, 1868.

82. Felton, *My Memoir of Georgia Politics*, 55–60.

83. *Columbus (Ga.) Daily Enquirer*, September 18, 1875.

84. *Columbus (Ga.) Sunday Enquirer*, April 16, 1876. The narrative persisted into the twentieth century. In 1978, local historians Margaret Laney Whitehead and Barbara Bogart characterized the defendants' unjust treatment at the hands of the prosecutors in the Ashburn murder trial as "an abominable miscarriage of military justice." Whitehead and Bogart, *City of Progress*, 118–20.

85. *Columbus (Ga.) Daily Enquirer*, April 18, 1876.

86. *Columbus (Ga.) Daily Enquirer*, August 4, 1876.

87. "Roanoke," "Why Ex-Gov. J. E. Brown Hates Senator Gordon," *Columbus (Ga.) Sunday Enquirer*, April 29, 1877.

88. "Striking Higher, and Reaching for the Governor," *Atlanta Daily Constitution*, September 20, 1879; "The Nelms Investigation," *Columbus (Ga.) Sunday Enquirer*, September 21, 1879.

89. Joseph E. Brown, "The Days of '68," *Atlanta Constitution*, October 2, 1879.

90. Joseph E. Brown, "The Case Re-Opened: The Facts of the Ashburn Trial," *Atlanta Constitution*, September 24, 1879; Joseph E. Brown, "Methods Compared," *Atlanta Constitution*, September 25, 1879.

91. Henry McNeal Turner, "On the Eligibility of Colored Members to Seats in the Georgia Legislature," September 3, 1868, in Redkey, *Respect Black*, 16.

92. *Christian Recorder*, March 25, 1880, in Redkey, *Respect Black*, 49.

93. "The Bull Run Celebration," *Atlanta Constitution*, July 22, 1870; "The Celebration of the 15th Amendment," *Atlanta Daily Intelligencer*, July 22, 1870.

94. *Atlanta Daily Sun*, November 5, 1871; Bacote, "William Finch, Negro Councilman."

95. "Atlanta," *Atlanta Constitution*, June 23, 1868.

96. "Kimball's Opera House," *Atlanta Constitution*, December 9, 1868; "The New State Capitol," *Atlanta Constitution*, January 7, 1869.

CHAPTER 5

1. Quoted in Bacote, *The Story of Atlanta University*, 11–12.

2. Ibid.

3. Alvord, *Letters from the South*.

4. Jacqueline Jones, *Soldiers of Light and Love*, 127.

5. Wright, *Eighty-Seven Years behind the Black Curtain*, 16–17.

6. Richard R. Wright, address, *American Missionary* 35 (January 1881): 380; Anderson, *The Education of Blacks in the South*, 29–30.

7. Bacote, *The Story of Atlanta University*, 11–12; Dittmer, *Black Georgia in the Progressive Era*, 168–69; Wright, *Eighty-Seven Years behind the Black Curtain*, 19, 41–49.

8. Fred Mosebach to C. C. Sibley, August 7, 1867, FB/FO, reel 43.

9. *American Missionary* 11 (November 1867): 247–48. On freedpeople's education, see Anderson, *The Education of Blacks in the South*; Williams, *Self-Taught*; Butchart, *Schooling the Freed People*.

10. Joe M. Richardson, *Christian Reconstruction*, vii, 37, 75.

11. Edwin P. Smith to Edmund Asa Ware, July 22, 1868, Edmund Asa Ware Papers, AUL.

12. Bacote, *The Story of Atlanta University*, 14–15; E. A. Ware to E. P. Smith, August 15, 20, 1867, AMA.

13. Du Bois, *The Souls of Black Folk*, 100.

14. "Erasmus M. Cravath," in Johnson and Malone, eds., *Dictionary of American Biography*, 4:516.

15. *American Missionary* 11 (November 1867): 247–48.

16. A. P. Eberhart to E. P. Smith, April 8, 1867, AMA.

17. Rebecca M. Craighead to E. P. Smith, May 9, 1867, AMA.

18. —— Phillips to E. P. Smith, April 9, 1867, AMA.

19. Lucy C. Kinney to Samuel Hunt, January 27, 1866, AMA.

20. E. M. Cravath to S. L. Eberhart, November 24, 1865, FB/SE, reel 8.

21. Bacote, *The Story of Atlanta University*, 1–8; *American Missionary* 11 (November 1867): 257–58.

22. Frederick Ayer to Ninth Street Sabbath School, June 1, 1866, Frederick Ayer Papers, AUL.

23. Frederick Ayer to Samuel Hunt, January 1866, AMA.

24. Elizabeth Ayer to Samuel Hunt, April 30, 1866, AMA.

25. *New York Tribune* story, reprinted in *American Missionary* 11 (February 1867): 28–29.

26. "The First Colored School House in the South," *Atlanta Daily Intelligencer*, February 13, 1867; Bacote, *The Story of Atlanta University*, 1–8; Jewell, *Race, Social Reform, and the Making of a Black Middle Class*, 90–91.

27. The orphan asylum was named for Worcester, Massachusetts, industrialist and philanthropist Ichabod Washburn. Undated manuscript history of Atlanta University, Edmund Asa Ware Papers, AUL.

28. Rebecca Craighead to E. P. Smith, May 8, 1867, AMA; Garrett, *Atlanta and Environs*, 1:742–43; undated manuscript history of Atlanta University, Edmund Asa Ware Papers, AUL; "The Atlanta Mission," *American Missionary* 12 (November 1868): 243–44.

29. E. A. Ware to Samuel Hunt, September 26, 1866, AMA; extract of an AMA report from Atlanta, December 1867, AMA; *New York Tribune*, December 10, 1866, in *American Missionary* 11 (February 1867): 28–29 (quotation); Rebecca Craighead to S. L. Eberhart, April 10, 1867, FB/SE, reel 8; case of Tom Robison, orders sent to local citizens and register of complaints, September 17, 1867, FB/FO, reel 45.

30. *American Missionary* 11 (November 1867): 257–58.

31. Bacote, *The Story of Atlanta University*, 13–14.

32. Edmund A. Ware to Samuel Hunt, November 29, 1866, AMA.

33. F. D. Duvall to Edmund A. Ware, July 16, 1867, Edmund Asa Ware Papers, AUL; Bacote, *The Story of Atlanta University*, 10–11.

34. "The Life of Edmund Asa Ware," undated, Edmund Asa Ware Papers, AUL; *American Missionary* 39 (November 1885): 300–301.

35. S. F. B. Morse, address on the death of Edmund A. Ware, September 1885, Edmund Asa Ware Papers, AUL.

36. Edmund A. Ware to E. P. Smith, August 23, 1867, AMA.

37. "The Life of Edmund Asa Ware," Edmund Asa Ware Papers, AUL.

38. Jacqueline Jones, *Soldiers of Light and Love*, 9.

39. McPherson, *The Abolitionist Legacy*.

40. *American Missionary* 14 (September 1870): 196.

41. *American Missionary* 14 (November 1870): 247.

42. *American Missionary* 14 (June 1870): 132.

43. George R. Waldridge to P. R. Phillips, May 9, 1866, FB/FO, reel 43.

44. Fred Mosebach to C. C. Sibley, September 7, 1867, FB/FO, reel 43.

45. Fred Mosebach to C. C. Sibley, August 7, 1867, FB/FO, reel 43.

46. Fred Mosebach to C. C. Sibley, April 9, 1868, FB/FO, reel 43.

47. Johnson, *Along This Way*, 66.

48. *American Missionary* 11 (October 1867): 225; *Atlanta Daily Opinion*, September 5, 1867.

49. "The Life of Edmund Asa Ware," Edmund Asa Ware Papers, AUL.

50. Fisk University, in Nashville, declared that its AMA supporters participated in the goal of "Universal Education for every Child of the Republic, irrespective of race, condition or color." *Fisk University Circular*, September 2, 1867, Edmund Asa Ware Papers, AUL; Richardson, *Christian Reconstruction*, 123.

51. *American Missionary* 13 (July 1869): 160–61.

52. Manuscript history of Atlanta University, undated, Edmund Asa Ware Papers, AUL; Edmund A. Ware to E. P. Smith, November 8, 1867, AMA; Jewell, *Race, Social Reform, and the Making of a Black Middle Class*, 109. The legislature made the same appropriation in 1871 and 1873, and in 1874 made it an annual appropriation. The university was required to admit one student without tuition for every member of Congress. According to C. H. Francis, Atlanta

University was to the "colored race what the university of Georgia is to the white race." "The Atlanta University," *Atlanta Constitution*, May 30, 1882.

53. S. F. B. Morse, address on the death of Edmund A. Ware, September 1885, Edmund Asa Ware Papers, AUL.

54. "Laying the Corner-Stone of the Atlanta University (Colored)," *Atlanta Constitution*, June 2, 1869.

55. *American Missionary* 13 (July 1869): 160–61.

56. Edmund A. Ware to George Whipple, September 19, 1868, AMA.

57. *American Missionary* 15 (April 1871): 283.

58. Ibid., 73–74.

59. Wooton, "New City of the South," 293.

60. *American Missionary* 14 (January 1870): 7.

61. Report of the Board of Visitors, Atlanta University, June 28, 1871, Edmund Asa Ware Papers, AUL.

62. Addison P. Foster, "Atlanta and Fisk Universities," *American Missionary* 22 (June 1878): 165–66. See also Emery, *Letters from the South*, 13–14.

63. "Atlanta University," *Atlanta Constitution*, December 8, 1884.

64. Emery, *Letters from the South*, 14.

65. Edmund A. Ware, "The Freedmen," *American Missionary* 22 (February 1878): 75–76; W. E. B. Du Bois, "Looking Seventy-Five Years Backward."

66. Edmund A. Ware, "The Freedmen," *American Missionary* 22 (February 1878): 75–76.

67. C. W. Francis, "Its Work," *American Missionary* 22 (February 1878): 76; Horace Bumstead, "Its Influence," ibid., 77.

68. *American Missionary* 11 (October 1867): 228.

69. Johnson, *Along This Way*, 70.

70. Towns, "Sources of the Tradition at Atlanta University," 122.

71. Johnson, *Along This Way*, 70.

72. "Life of Edmund Asa Ware," Edmund Asa Ware Papers, AUL.

73. Towns, "Sources of the Tradition at Atlanta University," 130.

74. Towns, "Horace Bumstead," 130.

75. Quoted in Jewell, *Race, Social Reform, and the Making of a Black Middle Class*, 95.

76. Quoted in Towns, "Sources of the Tradition at Atlanta University," 118, 121.

77. Alvord, *Letters from the South*.

78. *American Missionary* 14 (May 1870): 100–101.

79. Edwin P. Smith to M. E. Stieby, April 28, 1866, AMA.

80. Towns, "Sources of the Tradition at Atlanta University," 120–22.

81. Johnson, *Along This Way*, 65–66.

82. "Professor Ware Dead," *Atlanta Constitution*, September 26, 1885.

83. "Stone Hall in Mourning," *Atlanta Constitution*, September 30, 1885.

84. "Report of State Board of Visitors to Atlanta University," *Atlanta Constitution*, July 21, 1876.

85. W. E. B. Du Bois to George A. Towns, March 2, 1918, George A. Towns Collection, AUL.

86. "Whites and Blacks Being Educated Together in the Atlanta University," *Atlanta Constitution*, June 11, 1887; Jewell, *Race, Social Reform, and the Making of a Black Middle Class*, 119–26.

87. By June 1887, Horace Bumstead had taken over the permanent presidency, though Chase remained in the directorship.

88. "The Professor's Policy: The President of the Atlanta University Talks," *Atlanta Constitution*, June 12, 1887.

89. "The Message: Governor Gordon Pays His Respects to the Legislature," *Atlanta Constitution*, July 8, 1887.

90. "No Mixing of Races," *Atlanta Constitution*, July 12, 1887. On the controversy, see Bacote, *The Story of Atlanta University*, chap. 4.

91. "Atlanta University," *New York Times*, July 31, 1887.

92. Evarts Kent, "Why a White Youth Goes to a Colored University," letter to the editor, July 19, 1887, *Atlanta Constitution*, July 20, 1887.

93. "The University Side of the Controversy Growing Out of the Board of Visitors Report," *Atlanta Constitution*, July 20, 1887.

94. Ibid.

95. "What Will the Harvest Be?," *Atlanta Constitution*, December 15, 1887.

96. "Colored Schools and Colored Churches," *Atlanta Constitution*, July 21, 1887.

97. "Not Yet Paid: The Atlanta University Has Not Received That $8,000 Appropriation," *Atlanta Constitution*, December 24, 1887. For white opposition to Atlanta University, see "Georgian" to the editor, August 2, 1887, *Atlanta Constitution*, December 24, 1887.

98. "Badly Mixed: White Pupils Side by Side with Black in Atlanta," *Atlanta Constitution*, December 23, 1887; "The Glenn Bill," *Atlanta Constitution*, February 3, 1888; "Georgia's Colored Problem," *New York Times*, August 27, 1887.

99. *Atlanta University Bulletin*, no. 9 (April 1889): 1; *Atlanta University Bulletin*, no. 7 (February 1889): 1.

100. "The Usual Stuff, Which Is Annually Poured into New England Ears," *Atlanta Constitution*, February 27, 1888.

101. *Atlanta University Bulletin*, no. 7 (February 1889): 1.

CHAPTER 6

1. "The Gallant Dead," *Atlanta Daily Constitution*, July 23, 1878.

2. "Atlanta," *Atlanta Daily Constitution*, October 5, 1881.

3. "Atlanta of Long Ago," *Atlanta Daily Constitution*, November 25, 1883.

4. "Atlanta's History," *Atlanta Constitution*, April 12, 1885. The *Constitution* promoted the establishment of an Atlanta historical society, but this organization was not established until 1926. See "A Historical Society for Atlanta," *Atlanta Constitution*, April 20, 1885; "A Local Historical Society," *Atlanta Constitution*, July 29, 1885.

5. Old Colonel [pseud.], "Christmas in the Ashes," *Atlanta Constitution*, December 23, 1888.

6. Reed, *History of Atlanta*, 18–20.

7. *Pioneer Citizens History of Atlanta*, 400.

8. "Memorial Day," *Atlanta Daily Constitution*, April 25, 1880.

9. "Grady in New York," *Atlanta Constitution*, December 22, 1886.

10. "Greeting Grady," clipping in Henry W. Grady Scrapbooks, UGA. Sherman remembered the "very gloomy" days of the war. He grieved when "I saw the houses burning and other signs of desolation, the sufferers from which were in many cases innocent." Sherman, like Grady, preferred promoting a new culture of industrialism and northern investment to preserving the vestiges of the plantation economy, dependent on slavery.

11. Account in "Honor to the Puritans," *Chicago Daily Tribune*, December 23, 1886.

12. http://www.anselm.edu/academic/history/hdubrulle/civwar/text/documents/doc54.htm, accessed May 2, 2010. On Grady's speech, see Nixon, *Henry W. Grady*, chap. 11; Harold E. Davis, *Henry Grady's New South*, chap. 6.

13. Quoted in the *Atlanta Weekly Constitution*, January 18, 1887.

14. "Grady in New York," clipping, Henry W. Grady Scrapbooks, UGA.

15. "Henry W. Grady," *Atlanta Constitution*, December 23, 1889.

16. T. W. Reed, "An Early Member of the Constitution," *Atlanta Constitution*, March 26, 1939.

17. *Atlanta Sunday Gazette*, quoted in *Atlanta Daily Constitution*, August 30, 1881.

18. "Atlanta's Rush," *Atlanta Daily Herald*, July 13, 1873.

19. "Atlanta, Her Contrasts and Her Destiny," *Atlanta Daily Herald*, January 10, 1874.

20. Gaston, *The New South Creed*, chap. 1.

21. Edward DeLeon, "The New South, What It Is Doing, and What It Wants," *Putnam's Magazine* 5 (April 1870): 458–64.

22. Grady's piece responded to an article published in the *Boston Advertiser* calling for the South to urbanize and industrialize. In particular, the northern correspondent urged southerners to embrace "help from abroad." He advised that the South must "make it safe and attractive for strangers to unite with them in developing their resources." Disputing the suggestion that the South was not "safe" for northern capitalists, Grady urged them to investigate the opportunities for investment. "Favorable prospects of gain must be held out, they are here to speak for themselves. We can make them neither brighter nor darker, except so far as honest purposes to control them for good to the full extent of our power." "The New South," *Atlanta Daily Herald*, March 14, 1874.

23. "Boasting of Puritan Sires," *New York Times*, December 23, 1886.

24. "Down to the Sea," *Atlanta Daily Constitution*, January 25, 1879; "Matters of Memory," *Atlanta Daily Constitution*, January 31, 1879.

25. "The Last Visit," *Atlanta Daily Constitution*, January 30, 1879; "Wm. T., Come, Sir!" *Atlanta Daily Constitution*, January 31, 1879.

26. Quoted in Nixon, *Grady*, 109.

27. Reed, *History of Atlanta*, biographical section, 162–69; Russell, *Atlanta, 1847–1890*, 121–22; Reagan, *H. I. Kimball*; "What Grady Told Gath," *Atlanta Daily Constitution*, January 12, 1881.

28. "Wm. T., Come, Sir," *Atlanta Daily Constitution*, January 31, 1879; "Sherman's March through Georgia," *New York Times*, January 30, 1879.

29. "Down to the Sea," *Atlanta Daily Constitution*, January 25, 1879; "Matters of Memory," *Atlanta Daily Constitution*, January 31, 1879.

30. "General Sherman: He Will Be in Atlanta To-Day," *Atlanta Daily Constitution*, January 29, 1879.

31. "Hardly had the hoof ring of his horses died away," observed another reporter, remembering Sherman's departure after the Atlanta Campaign, "before the work of desolation and destruction was completed." Sherman's first visit to Atlanta had been "a healthy visit while it lasted—beginning with the booming of cannon and ending with the clangor of the fire-bell." Whenever Sherman felt "his bump of destructiveness feeling tender again," the reporter, observed, "we trust he will find it convenient to dodge Atlanta," as "one visit of that sort is about all a town can stand." "The First Visit," *Atlanta Daily Constitution*, January 30, 1879; "Two Receptions," *Atlanta Daily Constitution*, January 20, 1879.

32. *New York Tribune*, quoted in "General Sherman's Second 'March Through Georgia,'" *San Francisco Evening Bulletin*, February 11, 1879.

33. As Reardon, "Sherman in Postwar Georgia's Collective Memory" shows, over time Georgians blamed Sherman increasingly for wanton destructiveness.

34. "Sherman's March to the Sea—His Memory," *Georgia Weekly Telegraph and Georgia Journal and Messenger*, February 4, 1879.

35. "General Sherman's Opinion of Georgia," Sherman to E. P. Howell, February 4, 1879, *Georgia Weekly Telegraph and Georgia Journal and Messenger*, February 18, 1879; "The New South," *St. Louis Globe-Democrat*, February 11, 1879.

36. "Direct Questions," *Atlanta Daily Constitution*, January 1, 1881.

37. Ibid.

38. Ibid.

39. "The New South," *Atlanta Daily Constitution*, November 13, 1880. See also "A Grand Success," *Atlanta Daily Constitution*, March 25, 1881.

40. "Of Passing Interest," *Atlanta Daily Constitution*, March 16, 1881; Kimball, *Report of the Director-General*, 9–29. On the exposition, see Prince, "A Rebel Yell for Yankee Doodle," 340–71.

41. Kimball, *Report of the Director-General*, 96–99; "The Exposition," *Atlanta Daily Constitution*, June 29, 1881; Doyle, *New Men, New Cities, New South*, 155. Grady described Kimball's tour as the "apostles of the cotton exposition . . . abroad in the land." "Public Topics," *Atlanta Daily Constitution*, March 20, 1881.

42. Quoted in the *Atlanta Daily Constitution*, August 6, 1881.

43. "Cotton," *Atlanta Daily Constitution*, October 5, 1881.

44. Kimball, *Report of the Director-General*, 122; "Cotton," *Atlanta Daily Constitution*, October 5, 1881; Woodward, *Origins of the New South*, 124–25; Harold E. Davis, *Henry Grady's New South*, 172; Doyle, *New Men, New Cities, New South*, 151–58.

45. Quoted in Harold E. Davis, *Henry Grady's New South*, 168. For an account of the exposition, see ibid., 168–72. See also Blicksilver, "The International Cotton Exposition"; Doyle, *New Men, New Cities, New South*, 152–58.

46. *Augusta Chronicle*, quoted in "The Atlanta Cotton Exposition," *Atlanta Daily Constitution*, June 10, 1881.

47. Reed, *History of Atlanta*, 18–20; on the cotton exposition, see 472–76.

48. Jackson commanded state troops during the Atlanta Campaign. On Jackson, see the entry in the *New Georgia Encyclopedia*, http://www.georgiaencyclopedia.org/nge/Article.jsp?id=h-865, accessed February 23, 2010.

49. "At the Exposition," *Atlanta Daily Constitution*, November 16, 1881; Kimball, *Report of the Director-General*, 211–12. See also "General Sherman's Reception," *Atlanta Daily Constitution*, November 9, 1881; "Exposition Events," *Atlanta Daily Constitution*, November 15, 1881.

50. "The Old General At It Again," *Atlanta Constitution*, December 17, 1888.

51. Kennett, *Sherman*, 107.

52. Fellman, *Citizen Sherman*.

53. William T. Sherman, "Old Shady," 365–66.

54. "General Sherman's Unwisdom," *Atlanta Constitution*, December 23, 1888. For an account of the Wahalak violence, see "A Race War in Mississippi," *New York Times*, December 18, 1888.

55. *Bangor Daily Whig and Courier*, December 29, 1888.

56. "The Stage," *Atlanta Daily Constitution*, January 12, 1881. When Grady visited the St. Johns River and passed Stowe's home in 1876, he described how he "revenged himself" by "turning up his nose" at her. Nixon, *Grady*, 135.

57. Henry W. Grady, "The South and Her Problems," Shurter, ed., *The Complete Orations and Speeches*, 32–45.

58. "Extract from the Eloquent Address of Henry Grady at Dallas, Tex.," *New Mississippian*, November 7, 1888.

59. "Henry Grady on the Race Question," *New Mississippian*, December 5, 1888.

60. "The Old General At It Again," *Atlanta Constitution*, December 17, 1888.

61. Traveling by a special train from Atlanta, a delegation of southern whites accompanied Grady, and northern white dignitaries greeted them en route when they arrived in New York.

"Gone to Boston," *Atlanta Constitution*, December 9, 1889; "Southern Visitors to Boston," *New York Times*, December 12, 1889.

62. "Grady in Boston," *Atlanta Constitution*, December 15, 1889.

63. Nixon, *Grady*, 323–24.

64. R. D. Spaulding, "The Greatest Ever Delivered," *Atlanta Constitution*, December 13, 1889.

65. Quoted in the *Atlanta Constitution*, December 16, 1889.

66. Harold E. Davis, *Henry Grady's New South*, chap. 5.

67. "What Mr. Grady's Speech Means," *Boston Pilot*, in *Bulletin of Atlanta University* 15 (January 1890): 3.

68. "At the Exposition," *Atlanta Daily Constitution*, December 29, 1881.

69. Shadgett, *The Republican Party in Georgia*, 79–80; "The Port Surveyorship," *Atlanta Daily Constitution*, July 21, 1885. Pledger died in 1904 at the age of fifty-two. "Col. William Pledger," *Voice of the Negro* 1 (February 1904): 43.

70. "At the Exposition," *Atlanta Daily Constitution*, December 29, 1881; Hornsby, *Black Power in Dixie*.

71. "The Colored World's Exposition," *New York Freeman*, January 15, 1887.

72. See the petition of the Colored World Fair's association, January 5, 1887, 18 *Cong. Rec.* (1887), January 5, 1887, 352.

73. "Will It Come Here?," *Atlanta Daily Constitution*, June 23, 1887.

74. "The National Colored Exposition," *Atlanta Daily Constitution*, June 22, 1887.

75. "Another Indorsement," *Atlanta Daily Constitution*, April 7, 1888; "The Colored Industrial Exposition," *St. Louis Globe-Democrat*, October 12, 1887.

76. "To Stir Them Up," *Atlanta Daily Constitution*, June 15, 1888.

77. "A Charter Asked For," *Atlanta Daily Constitution*, July 17, 1887; "The Senate Bill," *Atlanta Daily Constitution*, July 31, 1888; 19 *Cong. Rec.* (1888), August 7, 1888, 7312.

78. "Dr. Edward Randolph Carter," *Spelman College Campus Mirror* 16 (June 1940): 2; *Morehouse College Bulletin, Morehouse Alumnus* 12 (November-December 1944): 6, in the Papers of Edward R. Carter, box 1, folder 3, AARL.

79. Mixon, "Henry McNeal Turner," 363–80; Ponton, *Life and Times of Henry M. Turner*.

80. Henry M. Turner, introduction to Carter, *The Black Side*, v–ix.

81. Carter, *The Black Side*, 10–11; Ellis A. Fuller to Rolfe Edmondson (copied to Carter), October 22, 1941; Louie S. Newton, "For Sixty Years His Fruit Faileth Not," *Souvenir Booklet of the Sixtieth Anniversary Celebration of the Pastorate of Dr. Edward Randolph Carter*, April 19, 1942; obituary, "Dr. Edward Randolph Carter," unidentified clipping, Papers of Edward R. Carter, box 1, folders 9 and 10, box 3, folder 3, AARL.

82. For further information about Ransom Montgomery, see Kaemmerlen, *The Historic Oakland Cemetery of Atlanta*, 34–35. See *Acts and Resolutions of the General Assembly, State of Georgia, 1882–1883*, 688.

83. Carter, *The Black Side*, chap. 3.

84. Ibid., chap. 4.

85. Brundage, "Meta Warrick's 1907 'Negro Tableaux,'" 1374; Doyle, *New Men, New Cities, New South*, 267–68.

86. Rydell, ed., *The Reason Why the Colored American Is Not in the World's Columbian Exposition*.

87. Perdue, *Race and the Atlanta Cotton States Exposition*, 18–20.

88. "Negroes Approve," *Atlanta Constitution*, April 4, 1894; "The Negro Exhibit," *Southern Workman* (December 1894), 211.

89. "Exhibits of Negro Progress," from the *Chicago Inter Ocean*, in the *Atlanta Constitution*, February 1, 1895.

90. Henry M. Turner, "To Colored People," *Atlanta Constitution*, January 13, 1895.

91. "The Colored Board," *Atlanta Constitution*, January 19, 1895.

92. "The Colored Committee," *Atlanta Constitution*, January 7, 1895.

93. Washington and Montgomery later helped to organize the National Negro Business League in 1900. "The Colored Board"; "Progress of a Race," *Atlanta Constitution*, January 19, 1895; "At a Mass Meeting," *Atlanta Constitution*, January 21, 1895.

94. Perdue, *Race and the Atlanta Cotton States Exposition*, 22–25.

95. Ibid., 48–50.

96. "Negroes' Congress," *Atlanta Constitution*, December 27, 1895.

97. "On the First Day," *Atlanta Constitution*, August 23, 1895; "Miles of Moving Soldiers," *Atlanta Constitution*, September 19, 1895; "Formal Opening of the Fair," *Chicago Tribune*, September 19, 1895.

98. On the exposition's layout, see Sharon Foster Jones, *The Atlanta Exposition*.

99. "Atlanta's Great Show," *New York Times*, September 19, 1895.

100. Ibid.

101. Blight, *Race and Reunion*, 325.

102. "Formal Opening of the Fair," *Chicago Tribune*, September 19, 1895.

103. *New York World*, September 18, 1895; Harlan et al., eds., *The Booker T. Washington Papers*, 4:3–9; "At Chickamauga," *Atlanta Constitution*, September 15, 1895. The best account of the speech remains that of Harlan, *Booker T. Washington*, chap. 11. But see also, more recently, Blight, *Race and Reunion*, 324–33, and Norrell, *Up from History*, 121–28.

104. Booker T. Washington, manuscript version of the Atlanta Exposition address, September 18, 1895, Harlan et al., eds., *The Booker T. Washington Papers*, 3:578–82.

105. *New York World*, September 18, 1895.

106. Booker T. Washington to the editor, *New York World*, September 19, 1895, Harlan et al., eds., *The Booker T. Washington Papers*, 4:15–16.

107. Du Bois, *The Souls of Black Folk*.

CHAPTER 7

1. Ray Stannard Baker, *Following the Color Line*, 3; Dittmer, *Black Georgia*, 123–31; Williamson, *The Crucible of Race*, 209–32; Mixon, *The Atlanta Riot*; Godshalk, *Veiled Visions*, chap. 4.

2. Godshalk, *Veiled Visions*, chap. 1.

3. Hornsby, *Black Power in Dixie*, 44–45, 48.

4. Henry M. Turner to the editor, January 28, 1904, *Atlanta Independent*, February 6, 1904, claims that there was no boycott. In this letter, he said that the Atlanta black community was too "cowardly" and "too much divided" to mount an effective boycott.

5. Dittmer, *Black Georgia*, 16–17, 20–21.

6. Ray Stannard Baker, *Following the Color Line*, 38–39. Baker consulted Du Bois extensively. Du Bois advised him that few northern whites perceived black people as "feeling" and "thinking." While northern whites spoke of southern whites in the "second person," they referred to southern blacks in the "third person." Du Bois to Ray Stannard Baker, April 7, 1907, W. E. B. Du Bois Papers (microfilm copy), reel 1, UMA.

7. Dittmer, *Black Georgia*, 48–49; "Atlanta Life Insurance Company Had an Humble Beginning in 1904," unidentified clipping, Papers of Edward R. Carter, box 2, scrapbook, ca. 1944, AARL.

8. Dittmer, *Black Georgia*, 12–13.

9. Ray Stannard Baker, *Following the Color Line*, 46–47.

10. Ibid., 50.

11. Mary White Ovington to the editor, *Outlook* 84 (November 17, 1906): 684.

12. Du Bois, "The Tragedy at Atlanta, 2: From the Point of View of Negroes."

13. Du Bois, *Autobiography*, 209.

14. Lewis, *Biography of a Race*, 231–33.

15. Booker T. Washington to Horace Bumstead, December 18, 1895, Horace Bumstead Papers, box 19, folder 5, AUL.

16. Du Bois, *Autobiography*, 212–13.

17. Ibid., 243.

18. Frances B. Clemmer, "Negro Football," December 17, 1900, Horace Bumstead Papers, box 21, folder 3, AUL.

19. Du Bois, *The Souls of Black Folk*, chap. 3.

20. Aptheker, ed., *Selections, 1877–1934*, 48–49; Puttkammer and Worthy, "William Monroe Trotter"; Fox, *The Guardian of Boston*, 13–29.

21. Booker T. Washington to Theodore Roosevelt, September 15, 1903, Harlan et al., eds., *The Booker T. Washington Papers*, 7:284–85.

22. Fox, *The Guardian of Boston*, 47–49.

23. Booker T. Washington to Francis Jackson Garrison, August 3, 1903, Harlan et al., eds., *The Booker T. Washington Papers*, 7:252.

24. Booker T. Washington to Timothy Thomas Fortune, September 10, 1903, ibid., 7:280.

25. Rudwick, "Race Leadership Struggle"; Lewis, *W. E. B. Du Bois: Biography of a Race*, 300–304; Rudwick, *W. E. B. Du Bois*, 72–76; Fox, *The Guardian of Boston*, 49–58.

26. Du Bois, *Autobiography*, 238.

27. In January 1904, Trotter wrote that Du Bois had become opposed to Washington "at last." Trotter to George A. Towns, January 2, 1904, George A. Towns Collection, box 2, folder 46, AUL.

28. Rudwick, "Race Leadership," 21.

29. W. E. B. Du Bois to George Foster Peabody, December 28, 1903, copy, Horace Bumstead Papers, box 19, AUL.

30. Ibid.

31. George Towns to William Monroe Trotter, draft of letter, ca. October 1903, George A. Towns Collection, box 2, folder 46, AUL.

32. Horace Bumstead to George Towns, July 13, 1903, George A. Towns Collection, box 2, folder 46, AUL.

33. Samuel Edward Courtney to Booker T. Washington, October 18, 1903; Booker T. Washington to Robert Curtis Ogden, October 20, 1903, Harlan et al., eds., *The Booker T. Washington Papers*, 7:295, 298. "I do not believe that the authorities of Atlanta University," Washington wrote, "will find themselves greatly pleased with the sympathy expressed by this teacher for so riotous a crowd as Trotter and his gang." Washington to Courtney, October 23, 1903, ibid., 7:307.

34. Horace Bumstead to George Towns, November 5, 1903, George A. Towns Collection, box 1, folder 22, AUL.

35. When Bumstead shared the contents of Du Bois's letter to Peabody with the members of the trustees' executive and finance committees, he described an "outburst of dissent from fully half those present—all based, I judged, on the closing portion." Bumstead defended Du Bois's "liberty of opinion and utterance on matters of vital interest to your race" and described him as one of the few blacks capable of speaking out with "ability, dignity, and courtesy." But Bumstead left the trustees with a "fresh sense of the difficulty of being honest with ourselves and at the same time being judicious in dealing with those who do not agree with us." Horace Bumstead

to W. E. B. Du Bois, January 26, 1904, Aptheker, ed., *Selections, 1877–1934*, 69–70; Rudwick, "Race Leadership Struggle," 21–22.

36. George Towns to Horace Bumstead, November 7, 1903, George A. Towns Collection, box 1, folder 22, AUL.

37. Horace Bumstead to George Towns, December 5, 1903, George A. Towns Collection, box 1, folder 22; minutes of the Atlanta University board of trustees, December 5, 1903, George A. Towns Collection, box 1, folder 22, AUL; Horace Bumstead to W. E. B. Du Bois, December 5, 1903, W. E. B. Du Bois Papers, reel 1, UMA.

38. W. E. B. Du Bois, "The Opening of the Library," *Atlanta Independent* 54 (April 3, 1902), 809–10.

39. W. E. B. Du Bois to Ray Stannard Baker, February 5, 1907, W. E. B. Du Bois Papers, reel 1, UMA; Rudwick, "The Niagara Movement."

40. Du Bois, "The Growth of the Niagara Movement," 43; Du Bois, *Autobiography*, 248–49. On Washington's relationship with Barber and *Voice of the Negro*, see Harlan, "Booker T. Washington and the 'Voice of the Negro.'"

41. W. E. B. Du Bois, newsletter of the Niagara Movement, October 7, 1905, June 13, 1906, W. E. B. Du Bois Papers, reel 2, UMA.

42. Barber, "The Niagara Movement," 403.

43. Du Bois, "Address of the First Annual Meeting of the Georgia Equal Rights Convention," 175–77.

44. Barber, "The Niagara Movement," 405–6.

45. "The Business Side of Law and Order," *Atlanta Constitution*, November 11, 1906.

46. "An Appeal to Reason—For Law and Order," *Atlanta Constitution*, September 24, 1906.

47. Alexander J. McKelway, "The Atlanta Riots, 1. A Southern White Point of View," *Outlook*, November 3, 1906.

48. Ray Stannard Baker, *Following the Color Line*, 4.

49. "Plays and Players," *Atlanta Constitution*, August 12, 1906. On Dixon, see Gillespie and Hall, *Thomas Dixon*. For another treatment of Dixon, see Williamson, *The Crucible of Race*, 151–76.

50. Barber, "The Atlanta Tragedy," 474.

51. "Atlanta Views on Riots," *Atlanta Constitution*, September 24, 1906. Atlanta newspaper editor John Temple Graves shared these views. He justified the mob as a practical tool to contain black crime. "John Temple Graves Discusses Cause and Effects of Riot," *Washington Post*, September 24, 1906; Graves, "The Tragedy at Atlanta, 1: From the Point of View of Whites," 1169–73.

52. "An American Kishinev," *Outlook* 84 (September 29, 1906): 241.

53. "Mob Murder in Atlanta," *Chicago Daily Tribune*, September 24, 1906.

54. "The Atlanta Riots," *New York Times*, September 25, 1906. "Atlanta is the most modern city in the South," said a writer in *Life*, "and the one least like a Southern city." "Atlanta and Its Warnings," *Life*, November 8, 1906.

55. "Atlanta Views on Riots," *New York Times*, September 24, 1906.

56. "Mob Violence, Rape—Their Baneful Consequences," *Atlanta Independent*, October 6, 1906.

57. "Why Mr. Barber Left Atlanta," *Voice of the Negro* 3 (November 1906): 470.

58. Ibid., 471.

59. "The Atlanta Massacre," *Independent*, October 4, 1906.

60. "John Temple Graves's Speech," *Atlanta Constitution*, December 29, 1889. On Graves, see Johnson and Malone, eds., *Dictionary of American Biography*, 7:508–9.

61. Graves, "The Promotive Power of the Southern Press."

62. Barber, "The Atlanta Tragedy," 475.

63. "He Defends Lynch Law," *New York Times*, August 12, 1903.

64. "Friend, Not Enemy, to the Negro," *Atlanta Georgian*, August 4, 1906; "As to Racial Prejudice," *Atlanta Georgian*, September 6, 1906.

65. "The Reign of Terror for Southern Women," *Atlanta Georgian*, August 21, 1906. See also "The Reign of Terror Must End," *Atlanta Georgian*, August 24, 1906.

66. "The Time for Action Has Come," *Atlanta Georgian*, August 29, 1906. See also "Let Us Find the Germ of the Rapist," *Atlanta Georgian*, September 22, 1906.

67. "Lest We Forget the Greater Crime," *Atlanta Georgian*, October 26, 1906.

68. "John Temple Graves Discusses Cause and Effects of Riot," *Washington Post*, September 24, 1906.

69. Graves, "The Tragedy at Atlanta, 1: From the Point of View of Whites."

70. Du Bois, "Looking Seventy-Five Years Backward," 244.

71. W. E. B. Du Bois, "Litany at Atlanta," *Atlanta Independent* 61 (October 11, 1906): 857.

72. Ray Stannard Baker, *Following the Color Line*, 4–5; Mixon, *The Atlanta Riot*, 76–77. Barber claimed that some of the rape cases were faked, some were relations by mutual consent, and others were perpetrated by white men disguised as black males. Only a "small percent" were real. Barber, "The Atlanta Tragedy," 479.

73. "Memorandum for Mr. Ray Stannard Baker on His Article about the Country Negro," May 1907, W. E. B. Du Bois Papers, reel 1, UMA.

74. Du Bois, "The Tragedy at Atlanta, 2: From the Point of View of Negroes."

75. Barber, "The Atlanta Tragedy," 479.

EPILOGUE

1. Hornady, *Atlanta: Yesterday, Today and Tomorrow*, 33–34.

2. Ibid., 31–32.

3. Ibid., 1–2.

4. Ibid., 4–5.

5. Ibid., 2–3.

6. Pyron, *Southern Daughter*, 46.

7. Ibid., 45.

8. Ibid., 40–41.

9. Margaret Mitchell, *Gone with the Wind*, 478–79.

10. Ibid., 555.

11. Bacote, *The Story of Atlanta University*, chap. 11.

12. Du Bois, *Autobiography*, 300–301.

13. Du Bois, "Apology," 3–5. On *Phylon*, see Bacote, *The Story of Atlanta University*, 327–28.

14. Du Bois, "Reconstruction and Its Benefits," 781; Lewis, *The Fight for Equality*, 351.

15. Lewis, *The Fight for Equality*, 350.

16. Du Bois, *Black Reconstruction in America*, chap. 17.

17. Karen L. Cox, *Dreaming of Dixie*.

Bibliography

MANUSCRIPTS AND ARCHIVAL MATERIAL

Georgia

Athens
Hargrett Rare Book and Manuscript Library, University of Georgia
Brown Family Papers
Henry W. Grady Scrapbooks
Key Family Civil War Papers
Charles A. James Martin Papers
Robert Goodwin Mitchell Papers
Horace Park Letter
Margaret Rhind Stokes Papers
Cyrene Bailey Stone Diary
Taft Family Papers
Robert T. Wood Papers
Atlanta
Auburn Avenue Research Library on African American Culture and History,
Atlanta-Fulton Public Library System
Papers of Edward R. Carter
Kenan Research Center, Atlanta History Center
Jennie Meta Barker Papers
Joseph E. Brown Papers
Colin Dunlop Papers
Holliday Family Civil War Correspondence
Diary of Thomas Maguire
Mayor's Court Record, Atlanta
Alonzo Miller Civil War Papers
James P. Wickersham Papers
Manuscript, Archives, and Rare Book Library, Emory University
Henry S. Campbell Papers
Robert W. Woodruff Library, Atlanta University Center
Atlanta University Presidential Records
Frederick Ayer Papers
Horace Bumstead Papers
Edmund Asa Ware Papers
George A. Towns Collection

Louisiana

New Orleans
Amistad Research Center, Tulane University
American Missionary Association archives

Massachusetts

Amherst
  Special Collections and University Archives, University of Massachusetts Amherst
    W. E. B. Du Bois Papers
Boston
  Historical Collections, Baker Library, Harvard Business School
    Georgia (Fulton County), vols. 13–14, R. G. Dun & Co. Collection

North Carolina

Chapel Hill
  Southern Historical Collection, University of North Carolina at Chapel Hill Library
    Edward W. Allen Papers
    George Washington Baker Papers
    Lucy Hull Baldwin Papers
    Clayton Family Papers
    John Kimberly Papers
    George Anderson Mercer Diary
    Benedict Joseph Semmes Papers
Durham
  David M. Rubenstein Rare Book and Manuscript Library, William R. Perkins Library, Duke
      University
    John Herr Papers
    William G. McCreary Papers
    Elizabeth Wiggins Papers
    Benjamin C. Yancey Papers

Washington, D.C.

Manuscripts Division, Library of Congress
    A. S. Bloomfield Papers
    James A. Congelton Diary
    James H. Goodnow Papers
    Diary of Henry Hitchcock
    Peter B. Kellenberger Papers
    John Wesley Marshall Journal
    Booker T. Washington Papers
National Archives and Records Administration
    Provost Marshal Records, Atlanta
    Records of the Assistant Commissioner for the State of Georgia, Bureau of Refugees,
        Freedmen, and Abandoned Lands, 1865–1869
    Records of the Field Offices for the State of Georgia, Bureau of Refugees, Freedmen, and
        Abandoned Lands, 1865–1872
    Records of the Superintendent of Education, State of Georgia, Bureau of Refugees,
        Freedmen, and Abandoned Lands, 1865–1869
    Southern Claims Commission Records

NEWSPAPERS AND PERIODICALS

American Missionary
Atlanta Constitution / Atlanta Daily Constitution

Atlanta Daily Intelligencer
Atlanta Daily New Era
Atlanta Daily Opinion
Atlanta History
Atlanta Independent
Atlanta Journal
Atlanta Weekly New Era
Atlantic Monthly
Bangor Daily Whig and Courier
Boston Daily Advertiser
Boston Guardian
Bulletin of Atlanta University
Chicago Tribune
Christian Recorder
Cincinnati Commercial Appeal
Cincinnati Daily Enquirer
Cincinnati Gazette
Columbus (Ga.) Daily Enquirer
Columbus (Ga.) Sun
Columbus (Ga.) Sunday Enquirer
Columbus (Ga.) Times
Daily Georgia Telegraph
Daily National Intelligencer
Daily Richmond Enquirer
DeBow's Review
Fayetteville Observer
Georgia Weekly Telegraph and Georgia Journal and Messenger
Houston Tri-Weekly Telegraph
Iowa Daily State Register
Life
Lowell Daily Citizen and News
Macon Daily Telegraph
Milwaukee Daily Sentinel
Natchez Daily Courier
Nation
New Mississippian
New Orleans Tribune
New York Evangelist
New York Freeman
New York Herald
New York Times
New York Tribune
North American and United States Gazette
Outlook
Peoria (Ill.) Democrat
Phylon
Putnam's Magazine
Richmond Daily Dispatch
San Francisco Evening Bulletin

Savannah Daily News and Herald
Southern Confederacy
Southern Workman
St. Louis Globe-Democrat
Vermont Chronicle
Voice of the Negro
Washington Chronicle
Weekly Columbus (Ga.) Enquirer
Western Christian Advocate
World To-Day

BOOKS, ARTICLES, DISSERTATIONS, AND THESES

Acts and Resolutions of the General Assembly, State of Georgia, 1882–83. Atlanta: J. P. Harrison, 1883.

Almand, Bond. "The Ashburn Murder Case and Military Trial." *Georgia Bar Journal* 10 (1947): 43–48.

Alvord, J. W. *Letters from the South, Relating to the Condition of Freedmen, Addressed to Major General O. O. Howard, Commissioner Bureau R., F., and A. L. by J. W. Alvord, Gen. Sup't Education, Bureau R., F., & A. L.* Washington, D.C.: Howard University Press, 1870.

Anderson, James D. *The Education of Blacks in the South, 1860–1935*. Chapel Hill: University of North Carolina Press, 1988.

Andrews, Sidney. *The South Since the War: Fourteen Weeks of Travel and Observation, Georgia and the Carolinas*. Boston: Ticknor and Fields, 1866.

Aptheker, Herbert, ed. *Selections, 1877–1934*. Vol. 1 of *The Correspondence of W. E. B. Du Bois*. Amherst: University of Massachusetts Press, 1973.

Ashburn v. Dempsey, Reports of Cases in Law and Equity, Argued and Determined in the Supreme Court of the State of Georgia. Athens: Reynolds and Brother, 1855.

Bacote, Clarence A. *The Story of Atlanta University: A Century of Service*. Atlanta: Atlanta University, 1969.

———. "William Finch, Negro Councilman and Political Activities in Atlanta during Early Reconstruction." *Journal of Negro History* 40 (October 1955): 341–64.

Baker, Bruce E. *What Reconstruction Meant: Historical Memory in the American South*. Charlottesville: University of Virginia Press, 2007.

Baker, Ray Stannard. *Following the Color Line: American Negro Citizenship in the Progressive Era*. New York: Harper Torchbooks, 1964.

Barber, J. Max. "The Niagara Movement at Harpers Ferry." *Voice of the Negro* 3 (October 1906): 402–11.

Bentley, George R. *A History of the Freedmen's Bureau*. Philadelphia: University of Pennsylvania Press, 1955.

Berlin, Ira, Barbara J. Fields, Steven F. Miller, Joseph P. Reidy, and Leslie S. Rowland. *Slaves No More: Three Essays on Emancipation and the Civil War*. New York: Cambridge University Press, 1992.

Berlin, Ira, Joseph P. Reidy, and Leslie S. Rowland, eds. *The Black Military Experience. Freedom: A Documentary History of Emancipation, 1861–1867*. Ser. 2. New York: Cambridge University Press, 1982.

Blair, William A. *Cities of the Dead: Contesting the Memory of the Civil War in the South, 1865–1914*. Chapel Hill: University of North Carolina Press, 2004.

Blicksilver, Jack. "The International Cotton Exposition and Its Impact on the Economic Development of Georgia." *Atlanta Economic Review* 7 (June 1957): 1–12.

Blight, David W. *Race and Reunion: The Civil War in American Memory*. Cambridge, Mass.: Harvard University Press, 2001.

Bonds, Russell S. *War Like a Thunderbolt: The Battle and Burning of Atlanta*. Yardley, Pa.: Westholme, 2009.

Bowlby, Elizabeth. "The Role of Atlanta during the War between the States." *Atlanta Historical Bulletin* 5, no. 22 (July 1940): 179–81.

Brady, Lisa M. *War upon the Land: Military Strategy and the Transformation of Southern Landscapes during the American Civil War*. Athens: University of Georgia Press, 2012.

Brundage, W. Fitzhugh. "Meta Warrick's 1907 'Negro Tableaux' and (Re)Presenting African American Historical Memory." *Journal of American History* 89 (March 2003): 1368–1400.

———. *The Southern Past: A Clash of Race and Memory*. Cambridge, Mass.: Harvard University Press, 2005.

Bryant, Jonathan. *How Curious a Land: Conflict and Change in Greene County, Georgia, 1850–1885*. Chapel Hill: University of North Carolina Press, 1996.

Butchart, Ronald E. *Schooling the Freed People: Teaching, Learning, and the Struggle for Black Freedom, 1861–1876*. Chapel Hill: University of North Carolina Press, 2010.

Carter, Edward R. *The Black Side: A Partial History of the Business, Religious and Educational Side of the Negro in Atlanta, Ga.* Atlanta, 1894.

Castel, Albert E. *Decision in the West: the Atlanta Campaign of 1864*. Lawrence: University Press of Kansas, 1992.

———. "Order No. 11 and the Civil War on the Border." *Missouri Historical Review* 57 (July 1963): 357–68.

Chapman Brothers. *Portrait and Biographical Album of Sedgwick County, Kan.* Chicago: Chapman Brothers, 1888.

Cimbala, Paul A. "The Freedmen's Bureau, the Freedmen, and Sherman's Grant in Reconstruction Georgia, 1865–1867." *Journal of Southern History* 55, no. 4 (November 1989): 597–632.

———. *Under the Guardianship of the Nation: The Freedmen's Bureau and the Reconstruction of Georgia, 1865–1870*. Athens: University of Georgia Press, 1997.

Cimbala, Paul A., and Randall M. Miller, eds. *The Freedmen's Bureau and Reconstruction: Reconsiderations*. New York: Fordham University Press, 1999.

Clark, Kathleen Ann. *Defining Moments: African-American Commemoration and Political Culture in the South, 1863–1913*. Chapel Hill: University of North Carolina Press, 2005.

Clayton, Sarah Conley. *Requiem for a Lost City: A Memoir of Civil War Atlanta and the Old South*. Macon: Mercer University Press, 1999.

Coffey, David. *Soldier Princess: The Life and Legend of Agnes Salm-Salm in North America, 1861–1867*. College Station: Texas A&M University Press, 2002.

The Condition of Affairs in Georgia, Statement of Hon. Nelson Tift to the Reconstruction Committee of the House of Representatives, Washington, February 18, 1869. Reprint, Freeport, N.Y., Books for Libraries Press, 1971.

Conway, Alan. *The Reconstruction of Georgia*. Minneapolis: University of Minnesota Press, 1966.

Conyngham, David P. *Sherman's March through the South*. New York: Sheldon and Company, 1865.

Cox, Jacob. *Atlanta*. New York: C. Scribner's Sons, 1882.

Cox, Karen L. *Dreaming of Dixie: How the South Was Created in American Popular Culture*. Chapel Hill: University of North Carolina Press, 2011.

Daniell, Elizabeth Otto. "The Ashburn Murder Case in Georgia Reconstruction, 1868." *Georgia Historical Quarterly* 59 (Fall 1975): 296–312.

Davidson, Henry Martin. *History of Battery A, First Regiment of Ohio Vol. Light Artillery.* Milwaukee: Daily Wisconsin Steam Printing House, 1865.

Davis, Harold E. *Henry Grady's New South: Atlanta, a Brave and Beautiful City.* Tuscaloosa: University of Alabama Press, 1990.

Davis, Jefferson. *The Rise and Fall of the Confederate Government.* New York: Appleton, 1881.

Davis, Robert Cott, Jr., ed. *Requiem for a Lost City: A Memoir of Civil War Atlanta and the Old South. Sarah "Sallie" Conley Clayton.* Macon: Mercer University Press, 1999.

Davis, Stephen. "How Many Civilians Died in Sherman's Bombardment in Atlanta?" *Atlanta History* 45, no. 4 (2003): 4–23.

———. " 'A Very Barbarous Mode of Carrying On War': Sherman's Artillery Bombardment of Atlanta." *Georgia Historical Quarterly* 79 (Spring 1995): 57–90.

Dean, Eric T. *Shook over Hell: Post-Traumatic Stress, Vietnam, and the Civil War.* Cambridge, Mass.: Harvard University Press, 1997.

DeCredico, Mary A. *Patriotism for Profit: Georgia's Urban Entrepreneurs and the Confederate War Effort.* Chapel Hill: University of North Carolina Press, 1990.

Dittmer, John. *Black Georgia in the Progressive Era, 1900–1920.* Urbana: University of Illinois Press, 1980.

Dorsey, Allison. *To Build Our Lives Together: Community Formation in Black Atlanta, 1875–1906.* Athens: University of Georgia Press, 2004.

Downs, Jim. *Sick from Freedom: African-American Illness and Suffering during the Civil War and Reconstruction.* New York: Oxford University Press, 2012.

Doyle, Don Harrison. *New Men, New Cities, New South: Atlanta, Nashville, Charleston, Mobile, 1860–1910.* Chapel Hill: University of North Carolina Press, 1990.

Drago, Edmund. *Black Politicians and Reconstruction in Georgia: A Splendid Failure.* Baton Rouge: Louisiana State University Press, 1982.

Du Bois, W. E. B. "Address of the First Annual Meeting of the Georgia Equal Rights Convention." *Voice of the Negro* 3 (March 1906): 175–77.

———. "Apology." *Phylon* 1, no. 1 (1st Qtr., 1940): 3–5.

———. *The Autobiography of W. E. B. Du Bois: A Soliloquy on Viewing My Life from the Last Decade of Its First Century.* New York: International Publishers, 1968.

———. *Black Reconstruction in America, 1860–1880.* New York: Harcourt, Brace, and Company, 1935.

———. "The Freedmen's Bureau." *Atlantic Monthly* 87, no. 521 (March 1901): 354–65.

———. "The Growth of the Niagara Movement." *Voice of the Negro* 3 (January 1906): 43–45.

———. "Postscript: Looking Seventy-Five Years Backward: Being the Personal Recollections of the Tower on Stone Hall." *Phylon* 3, no. 2 (2nd Qtr., 1942): 238-48.

———. "Reconstruction and Its Benefits." *American Historical Review* 15 (July 1910): 781–99.

———. *The Souls of Black Folk: Essays and Sketches.* Chicago: A. C. McClurg, 1903.

———. "The Tragedy at Atlanta, 2: From the Point of View of Negroes." *World To-Day* 11 (November 1906): 1173–75.

Du Bois, W. E. B., and Augustus Granville Dill, eds. *The Negro American Artisan.* Atlanta University Publications, no. 17. Atlanta: Atlanta University Press, 1912.

Dyer, Thomas G. *Secret Yankees: The Union Circle in Confederate Atlanta.* Baltimore: Johns Hopkins University Press, 1999.

Eddy, T. M. *The Patriotism of Illinois: A Record of the Civil and Military History of the State in the War for the Union.* 2 vols. Chicago: Clarke, 1866.

Ellison, Janet Correll, ed. *On to Atlanta: The Civil War Diaries of John Hill Ferguson, Illinois Tenth Regiment of Volunteers*. Lincoln: University of Nebraska Press, 2001.

Emery, E. B. *Letters from the South: On the Social, Intellectual, and Moral Conditions of the Colored People*. Boston: T. Todd, 1880.

Fellman, Michael. *Citizen Sherman: A Life of William Tecumseh Sherman*. New York: Random House, 1995.

Felton, Rebecca Latimer. *My Memoir of Georgia Politics*. Atlanta: Index Printing, 1911.

Ferguson, Karen. *Black Politics in New Deal Atlanta*. Chapel Hill: University of North Carolina Press, 2001.

Fleharty, S. F. *Our Regiment: A History of the 102d Illinois Infantry Volunteers*. Chicago: Brewster and Hanscom, 1865.

Foner, Eric. *Reconstruction: America's Unfinished Revolution, 1863–1877*. New York: Harper and Row, 1988.

Foster, Gaines M. *Ghosts of the Confederacy: Defeat, the Lost Cause, and the Emergence of the New South, 1865–1913*. New York: Oxford University Press, 1987.

Fox, Stephen R. *The Guardian of Boston: William Monroe Trotter*. New York: Atheneum, 1970.

Garrett, Franklin M. *Atlanta and Environs: A Chronicle of Its People and Events*. 2 vols. Athens: University of Georgia Press, 1954.

Gaston, Paul. *The New South Creed: A Study in Southern Mythmaking*. New York: Vintage Books, 1970.

Gildersleeve, Basil L. *The Creed of the Old South, 1865–1915*. Baltimore: Johns Hopkins University Press, 1915.

Gillespie, Michele K., and Randal L. Hall. *Thomas Dixon, Jr., and the Birth of Modern America*. Baton Rouge: Louisiana State University Press, 2006.

Glymph, Thavolia. *Out of the House of Bondage: The Transformation of the Plantation Household*. New York: Cambridge University Press, 2008.

Godshalk, David Fort. *Veiled Visions: The 1906 Atlanta Race Riot and the Reshaping of American Race Relations*. Chapel Hill: University of North Carolina Press, 2005.

Graf, LeRoy P., and Ralph W. Haskins, eds. *The Papers of Andrew Johnson*. 16 vols. Knoxville: University of Tennessee Press, 1967–2000.

Graves, John Temple. "The Promotive Power of the Southern Press." *Proceedings of the Southern Commercial Congress* (1911): 893–94.

———. "The Tragedy at Atlanta, 1: From the Point of View of Whites." *World To-Day* 11 (November 1906): 1169–73.

Hahn, Steven. *A Nation under Our Feet: Black Political Struggles in the Rural South from Slavery to the Great Migration*. Cambridge, Mass.: Harvard University Press, 2003.

Hahn, Steven, Steven F. Miller, Susan E. O'Donovan, John C. Rodrigue, and Leslie S. Rowland, eds. *Land and Labor, 1865*. Freedom: A Documentary History of Emancipation, 1861–1867. Ser. 3, vol. 1. Chapel Hill: University of North Carolina Press, 2008.

Harlan, Louis R. *Booker T. Washington: The Making of a Black Leader, 1856–1901*. New York: Oxford University Press, 1972.

———. "Booker T. Washington and the 'Voice of the Negro,' 1904–1907." *Journal of Southern History* 45 (February 1979): 45–62.

Harlan, Lewis R., et al., eds. *The Booker T. Washington Papers*. 14 vols. Urbana: University of Illinois Press, 1972–89.

Harwell, Richard, and Philip N. Racine, eds. *The Fiery Trail: A Union Officer's Account of Sherman's Last Campaigns*. Knoxville: University of Tennessee Press, 1986.

Hedley, F. Y. *Marching through Georgia: Pen-Pictures of Every-Day Life*. Chicago: Donohue, Henneberry, 1890.

Hewett, Janet B., et al., eds. *Supplement to the Official Records of the Union and Confederate Armies.* Part I, Series 7. Wilmington: Broadfoot, 1997.

Hickey, Georgina. *Hope and Danger in the New South City: Working-Class Women and Urban Development in Atlanta, 1890–1940.* Athens: University of Georgia Press, 2003.

Holzhueter, John O., ed. "William Wallace's Civil War Letters: The Atlanta Campaign." *Wisconsin Magazine of History* 57 (Winter 1973–1974): 99–100.

Hood, John Bell. *Advance and Retreat: Personal Experiences in the United States and Confederate Armies.* New Orleans: G. T. Beauregard, 1880.

Hornady, John R. *Atlanta: Yesterday, Today and Tomorrow.* Atlanta: American Cities Book Company, 1922.

Hornsby, Alton, Jr. *Black Power in Dixie: A Political History of African Americans in Atlanta.* Gainesville: University Press of Florida, 2009.

Howe, M. A. DeWolfe, ed. *Marching with Sherman: Passages from the Letters and Campaign Diaries of Henry Hitchcock.* New Haven: Yale University Press, 1927.

Hunter, Tera W. *To 'Joy My Freedom: Southern Black Women's Lives and Labors after the Civil War.* Cambridge, Mass.: Harvard University Press, 1997.

Janney, Caroline E. *Burying the Dead but Not the Past: Ladies' Memorial Associations and the Lost Cause.* Chapel Hill: University of North Carolina Press, 2008.

Jennison, Watson W. *Cultivating Race: The Expansion of Race in Georgia, 1750–1860.* Lexington: University Press of Kentucky, 2012.

Jewell, Joseph O. *Race, Social Reform, and the Making of a Black Middle Class.* New York: Rowan and Littlefield, 2007.

Johnson, Allen, and Dumas Malone, eds. *Dictionary of American Biography.* 20 vols. New York: Scribner, 1928–37.

Johnson, James Weldon. *Along This Way: The Autobiography of James Weldon Johnson.* New York: Viking, 1933.

Jones, Jacqueline. *Saving Savannah: The City and the Civil War.* New York: Vintage, 2009.

———. *Soldiers of Light and Love: Northern Teachers and Georgia Blacks, 1865–1875.* Athens: University of Georgia Press, 1980.

Jones, Sharon Foster. *The Atlanta Exposition.* Charleston: Arcadia Publishing, 2010.

Kaemmerlen, Cathy J. *The Historic Oakland Cemetery of Atlanta.* Charleston: History Press, 2007.

Kantrowitz, Stephen. *Ben Tillman and the Reconstruction of White Supremacy.* Chapel Hill: University of North Carolina Press, 2000.

Kennaway, John H. *On Sherman's Track; or, The South after the War.* London: Seeley, Jackson, and Halliday, 1867.

Kennett, Lee. *Sherman: A Soldier's Life.* New York: Harper Collins, 2001.

Kimball, H. I. *International Cotton Exposition (Atlanta, Georgia, 1881): Report of the Director-General.* New York: Appleton, 1882.

King, Edward. *The Great South; A Record of Journeys in Louisiana, Texas, the Indian Territory, Missouri, Arkansas, Mississippi, Alabama, Georgia, Florida, South Carolina, North Carolina, Kentucky, Tennessee, Virginia, West Virginia, and Maryland.* Hartford: American Publishing, 1875.

Kruse, Kevin. *White Flight: Atlanta and the Making of Modern Conservatism.* Princeton: Princeton University Press, 2005.

Lewis, David Levering. *W. E. B. Du Bois: Biography of a Race, 1868–1919.* New York: Henry Holt, 1993.

———. *W. E. B. Du Bois: The Fight for Equality and the American Century, 1919–1963.* New York: Henry Holt, 2000.

Liddell Hart, B. H. *Sherman: Soldier, Realist, American.* New York: Dodd, Mead, 1929.

Martin, Thomas H. *Atlanta and Its Builders: A Comprehensive History of the Gate City of the South.* 2 vols. Atlanta: Century Memorial, 1902.

Massey, Mary Elizabeth. *Refugee Life in the Confederacy.* Baton Rouge: Louisiana State University Press, 1964.

McCurry, Stephanie. *Confederate Reckoning: Power and Politics in the Civil War South.* Cambridge, Mass.: Harvard University Press, 2010.

McMurry, Richard M. *Atlanta 1864: Last Chance for the Confederacy.* Lincoln: University of Nebraska Press, 2000.

McPherson, James M. *The Abolitionist Legacy: From Reconstruction to the NAACP.* Princeton: Princeton University Press, 1975.

Miller, Brian Craig. *John Bell Hood and the Fight for Civil War Memory.* Knoxville: University of Tennessee Press, 2010.

Mitchell, Margaret. *Gone with the Wind.* New York: Scribner, 1993.

Mitchell, Stephens. "The Defenses of Atlanta." *Atlanta Historical Bulletin* no. 6 (February 1932): 32–35.

Mixon, Gregory. *The Atlanta Riot: Race, Class, and Violence in a New South City.* Gainesville: University Press of Florida, 2005.

——. "Henry McNeal Turner Versus the Tuskegee Machine: Black Leadership in the Nineteenth Century." *Journal of Negro History* 79 (Autumn 1994): 363–80.

Morgan, Lynda. *Emancipation in Virginia's Tobacco Belt, 1850–1870.* Athens: University of Georgia Press, 1992.

Neely, Mark, Jr. *The Civil War and the Limits of Destruction.* Cambridge, Mass.: Harvard University Press, 2007.

Nelson, Megan Kate. *Ruin Nation: Destruction and the American Civil War.* Athens: University of Georgia Press, 2012.

Nelson, Scott. *Steel Drivin' Man: John Henry, the Untold Story of an American Legend.* New York: Oxford University Press, 2006.

Newman, Harvey K. *Southern Hospitality: Tourism and the Growth of Atlanta.* Tuscaloosa: University of Alabama Press, 1999.

Nichols, George Ward. *The Story of the Great March from the Diary of a Staff Officer.* New York: Harper and Brothers, 1865.

Nixon, Raymond B. *Henry W. Grady: Spokesman of the New South.* New York: Alfred A. Knopf, 1943.

Norrell, Robert J. *Up from History: The Life of Booker T. Washington.* Cambridge, Mass.: Harvard University Press, 2009.

O'Donovan, Susan. *Becoming Free in the Cotton South.* Cambridge, Mass.: Harvard University Press, 2007.

Parks, Joseph H. *Joseph E. Brown of Georgia.* Baton Rouge: Louisiana State University Press, 1977.

Paskoff, Paul F. "Measures of War: A Quantitative Examination of the Civil War's Destructiveness in the Confederacy." *Civil War History* 54 (March 2008): 35–62.

Perdue, Theda. *Race and the Atlanta Cotton States Exposition of 1895.* Athens: University of Georgia Press, 2010.

Pioneer Citizens History of Atlanta, 1833–1902. Atlanta: Pioneer Citizens Society of Atlanta, 1902.

Ponton, M. M. *Life and Times of Henry M. Turner.* Atlanta: A. B. Caldwell, 1917.

Prince, Stephen K. "A Rebel Yell for Yankee Doodle: Selling the New South at the 1881 Atlanta International Cotton Exposition." *Georgia Historical Quarterly* 92 (2008): 340–71.

Puttkammer, Charles W., and Ruth Worthy. "William Monroe Trotter, 1872–1934." *Journal of Negro History* 43 (October 1958): 298–316.

Pyron, Darden Asbury. *Southern Daughter: The Life of Margaret Mitchell.* New York: Harper, 1992.

Radical Rule: Military Outrage in Georgia. Arrest of Columbus Prisoners. Louisville: John P. Morton, 1868.

Reagan, Alice E. *H. I. Kimball, Entrepreneur.* Atlanta: Cherokee, 1983.

Reardon, Carol. "William T. Sherman in Postwar Georgia's Collective Memory, 1864–1914." In *Wars within a War: Controversy and Conflict over the American Civil War,* edited by Joan Waugh and Gary Gallagher, 223–48. Chapel Hill: University of North Carolina Press, 2009.

Redkey, Edwin S. *Respect Black: The Writings and Speeches of Henry McNeal Turner.* New York: Arno, 1971.

Reed, Wallace Putnam. *History of Atlanta, Georgia.* Syracuse, N.Y.: D. Mason, 1889.

Reid, Whitelaw. *After the War: A Tour of Southern States.* New York: Moore, Wilstach and Baldwin, 1866.

Report of the Adjutant General and Acting Quartermaster General of Iowa. 2 vols. Des Moines: F. W. Palmer, 1863.

Report of the Joint Select Committee to Inquire into the Condition of Affairs in the Late Insurrectionary States, Made to the Two Houses of Congress, February 19, 1872. Washington, D.C.: Government Printing Office, 1872.

Richardson, Heather Cox. *The Death of Reconstruction: Race, Labor, and Politics in the Post–Civil War North, 1865–1901.* Cambridge, Mass.: Harvard University Press, 2001.

Richardson, Joe M. *Christian Reconstruction: The American Missionary Association and Southern Blacks, 1861–1890.* Athens: University of Georgia Press, 1986.

Roberts, Derrell C. *Joseph E. Brown and the Politics of Reconstruction.* Tuscaloosa: University of Alabama Press, 1973.

Rosen, Hannah. *Terror in the Heart of Freedom: Citizenship, Sexual Violence, and the Meaning of Race in the Postemancipation South.* Chapel Hill: University of North Carolina Press, 2009.

Royster, Charles. *The Destructive War: William Tecumseh Sherman, Stonewall Jackson, and the Americans.* New York: Vintage, 1991.

Rudwick, Elliot M. "The Niagara Movement." *Journal of Negro History* 42 (July 1957): 177–200.

———. "Race Leadership Struggle: Background of the Boston Riot of 1903." *Journal of Negro Education* 31 (Winter 1962): 16–24.

———. *W. E. B. Du Bois: The Voice of the Black Protest Movement.* Urbana: University of Illinois Press, 1982.

Russell, James Michael. *Atlanta, 1847–1890: City Building in the Old South and the New.* Baton Rouge: Louisiana State University Press, 1988.

Rydell, Robert W., ed. *The Reason Why the Colored American Is Not in the World's Columbian Exposition.* 1893. Reprint, Urbana: University of Illinois Press, 1999.

Salm-Salm, Agnes. *Ten Years of My Life.* New York: R. Worthington, 1877.

Sarris, Jonathan Dean. *A Separate Civil War: Communities in Conflict in the Mountain South.* Charlottesville: University Press of Virginia, 2006.

Savitt, Todd L. "Politics in Medicine: The Georgia Freedmen's Bureau and the Politics of Medicine, 1865–1866." *Civil War History* 28 (March 1982): 45–64.

Shadgett, Olive Hall. *The Republican Party in Georgia.* Athens: University of Georgia Press, 1964.

Sherman, William T. *Memoirs of Gen. W. T. Sherman, Written by Himself.* 2 vols. New York: Charles L. Webster, 1892.

———. "Old Shady, with a Moral." *North American Review* 383 (October 1888): 365–66.

Shurter, Edwin DuBois, ed. *The Complete Orations and Speeches of Henry W. Grady*. New York: Hinds, Nobel and Eldredge, 1910.

Simpson, Brooks D., and Jean V. Berlin, eds. *Sherman's Civil War: Selected Correspondence of William T. Sherman, 1860–1865*. Chapel Hill: University of North Carolina Press, 1999.

Singer, Ralph Benjamin, Jr. "Confederate Atlanta." Ph.D. diss., University of Georgia, 1973.

Taylor, Arthur Reed. "From the Ashes: Atlanta during Reconstruction, 1865–1876." Ph.D. diss., Emory University, 1973.

Testimony Taken by the Joint Select Committee to Inquire into the Condition of Affairs in the Late Insurrectionary States. 13 vols. Washington, D.C.: Government Printing Office, 1872.

Thomas, William G. *The Iron Way: Railroads, the Civil War, and the Making of Modern America*. New Haven: Yale University Press, 2011.

Thompson, C. Mildred. *Reconstruction in Georgia: Economic, Social, Political, 1865–1872*. New York: Columbia University Press, 1915.

Towns, George A. "Horace Bumstead, Atlanta University President (1888–1907)." *Phylon* 9, no. 2 (2nd Qtr., 1948): 109–14.

———. "Sources of the Tradition at Atlanta University." *Phylon* 3, no. 2 (2nd Qtr., 1942): 117–34.

Trelease, Allen W. *White Terror: The Ku Klux Klan Conspiracy and Southern Reconstruction*. New York: Harper and Row, 1971.

Trowbridge, John T. *The South: A Tour of Its Battle-Fields and Ruined Cities*. Hartford, Conn.: L. Stebbins, 1866.

Trudeau, Noah Andre. *Southern Storm: Sherman's March to the Sea*. New York: HarperCollins, 2008.

U.S. Army. Department of the South. *Report of Major General Meade's Military Operations and Administration of Civil Affairs in the Third Military District and Dep't of the South, for the Year 1868, with Accompanying Documents*. Atlanta: Assistant Adjutant General's Office, 1868.

U.S. Congress. House of Representatives. *Report of the Commissioner of the Bureau of Refugees, Freedmen, and Abandoned Lands, November 1, 1866*, in *Annual Report of the Secretary of War*, 39th Cong., 2nd sess., House Executive Document 1. Washington, D.C.: Government Printing Office, 1866.

U.S. Congress. House of Representatives. *Report by Brig. Gen. C. H. Howard of South Carolina, Georgia, and Florida, December 30, 1865*, in *Report of the Commissioner of the Bureau of Refugees, Freedmen, and Abandoned Lands, March 1, 1866*. 39th Cong., 1st sess., House Executive Document 27. Washington, D.C.: Government Printing Office, 1866.

U.S. Congress. Senate. *The Condition of the South: Extracts from the Report of Major-General Carl Schurz, on the States of South Carolina, Georgia, Alabama, Mississippi and Louisiana. Addressed to the President*. 39th Cong., 1st sess., 1866, Executive Document 2. Washington, D.C.: Government Printing Office, 1866.

U.S. War Department. *The War of the Rebellion: A Compilation of the Official Records of the Union and Confederate Armies*. 128 vols. Washington, D.C.: Government Printing Office, 1880–1901.

Venet, Wendy Hamand, ed. *Sam Richards' Civil War Diary: A Chronicle of the Atlanta Home Front*. Athens: University of Georgia Press, 2009.

Warren, Robert Penn. *The Legacy of the Civil War: Meditations on the Centennial*. New York: Random House, 1961.

Whitehead, Margaret Laney, and Barbara Bogart. *City of Progress: A History of Columbus, Georgia*. Columbus: Columbus Office Supply, 1978.

Williams, Heather Andrea. *Help Me to Find My People: The African American Search for Families Lost in Slavery*. Chapel Hill: University of North Carolina Press, 2012.

———. *Self-Taught: African American Education in Slavery and Freedom*. Chapel Hill: University of North Carolina Press, 2005.

Williamson, Joel. *The Crucible of Race: Black-White Relations in the American South Since Emancipation*. New York: Oxford University Press, 1984.

Wilson, Charles Reagan. *Baptized in Blood: The Religion of the Lost Cause*. Athens: University of Georgia Press, 1980.

Wilson, John Stainback. *Atlanta as It Is*. New York: Little, Rennie, 1871.

Woodward, C. Vann. *Origins of the New South, 1877–1913*. Baton Rouge: Louisiana State University Press, 1951.

Wooton, Grigsby Hart, Jr. "New City of the South: Atlanta, 1843–1873." Ph.D. diss., Johns Hopkins University, 1973.

Wortman, Marc. *The Bonfire: The Siege and Burning of Atlanta*. New York: PublicAffairs, 2009.

Wright, Richard R., Jr. *Eighty-Seven Years behind the Black Curtain*. Philadelphia: Rare Book, 1965.

Acknowledgments

I have incurred a number of debts which can never be repaid but should be fully acknowledged. I have relied on the assistance of numerous librarians and archivists, including the staff at the Atlanta History Center; Okezie Amalaha at the Auburn Avenue Research Library on African American Culture and History; Andrea R. Jackson and Kayin Shabazz at Archives and Special Collections, Robert W. Woodruff Library, Atlanta University Center; Katherine Fox at Historical Collections, Baker Library, Harvard Business School; Toby Graham and the archivists at Hargrett Rare Book and Manuscript Library, University of Georgia; Laura Clark Brown and Matt Turi at Southern Historical Collection, University of North Carolina at Chapel Hill Library; and Elizabeth Bramm Dunn at the David M. Rubenstein Rare Book and Manuscript Library, in William R. Perkins Library, Duke University.

I have also depended on a community of generous colleagues. Bill Blair provided a thorough and penetrating reading of an early version of the manuscript, and, as always, headed me in the right direction. Pete Carmichael and Keith Bohannon shared their wide knowledge and encyclopedic understanding of the Civil War era. Aaron Sheehan-Dean applied his critical eye to the manuscript, reading it twice and offering some very useful advice. Jim Broomall read the book manuscript critically and sympathetically. David Jackson very generously shared his knowledge of Atlanta history. The perspectives of Bruce Baker, Mary DeCredico, Matt Gallman, Michele Gillespie, John Inscoe, Susan O'Donovan, Richard Reid, Anne Sarah Rubin, Andy Slap, Frank Towers, and Wendy Venet were all very useful. My colleagues at the University of Florida provided intellectual stimulation and support, and I especially appreciate the assistance of department chairs Joe Spillane and Ida Altman. My graduate assistants were invaluable in the research, and I must especially thank Heather Bryson, Angela Diaz, Allison Fredette, Matt Hall, Shannon Lalor, Chris Ruehlen, and Angie Zombek for their invaluable help. Matt Hall provided especially important assistance during the later stages of the preparation of the book manuscript.

I also appreciate the enthusiastic support of David Perry, old friend and fellow racquetball fanatic, who caught on to what I wanted to accomplish in this book. I have always appreciated his assistance and interest, as I have the great people at the University of North Carolina Press, including Caitlin Bell-Butterfield, Chuck Grench, Ron Maner, and Kate Torrey. Shirley Werner, who copyedited the manuscript, spared readers a number of errors and infelicities.

I also appreciate my immediate and extended family's willingness to put me up during research trips. John, Jan, and Jack Douglas housed me in Atlanta, providing interesting conversation and the more-than-occasional glasses of craft beer. My sister and brother-in-law, Peggy Link and Michael Weil, have been always generous and hospitable during my many visits to the Chapel Hill-Duke area, providing a home away from home. As always, I have relied on Susannah's judgment, and value her as my most honest critic—and best friend.

The dedication is for my graduate students whom I've taught during twenty-three years at the University of North Carolina at Greensboro and eight years at the University of Florida. I often think that I've benefited more from them than they from me, and I've always appreciated their energy, inquisitiveness, and new ways of considering the past.

Index

Terrell, Joseph M., 184
Texas State Fair, 151
Third Military District in Reconstruction
    Atlanta, 79–80, 97
Thomas, William, 56
Thomaston, Ga., 45
Tillson, Davis, 74–75
Tolfson, E., 76
Tourgée, Albion, 179
Towns, George A., 177–78
Trelease, Allen W., 96
Trotter, William Monroe, 175–77
Trout House, 10, 13, 52
Turner, Henry McNeal, 94, 108, 158–59,
    162–63
Tuskegee Institute, 173–74

Uncle Tom's Cabin, 151
Unionists, 12, 13, 34, 79, 86–87
U.S. Army: Eighteenth Infantry, 143
United States Christian Commission, 116
U.S. Colored Troops: Forty-Third Regiment,
    126; First Regiment, 159
U.S. Military Railroad Corps, 56
U.S. Supreme Court, civil rights cases of 1883,
    162
University of Chicago, 112
University of Georgia, 158
University of Pennsylvania, Wharton School,
    112
Upson County, Ga., 93
Uxbridge, Mass., 115

Vicksburg, Miss., 32, 35
Vinyard, Cris, 78
Voice of the Negro, 183

Wahalak, Miss., 150
Waldridge, George R., 72, 74, 77, 80
Walker, William H. T., 136
Wallace, William, 22–23, 46–47
Walton County, Ga., 91

Ware, Edmund Asa, 117–22, 124–30
Ware, Edward Twitchell, 127
Warren, H. W., 156
Washington, Booker T., 162–65, 173,
    175–78, 180
Washington Post, 186
Watson, Tom, 105
Wells, John, 98, 101
Wesleyan Chapel (Atlanta), 48
Western & Atlantic Railroad, 8, 10, 11, 20, 24,
    41, 43, 46, 47, 48, 56, 144, 147, 160
Western Freedmen's Aid Commission, 115
Westmoreland, Greene, 92–93
West Point, Ga., 53
Whitaker, Elijah, 74
White, Walter, 195
Whitehall Street (Atlanta), 28, 190
Whitely, H. C., 98, 101
Whitfield, Ga., 132
Whittier, John Greenleaf, 111
Wiggins, James L., 102
Wilberforce University, 112, 162
William, James E., 74
Williams, J. E., 55
Williams' Mill Road (Atlanta), 28
Wilson, Charles Reagan, 2
Wisconsin (unit): Twelfth Regiment, 21
Women and wartime unrest, 14
Wood, Robert A., 102
Wood, Robert T., 24
Wood, William J., 31
Woods, W. B., 143
Woodward, C. Vann, 1, 148
Woodworth, C. L., 134
World To-Day, 187
Wright, Austin, 17
Wright, Mahaley, 82
Wright, Richard Robert, 111–12, 163
Wright, W. W., 20
Wylie, A. C., 51

Yale College, 121; Theological Seminary, 125

www.ingramcontent.com/pod-product-compliance
Lightning Source LLC
Chambersburg PA
CBHW020344270326
41926CB00007B/307